speech communication
for the
contemporary
 student

Under the advisory editorship of J. Jeffery Auer

speech communication
for the contemporary student

Third Edition

Wil A. Linkugel

E. Christian Buehler

University of Kansas, Lawrence

Formerly published
under the title
Speech Communication:
A First Course

Harper & Row, Publishers
New York   Evanston   San Francisco   London

Sponsoring Editor: Walter H. Lippincott, Jr.
Project Editor: Brenda Goldberg
Designer: James McGuire
Production Supervisor: Will Jomarrón

SPEECH COMMUNICATION FOR THE CONTEMPORARY STUDENT, Third Edition
Formerly published under the title *Speech Communication: A First Course*

Copyright © 1962, 1969, 1975 by Wil A. Linkugel and E. C. Buehler

All rights reserved. Printed in the United States of America. No part of this book may be used or reproduced in any manner whatsoever without written permission except in the case of brief quotations embodied in critical articles and reviews. For information address Harper & Row, Publishers, Inc., 10 East 53rd Street, New York, N.Y. 10022.

Library of Congress Cataloging in Publication Data

Linkugel, Wil A
   Speech communication for the contemporary student.
   Published in 1968 under title: Speech communication.
   1. Oral communication.   I. Buehler, Ezra Christian, Date,   joint author. II. Title.
PN4121.L48   1975   808.5   74-13481
ISBN 0-06-044002-3

contents

Preface vii

Part One: A Starting Point 1

Preliminary Perspectives 3
The Speech Profession 5
The Nature of Speech Communication 11
Social Contexts 16
A Model of Interpersonal Communication 20
The Need for Responsible Communication 30

Part Two: Four Integral Dimensions 37

dimension one: People as Communicators 39

People Are Symbolizers 40
People Are Inference Makers 45
Communicator Constraints 49
Communication and Human Motivation 58
The Speaker's Image 70
The Speaker's Poise and Confidence 81
The Reception of Messages 87
Characteristics of People in Audiences 99

dimension two: Circumstances of the Communication 102

Time 104
Place 108
Occasion 110

dimension three: Message Preparation—Thought and Its Form   114

    The Subject   114
    The Purpose of the Message   120
    The Form of the Message   144

dimension four: Message Presentation—Verbal and Nonverbal Cues   162

    Communicating with Language   165
    Communicating with Voice and Action   183

Part Three: Guided Experiences   195

    Participating in a Group   197
    Preparing Your First Speech   200
    A Program of Practical Experiences   203

    Index   225

preface

This book is an introductory text to the study and practice of speech communication. Its underlying philosophy is that the beginning student should be introduced to the basic rudiments of human communication in general before proceeding to specific contextual application. The first section, "A Starting Point," thus delves into the nature of speech communication, sets forth and elaborates an operational definition of speech communication, and depicts and explains a fundamental communication model which constitutes the basis for the theory in the remainder of the book. The book is tightly organized around this model. Perhaps the greatest merit of the book is its simplicity. Its bulk examines the four basic dimensions of the communication model: people as communicators, circumstances of communication, message preparation, and message presentation.

Most of the principles expounded are applicable to all types of contextual applications, be it dyadic, small-group, or speaker-audience communication. The focus of the application, however, is *speaking to groups and audiences*. This book is thus most suitable for a beginning course which has as its philosophy the introduction to human speech communication theory with practical projects designed to improve the student's ability to speak to groups and audiences. On the assumption that some teachers like to begin a course with a few group discussion-oriented projects, a short, concise section at the back of the book, "Participating in Groups," is devoted to discussion principles and practices. The class project section, "A Program of Practical Experiences," contains a few discussion-oriented projects. In addition, this section contains a short piece on "Preparing Your First Speech." The thought here is that the teacher will doubtlessly assign an oral project or two before the entire theory of the book will have been covered and that some basic guidelines should be helpful to the student as he is confronted with preparing his first class presentation. The teacher may want to assign this piece early in the course. The "Program of Practical Experiences" is intended not as a syllabus but merely as a reservoir from which the teacher may want to draw assignments for class projects. If the book is used in a course that already has a well-structured syllabus, the final section may be ignored.

If a teacher feels that the Dimensions of the book are too long to assign to students for any one class period, each of the Dimensions quite readily breaks down into sections which can be assigned separately. It is our philosophy that the student should see the various elements of each Dimension in concert. We feel that this approach enables the student to leave the course with a theoretical structure that he can easily remember and be able to apply for years to come. If a basic book is highly particularized in terms of chapters, it often fails to project a framework that the student will be able to absorb.

We hope that as a teacher using this book, you will not only discuss the model presented in "A Starting Point" at the outset of the course but will also frequently refer back to it and relate other material to it. We think that such a practice will heighten the instructional quality of the course.

Although this book is a revision of *Speech Communication: A First Course,* published in 1969, it is more than a minor overhaul. More than half of the content has been totally revised. In some instances we have borrowed directly from the previous edition, but for the most part this edition was written independently of the old one to assure fresh thinking on our part.

In preparing the book we have devoted ourselves to making it readable for the student. We have thus sought to limit footnoting. We have also made few specific references to research studies. In developing and writing the concepts, however, we have considered available research literature. It is our contention that in a basic textbook used in a practice course a discussion of numerous research studies only serves to clutter the book and that the student will not remember many of them. We feel that a discussion of pertinent research literature can be more profitable in an advanced course after the student has been initiated to the field and perhaps even has developed a degree of commitment to it. Neither have we tried to include all of traditional rhetorical theory. We drew heavily from classical writings when it served our purpose, but the attempt at all times has been to write a contemporary theory for the contemporary student.

W.A.L.
E.C.B.

part one
a starting point

Preliminary Perspectives

Henry Drummond, a late nineteenth century Scottish writer, once defined death as "that state of the body when it can no longer communicate with its environment." If we reverse this logic, we might reason that man comes alive as a person in that measure by which he is able to communicate with the world about him. Consider the developing infant. The greater the stimulation from his environment, the greater his awareness becomes; the greater his awareness, the more his personality develops. Babbling starts and soon he begins to speak. He not only receives messages but begins to send them. He becomes an *interacter*. Children who are deprived of these communicative contacts do not come alive in the same way as do their more fortunate counterparts. Their personalities do not develop properly, they turn inward, and they fail to acquire vital learning skills.

In adulthood, irregularities in human behavior can often be traced to the frustrations and feelings of inadequacy that are associated with communication. People who, for organic or psychological reasons, find it difficult to communicate often tend to withdraw further into themselves. A sociologist once said that if every person were completely articulate there would be no need for jails. In other words, the ability to communicate seems to be directly related to a well-organized personality.

The normally functioning adult, however, has been speaking all his life. His vocal quality is good enough, and he has no severe articulation problems. He talks freely in social situations; listeners seem to understand him; and he gets along well enough with most people. To be sure, when he is called on to address a large audience, he may experience a good deal of anxiety, but the speech may not seem as bad to him in retrospect. He may even feel he did pretty well, everything considered. Even though he thinks, visits with friends, rears and educates children, prays, and carries on all kinds of commerce through the medium of speech communication, he tends to be appallingly unaware of how much speech is tied to his normal process of living. It may seem as common to him as breathing. Yet, in the words of Andrew Weaver:

> Were speech to fail, our intelligence would lapse to the level of beasts, each individual would dwell apart from his fellows, the structure of society would crumble, the very fabric of life itself would disintegrate, all the vital processes of civilization would grind to a faltering stop.[1]

People come to know us largely by the way we talk. A stranger steps into our midst, and one word from him tells us something about him. Lee Travis, a prominent speech pathologist, once wrote: "Speech is a reflection of the personality of the speaker. With every utterance, the speaker gives himself away. His speech is a microscope directed towards his own inner self, through which others may get the most intimate glimpses."[2] Whether we like it or not, we cannot escape the fact that we do make impressions, favorable or unfavorable, on our listeners, both in private conversations and before groups. When we talk, our beliefs, mental attitudes, emotional balance, sense of justice, educational background—the countless attributes that form an impression of our total character and personality—are reflected in the listener's mind. No wonder Seneca the Elder of ancient Rome remarked, "As a man speaks, so is he." Whether this speech-created impression is accurate or erroneous is not the issue. The point is that the impression *is made*.

In the process of making a living, effective speakers have an advantage over poor ones. Those who speak easily and well make more sales, get more votes, secure better jobs and more promo-

---

[1] Andrew Weaver, "What Is Speech? A Symposium," *Quarterly Journal of Speech* (April 1955), p. 153.
[2] Lee Edward Travis, "A Point of View in Speech Correction," *Quarterly Journal of Speech* (February 1936), p. 57.

tions, are the best teachers, and, in a competitive society, generally outdo those who speak poorly. That speech-communication skills are vital in the business and professional world is well illustrated by the general popularity of adult speech courses. College night classes in speech communication enroll well, and Toastmaster's International and Dale Carnegie courses have flourished for years.

We must come to appreciate that there is far more to speech communication than just talking. Communication involves interaction between people, and people are extremely complex creatures, which means that communication is complex also. This book aims to help you understand the basic aspects of human speech communication and to apply them specifically to speaker-audience situations. Hopefully, by learning the basic principles expounded in this book and through the guided practical experiences of your course, you will get a truer picture of yourself as a communicator and will improve your ability to make more effective use of your personal resources.

The Speech Profession

Winston Churchill wisely observed, "The further backward we can look, the further forward we can see." To help focus our learning in speech communication, we feel it useful to look back to the older aspects of the profession, for we believe that "what happened yesterday gives the shape of things tomorrow."

This historical look at the speech profession takes us a long way back. Evidence shows that there was some speech instruction among the Egyptians in 2500 B.C., but few artifacts remain to tell us much about their theories and practices. However, the ancient Greeks of the fourth and fifth centuries B.C. left as our heritage both texts of speeches delivered and textbooks of speech theory. Athenian history tells us that rhetorical communication gave life and vitality to their way of life. The public assembly and the court of law provided exigence for rhetorical address. The Attic orators, among whom Demosthenes seemed to tower, delivered orations that are still studied for their style and beauty. The Greeks wrote numerous handbooks of speech principles, but Aristotle produced the most definitive statement when he published his *Art of Rhetoric* in 336 B.C. This work probably constituted a complete theory of communication in the Grecian world. Since it was public address that gave the Grecian system vitality, it was the focus of Aristotle's writing. If small group discussions or personal interviews had been of vital essence to the Greeks, it is likely that Aristotle would have addressed himself to these levels of communication also. In his *Rhetoric*, he even mentions that some of the principles he sets forth apply to personal interactions as well. It is from ancient Greece that we get many of our theoretical principles concerning argument, style, and rhetorical invention.

The Romans stressed instruction in oral discourse at all levels of education. In fact, Quintilian's *Institutes of Oratory*, published in 95 A.D., discussed speech training from the cradle to adulthood. Every Roman schoolboy was required to study rhetoric and engage in a series of exercises for his personal development. For theory, he read such handbooks as Cicero's *De Inventione*. In ancient Athens, speech training was essentially a private matter; Aristotle, Isocrates, and other teachers set up private academies where young people fortunate enough to be able to attend received their instruction. Roman speech education, by contrast, had a broader base. Quintilian was hired and paid by the state as a speech professor. But as the world slipped into the Dark Ages, speech instruction and its meaningful practice lost their stature.

The advent of the British Parliament revived oratory in the Western world. Great speakers such as William Pitt, Richard Sheridan, Charles James Fox, and Edmund Burke thundered their orations in the British halls of government. Learned writers, such as Richard Whately, George Campbell, and Hugh Blair, wrote new books on rhetorical theory. Although heavily influenced by the classical tradition, they contributed to the flow of rhetorical thought. Their books were most often used in British schools throughout most of the nineteenth century.

From colonial days to the twentieth century, American speech education in the context of curricular status was limited, sporadic, and marked by shifting trends. Rhetoric courses, at first integral to the core curriculum, gradually became oriented toward the study of written composition, and professors of rhetoric turned their attention to literature. Nowhere was this more apparent than at Harvard University. When John Quincy Adams, the nation's sixth president, occupied the Boylston Chair of Rhetoric at Harvard, he gave lectures on classical rhetorical theory, but later occupants of the Boylston Chair became outright professors of literature. The need for speech education has been so keenly felt by students throughout our history, however, that whenever the college curriculum lacked course work, students have sought speech training in other ways. By the mid-nineteenth century, literary societies and debating clubs sprang up, and advanced students gave declamations and orations at college chapel exercises, class-day functions, literary programs, and commencements. While some of this was integrated with regular classroom work, the larger portion of the performance activity was of a noncurricular nature.

Debate and forensic activities that emerged in the latter part of the nineteenth century did much to pave the way for speech as an academic discipline. Forensics appealed particularly to the bright, industrious, and ambitious students. Before the popular rise of basketball and football, intercollegiate forensic contests were in the spotlight on many college campuses. Railroads often chartered special trains to transport crowds of students to and from forensic events. Their victories were celebrated by playing bands, bonfires, and parades. Cash prizes for a single winner of a high school regional meet reached the $500 mark, and a state or regional college oratorical contest might enlist up to $1500 in cash prizes. Not unlike star athletes of our time, star orators and debaters enjoyed a hero worship, and forensics was looked upon as a richly rewarding educational experience for both speakers and listeners.

Two prevailing approaches to speaking existed in the nineteenth century: rhetoric and elocution. Rhetoric ultimately survived, for it had more to offer in academic circles. Yet, because of the poor quality of performance among preachers, lawyers, and politicians, elocution—which is mainly concerned with speech delivery—had wide popular appeal. Elocution thrived for four decades following the Civil War. Dozens of authors wrote books on the subject, setting forth systems of speech expression. Private schools of expression or elocution sprang up all over the country.

Elocution lessons were offered in many colleges, especially the privately endowed denominational schools. However, public performers trained by hard-core elocutionists seemed unnatural and mechanistic when they spoke, and their style of delivery seemed artificial.

In 1914, the modern speech profession was born when a group of 17 men from 13 different academic institutions broke away from the National Council of English Teachers and formed a separate National Association of Academic Teachers of Public Speaking. These men did not see how elocution could ever become a well-established academic discipline; they also believed the manifest destiny of the spoken word could not be fulfilled in the confines of college English departments. English teachers generally held the view that anyone able to write should be able to speak. The rebellious few insisted that skills required for speaking, though related to written communication, were very different. Even Aristotle had maintained that the "style of written prose is not the same as that of conventional speaking." One of the founders of the new speech association expressed the same thought somewhat differently: "A speech is not an essay on its hind legs."

At first, there were no speech departments, no speech majors, no graduate programs to offer a master's or doctor's degree. There were no speech texts to speak of; no one taught only speech-related subjects; there was no body of research and no cross fertilization of minds to provide the profession with an adequate basic philosophy to lend prestige in an academic environment. But by 1920, the newly formed Speech Department at Cornell University revived the teaching of classical rhetoric. Students in their courses read Aristotle's *Rhetoric*, Cicero's *De Oratore*, and Quintilian's *Institutes of Oratory*. Cornell graduates began taking posts at other colleges and universities and implanted the teaching of rhetoric in the curricula. Soon, graduate degrees were offered at several institutions, and professional growth occurred. Initially, almost all practical undergraduate training in speech departments dealt with some form of public address—debate, oratory, extempore speech. Graduate research focused on the study of rhetoric and public address, with some attention to debate.

The 1930s saw the advent of group-discussion courses in the

curricula of progressive speech departments. Group discussion, which emphasized cooperative, reflective thought, was held by many to be more meaningful than debate, which emphasized competitive argument. A controversy sprang up in certain quarters over the issue. However, the more reflective people of the discipline saw the two forms of communication as being compatible instead of divergent. They argued that group discussion preceded debate and that debate was essential in a free society when groups failed to reach a consensus and needed to present their differences to a third party for arbitration. They said that debate additionally played a vital role in the enactment of all kinds of legislation.

World War II may be considered the halfway point in the modern speech profession. Spectacular growth and change occurred after the conflict. Early in the war a National Defense Research Committee was formed by executive order, with James Conant, President of Harvard, as chairman. The central purpose of this committee was to set up guidelines for the training and education of 2 million servicemen from the army and navy doing special course work in nearly 300 colleges and universities across the nation. The guidelines the committee set up called for seven basic required courses. One of them was called communication whose purpose was to improve performance skills in both writing and speaking. This action seemed to stamp the image of communication on the public and academic mind. Within five years after the war many colleges made a basic course in speech a requirement for graduation. Almost concurrently, learning about human communication became vital in the fields of psychology, psychiatry, sociology, human relations, journalism, anthropology, and broadcasting. By 1949 the interdisciplinary National Society for the Study of Communication (since renamed International Communication Association) was founded; its chief purpose was to search for academic manpower to uncover hidden information concerning the problems and dimensions involved in human communication. Since so much of communication is related to speech processes, much of the realistic and dynamic leadership of the new society came from the speech communication field.

Americans as a whole became communication conscious during this time. Whenever a problem existed, it became fashionable to call it a communication problem, or attribute the problem's existence to a breakdown in communication. We began to hear much about communication barriers. Human relations training became fashionable at mid-century. The Harvard School of Business started to place heavy emphasis on the human relations aspects of business. Courses dealing with cases in human relations were developed in various colleges, and laboratory training groups, often called T-Groups, were inaugurated.

During the 1950s, speech departments grew, and many new courses were added. No longer did speech departments offer only performance-oriented, stand-up-and-talk courses; they now presented courses that dealt with the study of the history of public address and communication theory. Not all the graduate students in the field were doing historical research; some of them were engaged in experimentation. Because of their increased scope, numerous speech departments began to refer to themselves as speech-communication departments during the 1960s. These departments now were teaching about the entire communication spectrum, from dyadic to mass communication. Courses in small-group communication, business and organizational communication, intercultural communication, and public communication, as well as traditional rhetoric courses, were found in the college catalog. By 1970, even the Speech Association of America (the third-generation name for the National Association of Academic Teachers of Public Speaking) changed its name to Speech Communication Association.

Today there are more than 900 college speech departments graduating more than 5,000 speech majors annually, over 200 schools offering a master's degree, and more than 60, the doctorate. The growth and expansion of graduate study in speech communication has been spectacular. Graduate enrollments in speech communication at some schools are now among the largest within the university. We obviously are in another period of intense awareness of the importance of human communication. Protests and rebellions of the late 60s and early 70s, the so-called "generation gap," and the rapid pace of modern life have brought the dynamics of human communication front-stage center. The military is encouraging many of its officers to obtain advanced degrees in speech communication and human relations; business is searching for communication specialists; and social services want their personnel to be communication-trained.

The speech-communication profession, in the meantime, is heavily committed to exploring the nature of human communication. Scholars in the field are now examining such diverse subjects as nonverbal communication, interpersonal trust, campaign communication, source credibility, and situational effects on human interaction. Rhetorical scholars, who once only studied speakers and speeches, now address themselves to the rhetoric of song, cartoons, drama, pornography, and many other nonoratorical communication forms. The study of rhetoric in social movements also has become prominent, and courses such as Rhetoric of Black Americans, Rhetoric of American Feminism, and Rhetoric of War and Peace are found in the curricula of some departments. Even new journals have begun to appear; *Philosophy and Rhetoric*, for example, was first published in 1968. Many speech departments have been renamed communication departments.

This modern speech communication–education movement is an American phenomenon. And this is logically so. From the first we were embued with a spirit of freedom and human rights. The Bill of Rights added to the Constitution was careful to protect our right of free expression. Americans have truly shaped their destiny with their tongues. Discussion and debate, public opinion and voter education are essential to an open society. A closed society, by contrast, has no need of public dialogue.

The Nature of Speech Communication

The term *communication* has been defined at varying levels of specificity. In early usage, it referred to mechanical transmissions, such as telephone and telegraph systems. Still today, if you are in communications in the military, chances are that you are involved with mechanical signal-sending systems and not with public speaking or interpersonal relations. This usage of the term *communication* is tied to the field of operation. Within the confines of human communication, the term has been as broadly defined as "the discriminatory response of an organism to a stimulus."[3] This type of definition allows for almost any human behavior to fall into the category of communication and comes close to defining existence.

Etymologically, the word *communicate* is a transitive verb and has the Latin derivative of *communicare*, meaning "to share, to impart, or to commune." Although this type of definition tends to be rigid and artificially limited, we feel that a vital thought can come from the etymology of the word *communicate*, namely, that communication is an active process instead of a passive phenomenon. Communication doesn't just happen to us; we do it. If we actively engage in communication at some level of consciousness, we should be able, to some extent, to affect, change, or improve our communication habits. This thought is an essential assumption of this book: *With concerted effort and proper training we can improve ourselves as communicators.*

A second vital thought that comes from the etymological definition is that communication is the means to *community.* If communication is a sharing process, we may share both our ideas and ourselves. This thought is particularly meaningful when one emphasizes the infinitive *to commune.* It is safe to say that communication, used well, has the potential for an extremely positive effect upon human existence. It is through communication that we conduct our affairs, be they personal or affairs of state, and it is through communication that we achieve meaningful human relationships. Therefore, *through improved communication abilities we should be able to become more effective citizens and achieve a more satisfying personal and communal existence.*

A definitive definition of speech communication is not our quest, especially when we consider the dozens that others have offered previously. Our purpose is to explain speech communication in a way that will help clarify the concepts found in this book and make them meaningful. We, therefore, define speech communication as being *that process by which people in a given situation generate meaning through symbolic interaction.*

The first term, *process*, indicates a state of flux or motion, as distinguished from being stationary, quiescent, or fragmentary. It

---

[3] S. S. Stevens, "Introduction: A Definition of Communication," *Journal of the Acoustical Society of America* (November 1950), p. 689.

further includes the notion of change, even as the process is occurring. It says that people as communicators are continuously evolving; they are never totally the same from one day to the next and their relationships with other people are never identical from one encounter to another. Even while two people are communicating, changes are taking place. With each exchange of messages, the relationships of people engaged in communication change, grow, and develop. They now know more about each other and they have new inputs of thought. In addition to messages they receive from each other, people communicating constantly receive sensory stimuli from their environment as well as from themselves. They hear sounds, sense the general aura of the room, and feel the comfort and texture of the chairs on which they are sitting. Internally caused sensations also impinge on the situation. People may be aware of their heartbeats if they are anxious or of mild headache if they are tired. It is, therefore, apt to say that communication is *dynamic* in that it is a process involving a variety of forces and activities interacting over time. Also the process is multidimensional.

The second vital term is *people*. Since our definition limits us to human speech communication, we are obviously dealing with people as communicators. People are very complex beings, which means that they are also complex communication agents. They may have anxiety about speaking; they have unique life-experiences; their knowledge differs; their perceptions of themselves, other people, and the world in general are not identical; and they have differing degrees of motivation to communicate. These and many other factors make up the most complex communication machine in existence. Even a computer, complex as it is, will produce fixed results when programmed in a certain way. Unless some extreme form of brainwashing has taken place, people are far less predictable.

The third important term is *in a given situation*. All communication is situational. A speech may be given before dinner or after, on the Fourth of July or on Labor Day, at a high school commencement or at a fund-raising dinner, in a spacious hall or in a crowded room. In the same way, the place where face-to-face conversation occurs may exert considerable influence on the communication, be it in the parlor, a bar, the garden, a train, or the boss's office. Sometimes the most meaningful communication occurs while riding in an automobile. Every time you speak in class you are influenced by the size and shape of the room, the furnishings, the lighting and ventilation, impending examinations, and approaching holidays. It is easy to see that situational factors may strongly influence the nature and outcome of communication by either constraining or aiding the process. *When*, *where*, and *why*—time, place, and occasion—seem to be the critical situational dimensions.

The fourth vital term is *meaning*. Since meaning embodies ideas, it is, in the last analysis, what communication is about. In a sense, meaning is communication itself. If a person sends a message and no one assigns meaning to it, be it the meaning the speaker intended or an entirely different one, no interpersonal communication has occurred. Language and nonverbal symbols are external to people in that they have no intrinsic meaning, but the meanings that people assign to verbal and nonverbal symbols are internal. What symbols mean to people depends on their past experiences, the circumstances in which given symbols are encountered, and the sources from which they emanate.

The fifth term that needs consideration is *symbolic*. Symbols represent things. Although words are the most common symbols used in human communication, symbolic action is by no means limited to verbal communication. Facial expressions, insignias, or vocal rhythms all can be used symbolically. Words are uniquely human, since no other animal life has been able to invent verbal languages, but many animals are able to think symbolically. A dog, for example, sees his supper dish and starts barking for his food. The meaning is not inherent in the symbol itself, but symbolic meaning is learned by association; the dog has come to associate his supper dish with food. Likewise, people learn to associate the word *bed* with the object they commonly sleep in. Although one person may call to mind a water bed, another a foam rubber mattress, and, a young girl, a bed with a canopy, still such symbols refer to relatively concrete items and thus ordinarily mean about the same thing from one person to the next. Conversely, the words *idea* or *justice* suggest abstract concepts and almost never mean totally the same thing to different people. Our ability to symbolize makes interpersonal communication possible, problematic as it may be from time to time.

Finally, the concept of *interaction* suggests a circular response pattern. Both communication agents are involved in the interpretation of verbal and nonverbal message cues. This notion of interaction is by no means limited to conversations or small-group communication. Public speakers and their audiences interact also. The audience receives the speaker's message cues, assigns meanings to them, and reacts. Sometimes the reaction is definite—listeners may break into spontaneous applause or call out "hear, hear," thereby expressing strong approval—and at other times the feedback cues of the audience are much more subtle. Raised eyebrows, frequent shuffling of feet, shifts in posture, or smiles also contain messages. Even a cold and stony silence, assuming that the listeners are attending to the speech and are assigning meaning to its message, constitutes feedback for the speaker and illustrates the circular aspects of the communication process. Interaction occurs when two or more people maintain a shared frame of reference and it happens when there is a unit of behavior that links the parties of communication.

Although human communication is a process, our interpersonal relationships come in segments; we do not have continuous contact with anyone, including those closest to us. Thus, interpersonal communication takes on *many of the characteristics* of an act. Each encounter with another person has a beginning, a middle, and an end. Expressed differently, there is an introduction, a message, and a termination. Even in phatic communication, when we meet someone and say, "Hi, how are you," the three elements of an act are present. We make some initial contact with the person, either verbally or nonverbally; we send the essence of our message, which in this case is simply a demonstration of recognition and some degree of friendliness; and we terminate the encounter by moving on. Since we can decide how to introduce each encounter, how to order and encode the message, and how to terminate the encounter, choice seems to be intrinsic to interpersonal communication. The element of choice—or strategy—is a third underlying assumption of this book: We think *much can be learned about how to achieve effectiveness in interpersonal communication.*

Social Contexts

Intrapersonal Communication

Human communication occurs at various levels of social contexts. Our talks with ourselves constitute the most basic level—intrapersonal communication—which involves perception and processing of stimuli. A man mowing a lawn, a car rushing by, the roar of a freight train in the distance, the cardinals singing in the trees, the soft warm breeze with the fragrance of lilacs in bloom, the taste of chewing gum, the laughter of children playing next door, and the radio newscaster telling us about world events—all involve perception. This free flow of information reaches us through our senses, by what we see, taste, hear, smell, touch. We may be aware or unaware of the source of the sensory stimuli about us; nevertheless, the volume of sensory intake for one day is staggering. Some researchers contend the brain has the capacity to store one quadrillion bits of information in a lifetime. Memory has measureless value for storing information from which the individual can draw in his communicative endeavors.

At the same time, there are limitations to our recall abilities. For example, we have all had the experience of having the answer to a test question in our minds, but we could not draw it out and write it down. As soon as the exam was over, to our complete frustration, we could recall it clearly. For some people pressure seems to inhibit their ability to recall information; for others, shame, fear, or pain may have inhibitory functions. As a general rule, most of us can recall information that we got from multiple experiences better than that from a single encounter. If we have driven on a certain road repeatedly over a period of time, we can later in life recall that road better than one that we traveled only once. Intensity of experience seems to be another vital recall factor. One single, very intense experience may make an extremely memorable impact upon us. We may, for example, remember with great vividness the details of a scrape with death for years to come.

Another troublesome recall factor is the accuracy of information recalled. We have a tendency to forget certain details concerning an event, and at times we alter them slightly over a period of time. We may, for example, attach undue importance to one aspect, forget or de-emphasize other equally vital aspects, and thus distort what actually happened. In this manner two people may recall an event, only to have it seem that they are recalling two different events. It is apparent that our minds have phenomenal abilities to store information but that there can be problems attached to recall. The selective remembering we engage in greatly determines the frame of reference from which we communicate.

Inner speech, or intrapersonal communication, is more than just perception or the intake of information. It also involves processing the stimuli, or telling ourselves things about the information. Language seems to play a decisive role in our mental processes. We are constantly editorializing within ourselves about the information we take in. This is how we develop our self-concepts and our views of the world and of other people. Two people may have similar negative experiences regarding giving a speech, for example, and one person tells himself it is because he is an inferior individual and the other simply passes it off as a lack of training and thinks that he will doubtlessly master the art at some future time. We also form our prejudices and stereotypes through our inner speech. If we encounter three or four people from the same school, for example, and they all are "party" people, we often are led to conclude that their school is a "party school." The entire process of encoding messages in interpersonal communication is involved with perception, information recall, and thinking about the information. Intrapersonal communication always precedes, and is fundamental to, interpersonal communication. The role of language in intrapersonal communication will be discussed somewhat further under the subject of Language.

Interpersonal Communication

At all other levels of communication the speaker is reaching out to share thoughts and feelings with other people. Interpersonal communication is a term often used to refer to two-person or small-group communication—in other words, those instances of communication where an exchange of messages takes place, or where a person alternates rapidly in the roles of sender and receiver. We prefer to use the term in a broader and more basic sense. We think that *interpersonal* is the complementary term of *intrapersonal*; in a geometric sense, interpersonal coupled with intrapersonal completes the communication spectrum (see Figure 1). Interpersonal communication refers to the talks we have with other people, regardless of the form of these communications.

The terms *intrapersonal* and *interpersonal communication* can be compared to commerce. Intrastate commerce is that trading which takes place inside the boundaries of a given state; interstate commerce involves the sending and the reception of goods from one state to another. It is not necessarily limited to one state;

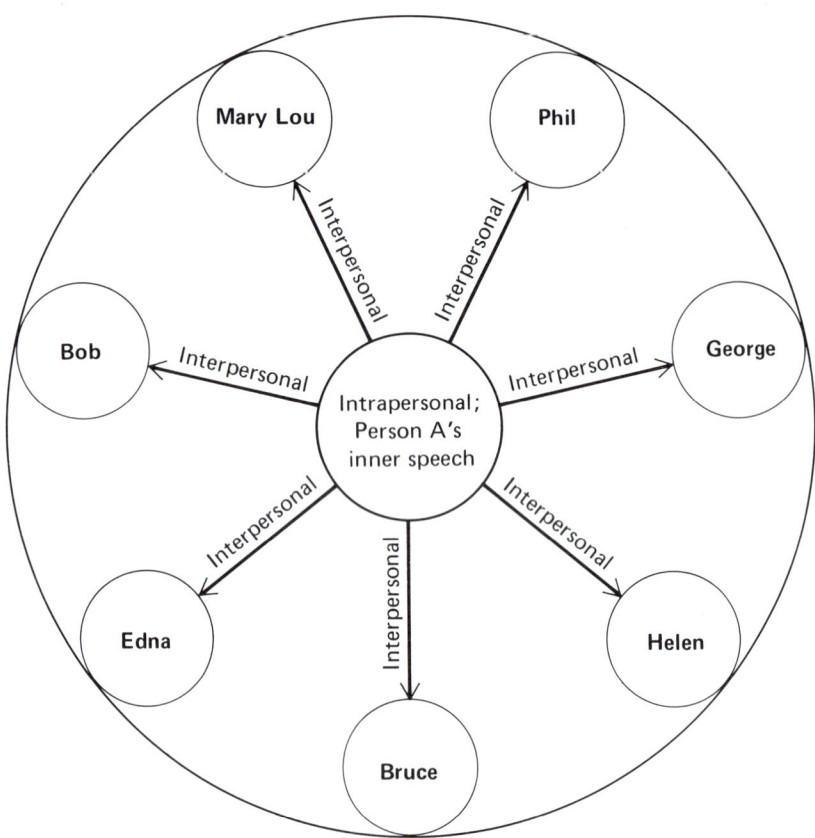

Figure 1—Interpersonal Communication

the same product may be sent to twenty states simultaneously. Not always is there an exchange of goods in interstate commerce; one state may do all the sending and another state do all the receiving. Dialogue, implying a definite communication exchange, is interpersonal communication, but not all interpersonal communication is dialogical. A public speech to an audience of a thousand people, though quite impersonal, is between people. Feedback, of course, is not as direct or as pronounced in most such instances as it is in two-person conversation. Interpersonal communication, then, is a process of building communication bridges between people. The diagram in Figure 1 illustrates this thought. Person A may speak with each person in the diagram individually or he may do so collectively. In other words, the communication arrows may move out to one person at a time, or they may all move out at once.

In its simplest form, interpersonal communication consists of *dyadic* situations—two persons engaged in conversation or one person interviewing another. Dialogue occurs at this level when the communicators genuinely interact, with each person listening to the other and responding to him openly. The second social level of interpersonal communication occurs when an individual participates in a *small-group discussion*. Small groups are similar to dyads in that people talk directly to each other, but the social context is different, for the increased number of people participating constrains the communication flow. We seldom are as open in expressing our feelings in small groups as we are in a private two-person conversation. We move to the next level of interpersonal communication when one person speaks to a group of people. At that point we have a speaker-audience situation, regardless of the number of people in the audience, and direct communication exchange is difficult. Although interaction may occur in a forum period after the presentation, intense interaction is hard to achieve because members of the audience usually have only limited chances to ask questions or reply to the speaker's points. Moreover, listeners tend to ask questions, with the speaker giving answers. Seldom is there much of an *exchange* of ideas. Although we touch briefly on participating in group discussion, our focus in this book will be upon interpersonal speech communication in the form of *speaking to groups*.

A Model of
Interpersonal Communication

Models are systematic representations of objects or events. They help us to picture and understand things better than we normally would from verbal description, which is why people commonly develop them. An architect rarely designs an important edifice without first building a model of his conception. Perhaps your first exposure was when you built a model airplane. Sometimes, too, we draw models. Communication scholars tend to do this, because it is difficult to develop a working model of communication that is more meaningful than a sketch on paper. Speech scientists have, of course, developed effective working models of the production of human speech, but that is a physical process rather than a mental one.

If, indeed, communication is a process, we must at some point stop the process in order to draw a model of it. It has been compared to a motion picture, which is always moving, always changing. We can stop the projector and focus upon a still shot of one particular frame, but if we do this we no longer have a motion picture. At the same time, close inspection of several still frames might well give us considerable insight into how motion pictures function. The model we present (see Figure 2) is a still frame of interpersonal speech communication. Moreover, it will be limited to the four basic dimensions of the process. The next part of this book is geared toward an extensive elaboration of each of the dimensions, and we hope at the close of that section our relatively simple model will have become far more sophisticated and complete, giving you insight into the process in some depth.

Regardless of how the model is drawn, an interpersonal speech communication model must include four basic elements: people as communicators, circumstances of the communication, message content, and message cues. These four factors are involved at all times when people talk to one another. These factors are not separate from one another but are integrated; they interact with each other like atoms setting off a chain reaction with impact which cannot be precisely measured, predicted, or repeated, but

A Starting Point

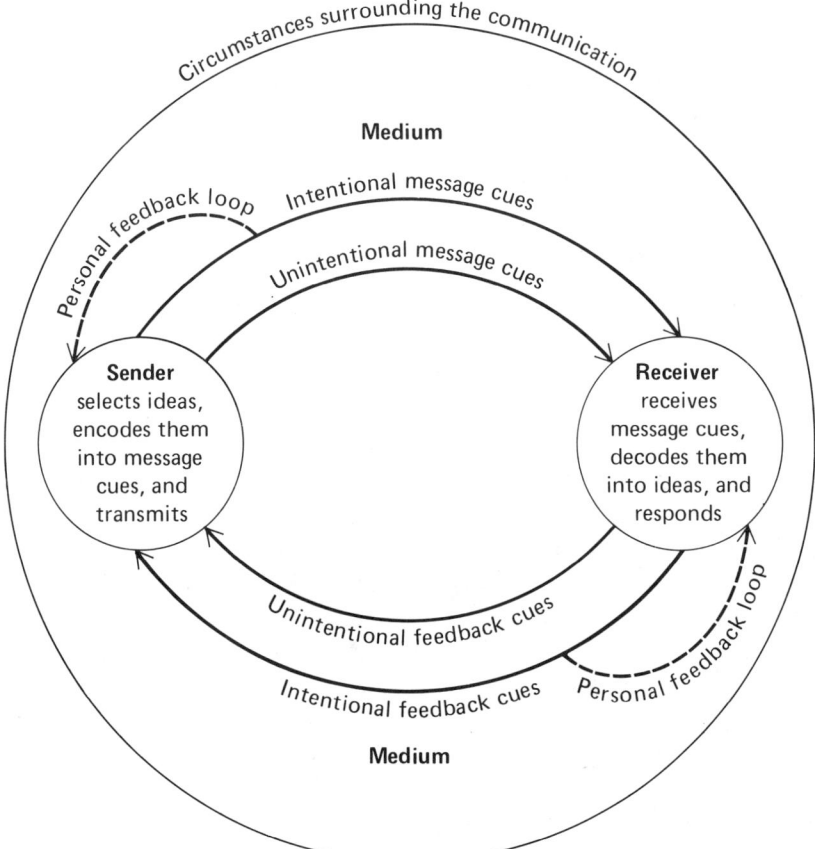

Figure 2—Interpersonal Communication Model

only approximated. This model, then, has the same disadvantage that all paper communication models do: It is static. It attempts simply to depict the factors that act upon each other when interpersonal communication takes place.

Communicators

Communication evolves around people. You and I as communicators are the most basic and important aspects of any communication model. The following diagram (Figure 3) represents a person

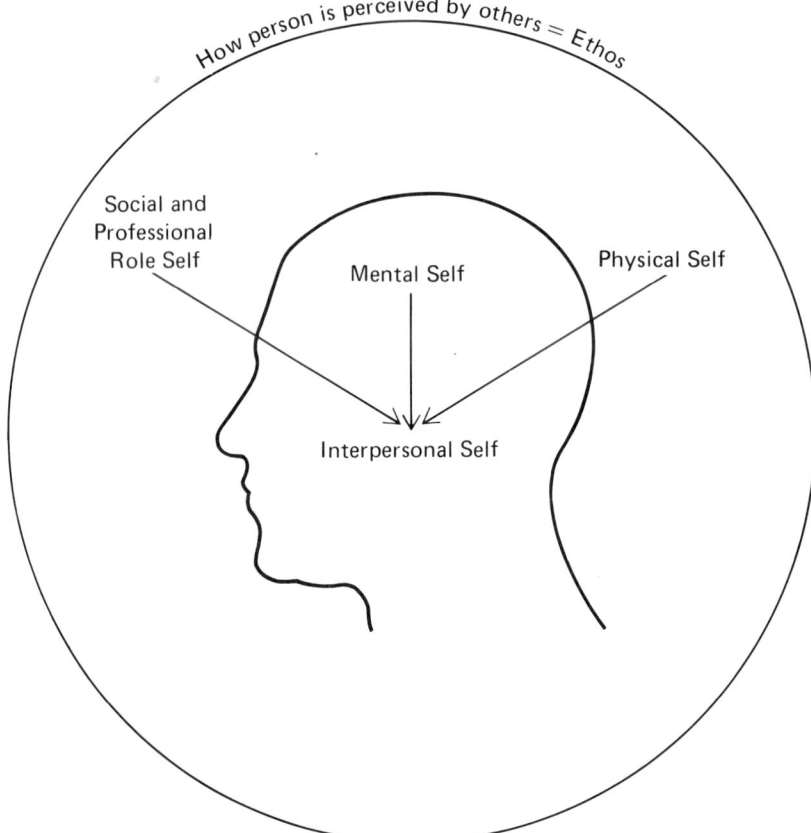

Figure 3—People as Communicators

as a communication agent. It is predicated on the notion that several different kinds of selves go into the makeup of a person's *interpersonal self*, and that each of these selves plays a role in communication and has a potential affect upon it. Fundamentally, each of us has two kinds of selves, mental and physical, which are closely related in that they tend to affect each other. How we feel physically affects our mental outlook, and our mental dispositions can influence our physical well-being. Yet, in a sense, we have another self, our role self. We have jobs, play professional and social roles, and have group memberships and allegiances. These professional and social factors not only strongly influence how we are perceived by others and what relationships we have with others, but they also tend to influence how we feel about ourselves and how we view the outside world. So we see that our mental self, our physical self, and our social and professional selves determine how we function as communication agents. They provide us with the abilities to perceive and decode messages, to reason and to emote, to relate with others, and to communicate with them.

People, of course, function as both senders and receivers of messages. The same factors constrain them in each case. Their knowledge, their needs and wants, their anxieties, their self-perceptions, and so forth, are constantly interacting with the messages they send and receive. Of course, our communication skills are two-fold. As senders of messages we need the ability to speak well and as receivers we need the complementary skill of listening, both of which are vital to the communication process.

Finally, the image we project to others determines our credibility as communicators. The Greeks used the term *ethos* to designate the persuasive effect of the personal character of the speaker. Although ethos is said to refer to the speaker's *personal persuasiveness*, in reality a speaker possesses ethos only as it is perceived through the eyes of others. A public speaker, for example, may be a genuine authority on his subject, but if his audience fails to perceive his expertise it will not contribute to his ethos. At the same time, a person may have the very best intentions toward his auditors, but if the audience does not perceive him as a man of good will his image may not be a favorable one in that rhetorical setting. Because of this factor, the diagram of people as communicators is encompassed by the statement, *How a person is perceived by others = ethos*. Message cues a listener receives from a speaker will always be interpreted and modified in terms of his perception of the sender. The potential impact of such modification is great.

Circumstances

Shakespeare dramatically demonstrated the impact situational atmosphere may have upon communication. Note a scene in *Hamlet*. It is near midnight. [In the darkness of the platform] Hamlet says,

"The air bites shrewdly; it is very cold." Horatio responds, "It is a nipping and an eager air." These lines create the proper environment for Hamlet's ghost to appear.

Time, place, and occasion are circumstances that bind every

> *Time*: In relation to clock and calender
> In relation to the subject of the communication
> In relation to the personal relationships of the communicators
> In relation to world events
>
> *Place*: In terms of locale
> In terms of the meeting facility
> In terms of the proximity of the communicators
>
> *Occasion*: In terms of the purpose of the meeting
> In terms of the rules and customs of the event

communication, as shown in the table. They are, in effect, the cocoon in which the communicators operate.

Message Preparation: Thought and Its Form

The preparation of a message involves thought and its form. This is the encoding process in the communication model. Messages have two kinds of content: logical and emotional (see Figure 4). We cannot draw a clear line between what is logical and what is emotional; moreover, what is essentially emotional will vary from one person to another. Yet cognition is more important at some moments and attitudes and feelings at others. Logical materials essentially consist of factual information and reasoned statements

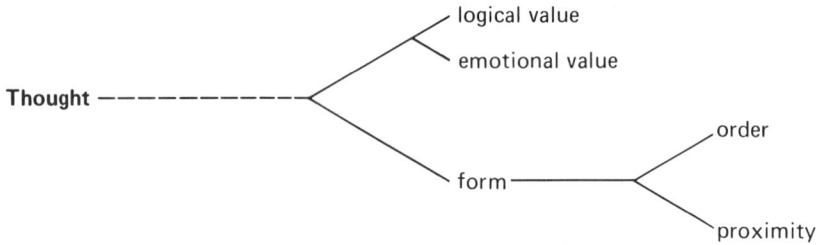

Figure 4—Message Content

which seek to emphasize rationality. Emotional materials emphasize feelings, which may range from very positive to very negative, from love to hate. Aristotle in his *Rhetoric* listed three kinds of proofs: logos, pathos, and ethos. On the assumption that ethos is essentially a speaker-oriented dimension instead of a message factor, and that any *ethical proof* found in a speech can be labeled as either logical or emotional, we think it reasonable to limit message content to logic and emotion. In preparing a message a speaker must first find or uncover the best available information, select the information he wants to use in his message (which means selecting ideas and giving them the most suitable blend of logical and emotional value), and arrange the materials in terms of his purpose.

Thought always has some kind of form, although sometimes there seems to be no discernible pattern. One statement must precede another; a phrase must be placed first, last, or in the middle of a statement. Whenever a speaker arranges ideas and statements purposefully, we can say that he has *strategically designed* his message. The order of thought may be so powerful that it can control the effect of the message. What we say first may so overpower the listener that what we say later may not even be heard. If a doctor tells a patient that he may have leukemia but that there still is a chance it may be something else, there is a good possibility the patient will not listen beyond the word *leukemia*. The notions of primacy and recency—which ideas to put first and which last—has been the subject of a good deal of research. The results are conflicting, but people are sure that it makes a difference. Another aspect of arrangement is the proximity of ideas. Ideas that are expressed closely together tend to be associated. This has always been a favorite device of propagandists who have tended to express the subject of their attack in proximity with an ideology, or an ism, certain to be unpopular with the audience.

Message Presentation:
Verbal and Nonverbal Cues

Our raw ideas do not constitute interpersonal messages. They must be translated into verbal and/or nonverbal cues. Usually verbal and nonverbal cues occur simultaneously and complement (or supplement or contradict) each other. Messages can, of course, be sent entirely without spoken words, as in the case of smoke signals. It is also possible for verbal and nonverbal cues to imply contradictory messages. Someone may say, for example, that he is glad to be present somewhere and have virtually all his bodily cues contradict that statement. A few years ago Jerry Lewis, hosting the *Tonight* show in the absence of Johnny Carson, observed that while flying to New York he had used the rest room over Mississippi, thereby fulfilling a long-standing ambition. Governor John Bell of Mississippi took offence at this remark and demanded that the National Broadcasting Company apologize. Lewis went back on the air and said, "We did a joke which I suspect, in reflecting, wasn't terribly funny and we did offend some of our friends in Mississippi. I openly, publicly and humbly apologize. That certainly was not my intention . . . to offend." The oral apology seemed adequate enough. However, the next day a Hattiesburg, Mississippi, television station announced that it was cancelling the *Tonight* show. "We feel that the oral part of his apology last night would have been acceptable," Marvin Reuben, the station's general manager, explained, "had Mr. Lewis not cast doubt on his sincerity by a careless gesture at the end of his remarks."[4] Our communication model in Figure 2 shows a double track for messages. One track consists of intentional cues and the other of unintentional cues. Verbal cues—except for a rare slip of the tongue—run on the intentional track, whereas nonverbal cues run freely on both the intentional and unintentional tracks. Most of our vocal inflections, for example, we intend; however, an anxious quiver in our voices is certainly unintentional. In some cases, unintentional cues may be so minimal that they play virtually no role at all; but in other instances, the unintentional cues may be so strong that they completely negate the speaker's intent or else virtually constitute the messages the listener receives. Not that the listener's feedback cues also run on double tracks. Much of our feedback is intentional, but some of it certainly is unintentional. For example, we sometimes yawn even though we are vitally interested in what the speaker is saying.

---

[4] Reported in the *Kansas City Star* (March 26, 1969).

A Starting Point

Verbal messages require a common language code (see Figure 5). Quite obviously, if the sender speaks French and the receiver does not, a communication problem exists. The receiver, in this case, may assign meanings to what he hears the sender say, but the likelihood is great that his meanings and those intended by the speaker will not be congruent. The same problem may exist in a more subtle manner. Both communication agents may speak English, but the speaker may use terminology or expressions that are not common to the experiences of the listener. The Black culture, for example, has generated modes of speech that are unfamiliar to white listeners.

Verbal cues
- common language
- grammar
- style
  - clarity
  - appropriateness
  - impressiveness

Nonverbal cues
- smell
- visual
- auditory
- tactile
- taste

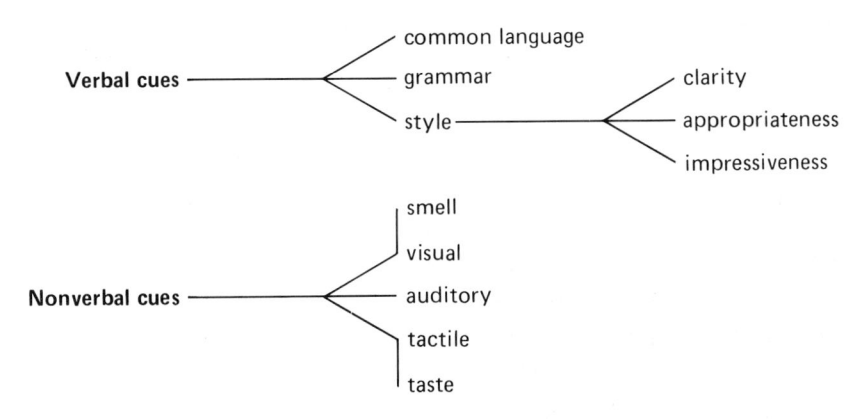

Figure 5—Message Cues

Nonverbal message cues essentially are visual, auditory, and tactile, although taste and smell certainly may be factors. The scent of perfume has assuredly been a factor in romance for years. Our facial expressions, the quiver in our voice, the shuffling of our feet, the way we dress, and dozens of other physical factors contain message cues. The speaker's posture quite often tells a person a great deal about his attitude. At the same time, there are moments when a simple touch of the hand may provide more meaning and send a clearer message than will ten minutes' worth of speech.

Interpersonal communication is an interactive process. Person A sends out message cues which are perceived by Person B, who assigns meanings to them. Notice that although messages are sent, *meanings*, as such, cannot be transferred from one person to another. Meanings are always assigned to message cues in terms of a receiver's frame of reference, mainly his past experiences and what he has told himself about those experiences. When a person assigns meaning to a message he is *responding* to message cues. Response is the key to communication, and whenever a receiver's response is at least reasonably congruent with the meaning the sender intended, communication is effective. One way of checking the degree of congruency in communication is by observing the *feedback* of the receiver. If Bill Jones and Henry Brown, two friends, are talking, Bill may say that he feels absolutely rotten. Henry will respond by calling to mind how he has felt when he felt absolutely rotten. He may have had a bad cold, a stomach upset, or perhaps he was emotionally distressed. He may simply select the worst he ever felt and assume that is how Bill must feel. On the other hand, he may be the type of person who does not want to make hasty generalizations and engage Bill in dialogue. "What do you mean, Bill? Are you emotionally upset or do you feel ill physically?" Bill may place a hand to his head and say, "I have a very bad sinus headache." Henry, who is a chronic sufferer of sinus conditions, responds, "Oh! I know exactly how you must feel," being fully certain that he does. In this interaction between Bill and Henry, feedback, both visual and oral, played a vital role in determining the ultimate meaning of Bill's message.

This same process occurs, in some form, when a single person is addressing a group of people. All audiences send feedback to the speaker: They may applaud; call out, "No, no"; smile; stamp their feet; or sit in stony silence. The effectiveness of the communication interaction depends, at least partially, upon how accurately the speaker perceives and assigns meaning to the feedback he gets from his listeners.

Feedback has a second vital dimension. When our mythical Bill Jones speaks, he hears himself say that he feels rotten, and he will react to himself. He may now think that he feels even worse than he did earlier. The public speaker also is aware of this internal feedback loop. He may hear that his voice seems unclear and clear his throat. He may realize that a statement he just made may seem confusing or contradictory and try to elaborate on it. He may feel that he used words in expressing an idea that he didn't mean to use and will repeat the same thought using different words. He may also like what he hears himself say, feel successful, and have increased confidence. The speaker experiences a constant *inner speech* in which he checks words he uses with the ideas he is trying to present. This internal feedback loop can be as vital to success in interpersonal communication as external feedback from listeners.

Media

A final dimension of an interpersonal communication model is the *medium* of transfer. A person may choose one of three basic options for sending interpersonal messages (these options, of course, may be used simultaneously): the spoken word, the written word, or nonverbal signs and symbols. The spoken word, involving vocalization, employs sound waves as the medium of transmission. The sound medium may be used with or without electronic assistance. In most face-to-face speaking situations no electronic devices are used; microphones, however, may be practical when addressing audiences. Radio, television, and the telephone can be used to transmit the human voice. Electronic recordings may serve the purpose in some instances. At the same time, a memo or a personal letter are interpersonal communications. The nonverbal medium may consist of a simple wave of the hand, the elaborate sign language of the deaf, the intricate sounds of a telegraph, or a handshake and an embrace. Oftentimes dress and personal appearance will comprise a powerful message. Signal corps flags or smoke signals are good examples of nonverbal means of communication.

Selecting the right medium of communication can often be a critical factor. For example, should one discuss a matter personally with someone or should one write a memo or a formal letter? If the decision is to speak personally, should it be done face-to-face or over the telephone? Since this book is concerned with interpersonal *speech* communication with a particular focus on a single person addressing a group of people, we will not be directly concerned with media beyond this point. We will make a brief examination of some basic differences between speech and writing under the subject of Language; nonverbal elements will be examined as they relate to Message Cues; and signs and symbols will receive some attention under Circumstances.

The Need for Responsible Communication

The need for responsible communication has never been so great. Our pressure-packed contemporary society contains elements and trends which greatly complicate our communication efforts. Consider, first of all, the fantastic knowledge explosion of our time. Human knowledge has been escalating at a frantic rate in the past few decades. Unfortunately, as the volume of knowledge increases, the ratio of ignorance increases proportionately. We know much more now than our ancestors did, yet we know much less about what there is to know. Since communication and knowledge are interdependent, the risks of not talking from a common core of experience and interests are increased. The greater our tendency to become specialists in terms of knowledge, the less our chances of speaking from a similar frame of reference.

Population is another explosion that complicates our communication efforts. When there are large numbers of people they are frequently bumping into each other and getting into each other's hair. Our cities and suburbs grow more crowded and people contact each other with all kinds of clutter, noises, smells, movements, and territorial claims. These crowded conditions tend not to produce neighborliness but loneliness and antisocial attitudes. No wonder youth groups emerge to form their own special kinds of polarized communities made up of peers and thereby harden the so-called generation gap.

The crime rate keeps exploding also. More people are ill from drugs and alcohol. A steady stream of violence is fed us by the press, radio, television, and film. Violence in the form of fists, knives, guns, and arson is common. So are vulgarity, profanity, and abrasive language. Physical violence and verbal violence often complement each other and act as circular stimuli. The result is communication breakdowns we never dreamed of a generation ago. Friendly discussions often turn into bitter personal arguments that wind up in violence. More than half of our homicides are committed not by thugs and criminals but by friends, relatives, and acquaintances who overreact to anger and intense individualism.

Technological developments have produced an enormous output of machines, electronic devices, and computers creating an environment which has a dehumanizing effect upon human beings. If a company's billing system goes awry, the victim's letters of complaint may be answered by a computer, which gives little satisfaction and causes much frustration and irritation.

When one considers these factors, along with the great pollution problems of dirt, chemicals, odors, and noise, as well as the great racial problems that linger with us, the call for responsibility in communication is clear.

Many established professions are alert to matters of ethics. Law, medicine, engineering, and journalism have their codes of ethics. Guidelines for responsible and ethical conduct are reflected in oaths of all sorts when people take public office, enter armed service, join the police force, become naturalized citizens, or join a secret fraternity. But the average communicator is on his own with only his conscience to guide him. He can incite a riot, assassinate a character, indulge in plagiarism, engage in brinksmanship or slander, and attempt all manner of fraud. Little tricks and petty practices such as quoting a passage out of context, padding an argument with a fictional authority or fact, or plagiarizing someone else's materials are readily available to everyone.

Responsible speech communication, the lifeline of a free society, requires the joint effort of speaker and listener. Much of the following discussion, therefore, applies to both phases of speech communication. We include it at this point to emphasize that the listener has at least as great a responsibility as the speaker. Responsible listening is integral to wise decision-making. It is just as essential for the listener to look for and detect the truth as it is for the speaker to be free to speak it.

Hitler once cynically observed, "It is in their listening that people are the most vulnerable." This statement by history's greatest demagogue highlights the importance of alert and discriminating listening. Too many of us, even the informed and the educated, gullibly accept the utterances of unscrupulous demagogues, lobbyists, radio and television advertisers, and supersalesmen. We either lack the ability to be discriminating or else are too apathetic or unsuspecting to expend the effort. Wendell Johnson pinpoints the problem: "As speakers, men have become schooled in the arts of persuasion; and without the counter-art of listening a man can be persuaded . . . to eat foods that ruin his liver, to abstain from killing flies, to vote away his right to vote, and to murder his fellows in the name of righteousness. The art of listening holds for us the desperate hope of withstanding the spreading ravages of commercial, nationalistic, and ideological persuasion."[5]

Responsible citizens must be willing to accept the basic responsibilities of communication if they want their society to remain free. When people shrink from these duties, demagoguery and totalitarianism make insidious gains. In order to perpetuate our democratic way of life, we should accept the following responsibilities:

Uphold the Right to Speak

Our precious right of free speech is based upon the First Amendment to the Constitution: "Congress shall make no law . . . abridging the freedom of speech. . . ." The framers of our government believed man to be endowed with the inalienable rights of life, liberty, and the pursuit of happiness, not the least of which was the right to formulate and express opinions freely. They wished the government to permit and even encourage dissemination of public opinion without threat of reprisal. This condition is essential for a democratic government to flourish. It is platitudinous to say that our government is government by talk, but it is still true. The ablest and wisest decisions are usually made after intensive discussion of issues. "Men are never so likely to settle a question right," wrote Macaulay, "as when they discuss it freely." It is the freely expressed ideas of able thinkers that produce laws for the common welfare. John Stuart Mill in his essay *On Liberty* succinctly expressed the need for free speech: ". . . the peculiar evil of silencing the expression of an opinion is that it is robbing the human race; posterity as well as the existing generation; those

---

[5] Wendell Johnson, "Do You Know How to Listen?" *ETC*, 12 (1949), p. 3.

who dissent from the opinion, still more than those who hold it. If the opinion is right, they are deprived of the opportunity of exchanging error for truth: if wrong, they lose, what is almost as great a benefit, the clearer perception and livelier impression of truth, produced by its collision with error."

It is our responsibility as citizens to uphold the right of everyone to air his views. We must guard our sacred trust of freedom of speech zealously by always giving people a fair hearing, and a good place to begin this practice is in your classroom. Show a proper respect for ideas. Don't close your mind to controversial issues, but encourage classmates to express their thoughts fully, so long as their speech is in good taste. The critical listener must stand as guardian of wise thought and action, which, as Macaulay so wisely observed, are most often arrived at when people speak their minds freely and openly.

Study All Sides of a Controversial Question

Enlightened public opinion is the dynamo of a republic. We make our best decisions when we understand the question at hand most fully, and a proper study of a controversial issue requires the probing of all sides of the question. Cicero, as a famous Roman trial lawyer, assiduously studied the other side of his cases. Aristotle listed this as one of his four purposes of rhetoric. The more diligently speakers and listeners study the other aspects of a question, the better will they understand their own. If we know only our side, we frequently know little of that. We will make far more rational decisions if we put aside our biases and try to understand the other person's point of view, if we suspend judgment until we understand the question fully. Indeed, the best way to acquire proper understanding is by listening to speakers who present points of view not in accord with ours. As Milton said in his *Areopagitica*, the truth is to be discovered through the conflict of differing ideas. A truly critical listener will try to find arguments in their most plausible form, and that means hearing them from persons who actually believe them. In class as well as out, we cannot be termed responsible, effective citizens unless we demonstrate a willingness to study and listen to all points of view. Rational choices are made by sober and critical reflection, not by long-standing biases.

Demand High Ethical Standards

Just as in other phases of life, the problem of ethics also presents itself in speech communication. As potential speakers and listeners, sooner or later we all will have to make ethical decisions. When this happens, we should be prepared to act with responsibility. To be able to do so, we must find the best available answer to the question: What are the ethics of speech in a free society?

Machiavelli in *The Prince* and Hitler in *Mein Kampf* were interested *only* in getting results, not in what is morally justifiable. No *responsible* speaker can use this approach; what works must be limited by what is ethical or there is no such thing as a meaningful public dialogue. Yet it is difficult to list the ethical obligations of a speaker in chronological order. Ethical concepts are so relative to situations that they almost defy such identification. Nonetheless, it is helpful to try to isolate as many unethical practices as possible.

Historically there have been two primary approaches to judging the ethics of speech: the *end* sought by the speaker and the *methods* used by the speaker. Both approaches have limitations. If we are to use the end of the persuader as our guide, who is to answer the question whether or not the end is justifiable? And if we set apart certain methods as inherently unethical, then are we never justified in using them—for instance, in telling a white lie?

Despite these problems, we must try to differentiate between unethical and ethical practices and set down relatively useful criteria for judging ethics in speech communication. The present authors choose to present a code concerning the ethical responsibility of a speaker prepared by an honors class in Fundamentals of Speech at the University of Kansas. Each semester one author divides his class into committees which prepare and submit to the class a resolution concerning ethics in speech communication. The class hears these committee reports and then tries to adopt a code which they will use as an ethical guideline for classroom presentations as well as for speech in society. One class adopted the following resolution:

> Whereas, in modern society, due to technological developments in the field of communication, speech has become one of the major means of disseminating ideas, and

A Starting Point

Whereas, the opinions of people are influenced heavily by the words of public speakers, and

Whereas, all communication presupposes a premise of ethical participation, and

Whereas, the listeners cannot always have at hand the facts necessary to distinguish distorted or biased materials, and

Whereas, our society is founded upon the vital dignity of each individual in it, and

Whereas, a free and open society relies upon a sincere, meaningful, and responsible public dialogue in its decision-making process,

BE IT RESOLVED that the speaker should recognize his ethical responsibilities and conduct himself accordingly, these responsibilities being as follows:

1. That he examine his motives to assure that they are not harmful to others or to society;

2. That the idea he wishes to promote likewise not be harmful to others or to society, that he be responsible for the consequences of his idea, and that he recognize the limitations of his own perception;

3. That he seek a productive end (such as sharing valid information, helping to solve common problems, and helping to lift the spirits of others), and not merely to manipulate and exploit his listeners;

4. That he use emotional appeals to support his point only if the appeals have a logical basis;

5. That he truly have something worthwhile to say and have convictions of his own, and not speak glibly without thought or merely parrot the ideas of others;

6. That he avoid methods which would distort, falsify, or misrepresent the truth, or would personally devaluate his opposition instead of his opposition's arguments, or would make himself (the speaker) appear as an authority on the subject when in reality he is not, or would attempt to conceal his motives or the interests he represents;

7. That in all his communicative efforts—both public and private—he employ only methods which never reject or attack the value of human beings but instead seek to enhance the human personality.

BE IT FURTHER RESOLVED that both speakers and listeners must assume responsibility for ethics in communication. Since most people sooner or later find themselves in both roles, everyone has the obligation to develop definite standards. Ethics are usually lowest when people have no concept of what they should be. But if the majority of people have formulated ethical principles and have the courage to proclaim them and seek adherence to them by people engaged in communication, then the ethical level can be raised.

Listeners, probably more than speakers, determine ethical standards of speech communication in a free society. Listeners have freedom of choice and can accept or reject both the speaker's message and his practices. This freedom brings with it the responsibility of independent thinking. Too often people find it easier to let others make their decisions for them, often because of apathy and sometimes because they are afraid to stand alone. They fear being isolated and do not have the strength to be free. Such fear of freedom is a dangerous threat to democracy.

The enlightened listener who through his critical faculties is able to detect unethical practices or specious reasoning has a moral obligation to speak out and expose it. Silence is not always golden; it can be gross irresponsibility. As one author states it, "Speaking out against what one thinks wrong is more than a citizen's privilege in a free society, it is his bounden duty."[6]

Ethics of communication should begin in the classroom. As a speaker you will have the obligation to speak ethically, and as a listener you should expect your classmates to observe ethical principles. If a speaker is distorting facts or plagiarizing materials, you should make this known. As a responsible listener outside of the classroom you need to be even more vigorous in demanding high ethical standards. The demagogues history has known have been successful chiefly because they had undiscriminating and apathetic listeners.

---

[6] Theodore Clevenger, Jr., "The Teacher of Speech and Freedom of Speech," *Speech Teacher* (March 1956), pp. 91–101.

part two two two two two two two two two
four integral dimensions

dimension one
people as communicators

Speech communication finds its being in people. This is the most obvious yet the least predictable dimension in the communication process. At each end of the human communication poles, for each speaker and each listener, there is a mind, turbulent and dynamic, ready to take off in any direction. And what is the makeup of that mind? Mark Twain said it is something nobody knows except the one who has it. The psychic self, psychiatrists say, is a phenomenon that a person himself cannot really fathom. We all carry within us a complex set of wants, desires, motives, fears, hopes, and beliefs. When speaker and listener both feel and fumble for some kind of inner equilibrium there can be serious interference with communication. Like so many amoebas, people withdraw from one another or are attracted to one another, as if to protect or satisfy the social self which is always reaching for a kind of equilibrium. Thus, words alone spoken in a complex environment by a complex person to a complex listener make genuine interpersonal communication uncertain. Eric Fromm says, "In life's situations, anyone who judges a person solely by what he says is hopeless." If we confine our perceptions to a person's outward manifestations in speech communication, we may fail sadly to come to grips with a deeper reality of his message.

In an ultimate sense, our world is made up of human creatures somewhat like ourselves. Here lies, on the one hand, our salvation, but on the other, our greatest threat to life and happiness. People need each other. No one can be entirely a self-made person. We are all, in a sense, our brother's keeper. Even the simple act of putting on a coat involves hundreds of people, some from far-off lands, who help grow the wool, others who design, weave, tailor, and manufacture the coat. We are what we are largely because of what we have heard other people say about us, how they have reacted to us, and what they have done for us. We may, happily, discover that we are what we are largely because others have practiced being our brother's keeper on us. At the same time, when our interpersonal relationships break down and we develop a feeling of alienation, our lives become filled with turmoil and unhappiness. The social equilibrium we are reaching for has become upset. From this we can see how vital effective interpersonal communication is to each and every one of us. Ordinarily, when our interpersonal communication is healthy our intrapersonal communication is healthy also. The central purpose of this chapter, then, is to help you gain insights about people as communicators—both as speakers and as listeners.

People Are Symbolizers

People symbolize their experiences. These symbols may take different forms: perhaps an insignia, a badge, a particular color, a flag, or a word. The meaning of the symbol cannot be determined from analyzing the symbol itself; it has meaning only as it calls to mind an object, event, relationship, or idea. People have used this symbolizing power to invent verbal languages. As a result, how effectively we use and manipulate language greatly determines how we think, live, and communicate. Language was our introduction to the world of symbols. In early childhood, it acted as an antenna by which we made contact with people around us and became aware of being. At first, as infants, we communicated by means of action—kicking, reaching, squirming, and batting our arms about—and by various types of vocalizations—crying, screaming, cooing, and so forth. After a year or so, we learned to associate a few sounds with objects. Then we discovered a kind of *selfhood* by means of a single word—our name. At first, the words we learned to use most were *I*, *me*, and *mine*. This was self-expression on an elemental level. Soon, other dimensions of self came into being: a biological self, a social self, and a rational self. By means of language, these dimensions expanded and grew to more advanced levels of maturity with their accompanying complexities of wants, desires, hungers, and emotions that are related to a normal, well-ordered personality.

Ultimately, language provided the key to learning, thinking, planning; it provided us with a tool for developing a sense of values and for making choices and judgments; it also provided us with a means of self-expression. All this probably occurred without our realizing how fortunate we were to be able to use language to relate to our environment. Most of our language experience was a part of routine living, like eating or sleeping. Parents, teachers, and playmates in various ways gave guidance and training in rudiments of language uses such as pronunciation, articulation, and simple grammar. Special guidance entered the picture when at school our attention was directed toward language as a communication tool for reading, writing, speaking, and listening.

As adults we use language in many ways: for conversation, memos, scientific reports, sportscasts, and many other purposes. But language serves each of us in a dual function: It is a tool for communication, and, through speech, a means of self-expression. The integration of these two functions often energizes the mind and generates a sense of self-discovery and personal growth.

Words Have Different Meanings
to Different People

People look at things from different experiences, from different frames of reference. They see the world not as it is, but as *they are*. Their opinions, interests, motives, and attitudes differ from those of their neighbors. The total of their experience, thinking, and feeling gives them unique abilities to conceive and grasp an idea. No two people witnessing the same automobile accident will give identical testimony about it. A mountain means different things to a ski enthusiast, a lumberman, an artist, and a miner. The four-year-old boy, when asked where the sun sets, may reply with assurance, "On the highway." Ask twenty adults to define the word *happiness* and you will get twenty different definitions, a fact that has been insightfully depicted by the cartoonist Charles Schulz in his book *Happiness Is a Warm Puppy*.

People vary widely in life experiences related to culture, religion, race, politics, morals, and family backgrounds. They also vary widely in personality and character, which affect their mental and emotional reaction to words. What is ugly to one person may be beautiful to another. Certain words may bring joy to some and misery to others. Language used by children may be a far cry from what we hear from adults.

Words Have Two Fundamental Kinds of Meanings

People attach *denotative* and *connotative* value to words. Denotative meanings are logical, objective, and extensional; connotative ones are emotive, subjective, and intensional. A denotative meaning points beyond a person's mind to the reality of the outside world. Denotation has an explicit referent, like a section on a map that represents a definite territory. We often associate denotative meanings with concrete or *name* words, such as "cow," "chair," or "wall." Yet the terms *denotative* and *concrete* are not the same, for an individual's frame of reference will determine whether words have implications beyond the naming of a real object. Clearly, to a prison inmate, *wall* will have meanings different from what it has for most of us.

Human emotions give rise to connotative meanings. If someone tells a child, "The goblins will get you if you don't watch out!" what he says contains emotive intensional, but not extensional, meaning. There is nothing in the content that is verifiable; we cannot see, hear, touch, or photograph the goblins. The referent must reside in the emotions of the child. Whether you believe in goblins or not, there is no way of settling the dispute by endless argument. However, if there is an argument about the height of the table in your room, the dispute will come to an end when someone measures it with a yardstick. Statements that have extensional meanings can be verified, and agreements can be reached; those containing only emotive intensional meanings afford no basis for logical agreement.

Intensity of experience produces connotative meanings. The word *mother*, for most people, is a supercharged value term because of the pleasant, warm, and comforting connotations it produces. To Americans, *democracy* is a highly connotative term because, through instruction and through practical experience, many have come to believe it to be the best form of government. Conversely, any term that is in direct and strong conflict with our basic values will have a potent negative connotation, for instance, the word *dictator*. Connotation is the affective quality of a word. And this affective value may have tremendous influence on a person's life. An individual may experience inner emotional turmoil because of his habit of using affective, self-deprecating words about himself. If he keeps saying to himself that he is inferior, he will probably end up believing it to be true because he anticipates the fulfillment of his prophecy. In speech communication, stage fright is an almost certain result of this autosuggestion.

People Change Language to Meet Their Needs

Language is a flexible instrument of communication. In a world of change, words often lose their usefulness and become archaic. People make up new words to replace them. Our vocabularies grow larger and larger. We hear about the special terminology of the military, the underworld, astronauts, doctors, lawyers, and scientists of all kinds. We tend to forget that the word *television* was not in our vocabulary fifty years ago. Obviously, new ways of doing things require changes in the tools of communication.

Language expressions coined in the process of change may endure for long periods of time. For example, farm animals affected the language of our pioneers. People from that era coined such expressions as "hold your horses," "put a halter on him," and "kick the bucket." Many of these expressions are still part of our vernacular today. Electronics came along and we now hear about "tuning in and tuning out," "getting on the right wave length," "static," and "clear channel."

With societal change and scientific development, words often take on new meanings and a newfound prominence. The word *orbit* was a relatively low-profile word until the Russians fired Sputnik I into the sky. During the past decade or so, words such as *liberation, establishment, relevance,* and *pig* have found new prominence and new meanings. Not too long ago, a deeply honest person was said to be *square*; today a square is someone who is not with it. Music that used to be considered *hot* is now *cool*. Something *bad* is really good. *Propaganda* originally meant instruction; now, for most people, it means distortion of the truth. *Rhetoric*, to the Roman, meant the noble art of public speaking; to many Americans, it means empty and flamboyant oratory.

Language always has had a hard time keeping up with changes brought on by research and new knowledge. A common term such as *communication*, which is now a kind of bread-and-butter word for the contemporary speech student, does not even appear in the index of many speech textbooks before World War II. Speech students now commonly use expressions such as *feedback, circular, response, group dynamics, nonverbal,* and *social distance*. When their parents took a speech course, they probably never heard these terms mentioned.

People Give Names to Things

People not only use language as a means of talking to each other, but they are also the products of that language. Because they have spent their lives giving *names* to their perceptions, they become the products of those names. This applies both to themselves and to things external to themselves. They may have designated themselves as clumsy, unattractive, smart, slow-witted, and various other things. They see the outside world largely in terms of how they have named it. They may have designated society as heartless, unchanging, indifferent, or responsive. Or they may feel that other people are essentially selfish, generous, hostile, or friendly. This naming process is the basis of all kinds of prejudices. Prejudice may be thought of as hardened categorization. Some of our categories become so rigid that when we have a new encounter with one of them we react without reflection because we have already named it. We all carry in our minds a long list of labels— emotion-laden words and phrases which act as emotional filters to our minds.

In summary, language constitutes a basic human equation. How people themselves think and how they relate to others is greatly determined by their language. Awareness of this phenomenon is vital to improved communication habits, both intrapersonally and interpersonally. We should, first of all, try to appreciate how we ourselves are bounded by language and then try to understand the role of language in others. We must understand that language is used not only for communication cues in transmitting messages to others, but that it also is the principle vehicle of our inner speech.

People Are Inference Makers

Not only are people symbolizers, they also are inference makers. The data we perceive come to us in their raw form, and such incoming data are often called observations. These observations may or may not correspond with reality. Two people may see the same bear and one person report that the animal was at least six feet tall, whereas the other saw it as less than four feet tall. Neither may be right, but it is certain that one of them has either distorted fact or is a poor judge of reality. Some of the best examples of erroneous observations occur in the baseball stadium, when a highly-partisan fan sometimes perceives a runner as having beaten the ball to first base when actually he was out by five steps. Assuming that we have perceptual problems, what are some of the factors that affect our ability to observe accurately?

We have already illustrated that bias or partisanship tends to distort our ability to see reality. One of the authors recently witnessed a television program about a San Francisco policeman who was a Vietnam war veteran. Because of his war experiences and because of the turmoil back home caused by dissident youths, he had developed an intense bias against long-haired young people. One night he answered a call for a robbery, spotted a car that fit the description, and followed the car to a house. He looked through the window of the house and saw a long-haired young man who fit the description of the suspect. The young man was holding a rifle, and when he turned around, the policeman burst into the room with his gun drawn, and told the young man he was under arrest and to put his rifle down. The startled youth started to comply, took one step forward, tripped slightly, and the rifle discharged into the ceiling. The officer responded by shooting and killing the youth. At a hearing, the police officer, a very sincere man, swore that the youth had made a tricky move and had fired his weapon. Another officer, who was a good friend of the one who entered the house, had remained outside and witnessed the event through the window. With a heavy heart, he testified that the young man had made no threatening move at all. This testimony was corroborated by a second youth who had entered the room just as the incident took place. Worse yet, the real robber was later apprehended. The officer's bias coupled with the pressure of the moment had distorted his ability to perceive reality.

Another vital question is the position from which we see an event. Our perceptions are never fully identical because two people never see a thing from exactly the same spot. Distance makes a difference. We all know that distance effects the size of an object; the farther away this object is, the smaller it appears. This phenomenon is operating at even relatively close distances. Angle of perception is another factor: A table looks different from one angle than it does from another.

Our ability to observe is also limited by our knowledge, appreciation, and experience with an object or event. Someone who is attending his first concert and has little appreciation for symphonic music may report that he saw nothing but a bunch of musicians wearing black suits and drawing violin bows back and forth; he heard nothing but loud music that sounded all the same to him. Yet an experienced observer of concerts will have an entirely different experience. He will know what to look for and will see and hear much more of what actually happened. The trained scientist is another good example. A botanist may look at a piece of bark and see many things that the layman would never notice.

Lastly, our observations are distorted by time. We tend to forget certain details, factors that especially caught our attention may grow in size and importance, and we may begin to confuse the event with another one and transpose aspects from one to the other, giving each an element of fiction. Courtroom witnesses are constantly confronted with this problem because they are always testifying about events that transpired some time ago.

Lest we despair too much, we should appreciate that people as

Dimension 1: People as Communicators

a rule do observe quite accurately. In fact, much of the time their observations are roughly akin to reality. The greater problem comes with the inferences they make about their observations. As we said at the outset, people are inference makers. As a matter of fact, we are so inference-prone that quite often we confuse inferences with observations. We see a fire truck coming down the street with its siren blowing and its lights blinking, and we report that we saw a fire truck on the way to a fire. The fact that we saw a fire truck with its siren blowing and its lights blinking is observation, but the statement that it was on the way to a fire is an inference. Since normally when fire trucks blow their sirens and blink their lights they are on the way to a fire, we assumed that this was the case. However, it is an inference—or judgment—because the firemen may only have been testing equipment in this instance. This observation-inference confusion can lead to all kinds of miscommunications and thus needs a more careful exploration.

We make three kinds of judgments: factual, value, and definitional. In an elemental manner, whenever we look out of the west window of our house, observe that it is raining and infer that it is raining on the east side of the house as well, we are making a factual judgment. The chances, of course, are very great that it is raining on the east side of the house; yet it is possible for the rain cloud to end right over the top of the house, making the statement "It is raining on the east side of the house also" an erroneous inference. We can test many of our factual judgments by taking a look at them. In the instance concerning the rain, we can walk to an east window and see whether or not it is raining there. At others times, it is difficult or even impossible to check out our factual inferences. For years, people inferred from their observations that the world was flat, and until their means of transportation became sufficiently sophisticated, they had no way of verifying the accuracy of their judgment.

By now it is apparent that our factual judgments are based upon probability. If it is raining on one side of the house, it is highly probable that it is raining on the other side also. We make such judgments about the past, present, and future. We observe that the cliff-dwelling Indians centuries ago built their houses on the sides of treacherous cliffs and conclude that they did this as a means of safety from hostile tribes and animals. This inference makes good sense, yet we have no means of verifying it. The *historical method* involves making intelligent inferences about the past from the best available data. This is useful activity, but we can never check its validity by observing it firsthand.

Every day we operate on the basis of inferences concerning present and future fact. Someone whom we trust and find reliable has told us that he will meet us at the corner of 8th and Vine at ten o'clock; we fully expect him to be there. We find no "bridge out" signs along the highway, so we assume that all the bridges are in their proper places. Our paycheck is sent regularly to the bank on the first of the month; we write a personal check on the thirty-first with the assumption that the next day our paycheck will resupply our account.

As Aristotle observed, some things are absolutely true whereas other things are only probably true. Water freezing at 32° F. is an absolute truth because no one has ever observed a contrary example. "All men are mortal" is thought to be an absolute truth, because we know of no counter-examples. The scientific method is always in search of absolute truth and in the realm of chemistry, for example, often provides us with certainties. At the same time, the scientific method is used to predict probable truths. Social science is filled with statements such as "almost always," "most of the time," and the 99 percent level of confidence, and so on. All these statements involve qualifiers that allow for exceptions.

A big problem in human thought and action is a tendency to confuse *facts* with *values*. Values have no roots in reality; they are products of the mind. They represent what people have decided to be good and bad, desirable and undesirable, tasteful or tasteless, and so forth. We have generally decided that a car is a good car when its motor runs, it performs efficiently, its tires are inflated, and it has no visible damage. Yet a car is still a car (linguistically) even if it meets none of these tests. When we say a car is a *good* car we have moved from the realm of fact to value. "That is a tasteless movie." "LeAnn is prettier than Mary Lou." "Kristin is a better piano player than Edna Mae." "Smoking is wrong."—All these statements have one thing in common: They include value terms—*tasteless, prettier, better, wrong*. Valuation is a distinctively human enterprise and constitutes a potential for human betterment. It is through such concepts as right and wrong and good and bad that we improve the human condition. At the same time, the value-fact confusion that people often make in their thinking and the propensity to pass off an evaluative inference as observation are data-processing problems that need correction.

Whether something is a horse or a cow is essentially a linguistic problem. In the last analysis, we can call the animal anything we want. However, definitional questions are vital in human thought and action because how we label and classify something essentially controls our attitude toward that object. The minute we have labelled a certain action as "fraud" we tend to be locked into that definition and will tend to view the action in a negative sense. This is probably harmless. However, when for various reasons we decide a certain group of people is "subhuman," as the Southern aristocrats did in our early history, the potential for harm is great. In the process of definition we infer from observed characteristics that an object, thing, or person fits into a certain word-category. It is vital to realize that this is linguistic activity rather than a fact of nature.

Quite obviously, we have to use inferences when we communicate. Our inferential powers enable us to transcend a very basic mode of life; they allow us to search for *justice*, for *the good life*, for *the good society*, and for many other desirable ends. At the same time it is useful to be aware of the fact-inference-judgment problem in our communications and in those of others. Treating inferences like facts can lead to grave consequences. It is the kind of confusion that, on the international scene, could lead to nuclear war.

Communicator Constraints

When we speak to each other we make contact, in a figurative sense, with one another. Each of us carries a style of sensitivity to persons about us who make an imprint on our personality and selfhood. We touch each other in mind, spirit, and attitude. When two people get together in a friendly, buddy-buddy way, each senses a new feeling of belonging, of mutual trust and loyalty, which creates a feeling of security. Personality and character traits interact with one another, affecting the selfhood of each. This is a positive reaction. We may also turn each other off in negative ways. We hear about personality clashes: "He or she rubs me the wrong way" is a common expression. We may walk a mile with a person but refuse to go any further with him. Shylock, in the *Merchant of Venice*, would cooperate with Bassanio only in certain ways, saying to him, "I will buy with you, sell with you, talk with you, walk with you, and so following. But I will not eat with you, drink with you, or pray with you." Skillful communicators realize that they must relate with others in terms of their sensitivities. All people, both as speakers and as listeners, bring constraints with them to their interactions. These constraints are a kind of framework in which people must operate if they wish to relate with one another.

To constrain means to confine, and by communicator constraints we mean those factors that people possess—cultural, attitudinal, intellectual, emotional, and so forth—that limit or influence their communications. Of paramount importance to any communicator is his ability to perceive the vital constraints of those people he is addressing and to adapt his presentation accordingly. Static on the communication channel is sure to occur if a person speaks without regard for listener constraints or if he fails to perceive them correctly. We have already discussed language as an important communicator constraint. What follows is an identification of other relevant constraints. Some of the items overlap somewhat, but they are sufficiently important to warrant separate discussion.

Culture

Robert T. Oliver, a prominent speech professor, tells the following story:

> It happens that some time ago I engaged over a span of months in a running discourse—you might even call it an argument—with a professor who was on our campus as a visitor from his native land of India. The subject of our discussion was the nature of certain qualities of the Oriental value system with which our own democratic

heritage could most readily interlock. For months he kept insisting to me that I had the ideas almost but never quite right. Then I had occasion to ghost-write a speech for a distinguished Oriental statesman on this very theme; and in a short time it appeared in print. A day or so afterwards the Indian Professor burst in to see me with the published speech in his hand and said, "I want you to read this. Here is a statement by one of my fellow Orientals that says exactly what I have been trying to tell you and says it so clearly I don't think you can miss the point."

Professor Oliver goes on to observe from this incident:

The point, I am afraid, is all too clear. When we peoples of the world try to address one another across cultural gaps, we encounter two serious kinds of difficulties. The first is that we may not and probably do not understand one another's point of view. And the second is that even when we do, we speak to one another essentially as strangers, as foreigners, as spokesmen for and from differing and even competing ways of life.[1]

Undoubtedly, cultural factors influence people as communicators. People from different cultures think differently. The most obvious of these differences are the international ones. We hear of a Western civilization, an Eastern civilization, an African civilization, and so on. And when people from one such culture try to communicate with people of another they may encounter considerable difficulty. It is common, for example, for an American to aspire to a higher status than that of his parents; in fact, it is almost part of the American tradition that he do so. Yet for an Oriental, this would be a matter of shame even to contemplate.

Vast cultural differences exist even within our own nation. We have heard much recently about Black culture; Chicanos and Indians also form subcultural groups. The Amish are very different from people living within ten miles of them. Even the New Englander's background is strikingly different from that of the Southerner.

Cultural factors are likely to be inconsequential in most of our interpersonal dialogues and speeches, for we usually communicate with people from our own or a very similar culture. Nevertheless,

---

[1] Robert T. Oliver, "Culture and Communication," *Vital Speeches of the Day* (September 15, 1963), p. 721.

cultural constraints are operative, for example, when middle-class suburbanites talk with people from the inner city. These factors are also vital in the great game of international politics. War and peace, perhaps even the preservation of mankind, may hinge upon our ability to communicate across cultures.

Values

People's values are their personal guides to thought and behavior. At the societal level, values shape the goals and means of collective human action. The rights of the common man and equality of opportunity, for instance, have had fantastic effects upon our national destiny. Many of our values are rooted in our cultural heritage. Most Americans cherish freedom. Our most basic values doubtlessly stem from our familial upbringing. From your mother you may have learned thrift, from your father, honesty. Our friends and associates, our teachers and ministers, also have helped shape our values. Most of those we have accumulated have probably not involved a conscious decision. Some of them, however, especially as we increase our education, we reflect about and decide to reject or to adopt.

Every individual has a hierarchical value-structure. Each of us prizes one value above all others, although we may not be sure which that is. We may think that self-preservation is our supreme value, yet when the occasion arises we may be willing to sacrifice our own lives to save that of a child. People, collectively, likewise have a hierarchy of values. Some of the Indian tribes of the Great Plains, for example, prized heroism in battle so highly that one's life had no meaning without it. Ancient Sparta and Athens were a graphic contrast of differing value-hierarchies; one city-state admired militarism, the other intellectuality.

People's values may be classified under different headings. They may be said to have social and economic values. They also have political, educational, spiritual, moral, and aesthetic values. What hierarchy is ascribed to these varies from person to person. We do, however, have certain national tendencies. For example, we have traditionally prized economic values more than aesthetic.

And we have a long history of believing in free and compulsory education for all.

Our values exert a strong influence on our interpersonal messages. When the political poster describes a gubernatorial candidate as a "rancher, veteran, and family man," it is saying nothing about the candidate's real qualifications for office but is capitalizing upon standard American values. Intensely-religious people may be quickly turned off by someone who expresses a strong preference for agnosticism. The problem of *longhairs* and *shorthairs* communicating with each other in our recent past stemmed greatly from an overt expression of value differences. Similar values, by contrast, have a strong unifying effect. Any Black person who believes that "Black is beautiful" is automatically treated as a soul brother by other like-minded Blacks.

Perception

Everybody has multiple perceptions: of himself, of the world in general; of the speaker's subject, of the person speaking, when listening; and of the people he is addressing, when speaking. Some people perceive themselves as downtrodden; others think of themselves as riding the crest of the times. Some perceive themselves as uneducated and uninformed, others as part of the intelligentsia. Some perceive themselves as inferior, others feel they are superior in most respects. The point is that we all have perceptions about ourselves that form our self-images. Some people perceive themselves quite realistically, but many do not. How people think of themselves will greatly influence how they receive messages. A person who feels himself to be inferior, for example, may feel threatened by any sort of challenge, whereas someone who thinks himself to be totally capable and on top of things in general may find a challenge strongly motivating.

The German word *Weltanschauung* means "world view," or "a perception of the purpose and meaning of the world." Our world view is strongly shaped by our culture, by our religious heritage, by our familial circumstances, and by the philosophical thoughts of educated men. If asked, most of us might find it difficult to state specifically our perception of the world, but we all do have a world view. Some of us see the world as being a jungle in which only the fittest survive; others regard it as a warm and friendly environment in which everyone has a place. Some of us equate life with great suffering; others think of it as a pleasant and beautiful experience. Some of us think that the purpose of man is to fulfill a divine plan; others think of mankind as aimless and wandering without any special destiny. Each individual's philosophy of the meaning of life forms a framework through which messages filter as they enter his mind.

A listener's perception of the speaker will be based on the impressions formed prior to the communication event and upon the direct impression the speaker makes when he speaks. As listeners we receive visual, auditory, and message images from the speaker. From these clues we decide whether he is competent or incompetent, expert or inexpert, wise or foolish, trustworthy or unreliable, well-intentioned or deceitful. It has been amply demonstrated, both by historical example and by experimental investigation, that a listener's perception of the speaker greatly influences the response he gives to the speaker's message.

On the other hand, when we speak we have perceptions of those we are addressing, vague as they may be sometimes. In conversations our impressions of the other are constantly evolving. We observe how the person listens, what nonverbal responses he gives, and how he sits or stands. In public speaking we have perceptions of the audience as a whole and may even develop a few impressions of specific people in the front of the room. Our perceptions of the audience will influence how we speak to them and, oftentimes, what we say. The inferences we have made about the audience may, of course, be extremely faulty, and we may fail in our communicative mission because of it. Yet the very fact that we have formed impressions about our listeners constrains our relationship to them.

Cognitive Knowledge

A person's general knowledge or education and his knowledge of the subject discussed and of the communication code are important factors in communication. A person's general level of education, his knowledge of science, history, psychology, world affairs, communication theory, and so forth, will have a bearing upon his communication. It is clear that a speaker is bound by his knowledge of the subject. At the same time, a listener with no familiarity with the speaker's immediate subject is going to be a different challenge to the speaker than a listener who has considerable knowledge of, and perhaps even experience with, the subject. Misinformation and/or incomplete information on the part of the listener will also have relevance to the speaker. It has been said that a little knowledge is a dangerous thing. Moreover, some listeners will have opinions about the speaker's subject and others will not. Some may have firm convictions about the topic; others may be much less sure. If a person speaks on a social problem to which he offers a solution, he may find that some listeners are very much aware that the problem exists; others are not aware at all. Some have already thought of possible solutions that are different from the one the speaker proposes; others may not have been exposed to possible solutions. A speaker oblivious to how much the audience knows about his subject may find himself talking to disinterested, bored, confused, or hostile listeners.

A critical factor in any communicative venture is the knowledge the listener has of the communication code the speaker is using. In speech communication the primary code is, of course, language. This being true, it is vital that the speaker present his message in a linguistic code familiar to his audience. If a person speaks in German and his auditors only understand English, the intended receivers obviously will not understand him. At a somewhat more subtle level, if an individual addresses this same audience in English but uses technical jargon foreign to the experience of his hearers, a communication breakdown will occur also. The same is true if people use a word in different senses. The word *dinner*, for example, may mean a noon meal or an evening meal. Visual cues and bodily and vocal expressions may often be an integral part of the communication code. A lifted eyebrow may mean a lot in some cases. A certain kind of gesture may often communicate more than words—provided the listener and the speaker have a common code derived from association and experience.

Emotions

Our values and our attitudes constitute emotional filters through which all messages must pass into our minds. Additionally, the general emotional makeup of the person is a factor. An emotionally unstable listener may feel himself easily threatened and feel sure that people are trying to take advantage of him. An easily excitable person probably needs to be addressed differently than does a calm and placid individual. The immediate emotional state of a listener or of an audience as a whole can also be a major communication constraint. Feelings of sadness, jubilation, love, or fear will influence our reception of, and perhaps our receptivity to, a speaker's ideas. A person saddened by the death of a loved one may be a very poor listener; an entire audience, jubilant over a great triumph, may be extremely receptive.

Physical Factors

The satisfaction of basic bodily needs, such as food and drink, strongly influences human behavior. In underdeveloped regions of the world it is quite apparent that hunger is a stronger drive than the desire for freedom. At another level of importance, it can be observed that a person who is physically uncomfortable is not likely to be a good listener. Someone who is suffering from a bad cold is not going to be as interested in listening to a speaker's ideas as he would be if he felt well. People in an overheated or badly-ventilated room will have a poorer attention span and a much worse disposition than they would if the room were more comfortable. Great physical discomfort is likely to block communication entirely.

Motivation

Every member of an audience has a degree of motivation to listen to the speaker's message. In some situations the motivation to listen may be at a high level among the entire audience. Members

Dimension 1: People as Communicators 57

of a flight squadron receiving a last-minute briefing of the details of a flying mission doubtlessly will be highly motivated to listen. On the other hand, audience motivation to listen at a humanities lecture on a university campus may vary tremendously from one person to the next. Most people, when they are well motivated, are good listeners. Concentration, at such moments, seems to be no problem. Motivating the members of an audience to listen is, therefore, a key problem that confronts every speaker.

Equally vital is the speaker's motivation to speak. If he has little or no interest in the task at hand, this attitude will certainly constrain his performance. At the same time, a highly motivated speaker will usually achieve a modicum of success on the basis of sheer effort. He tends to speak with vitality, respects his listeners, and tries to adapt to their feedback. The importance of motivation in communication can hardly be overemphasized. When people try very hard to understand each other, they usually can.

Communication Skills

Skill in listening as well as speaking is vital to effective interpersonal communication. Needless to say, a poor speaker—be his problem bad vocal quality or poor articulation, a lack of organization of ideas, insensitivity to feedback, or an inability to express ideas clearly—will experience limited success in interpersonal communication. At the same time, listening skills are as important to effective speech communication as are speaking skills. And although some people are very good listeners, many, unfortunately, are poor listeners. To compound the matter, educators for centuries have recognized the need to improve the skills of speaking, reading, and writing, but the art and skill of listening has largely been neglected in the schools. People tend to take listening for granted, and take a dim view of the notion that it can be taught. They view listening as a set, unalterable skill provided by nature, something akin to breathing. But we now know that listening is a multifaceted skill. We listen with our minds, our emotions, our hopes and fears, our experiences, the many sides of our personality; even the environment where listening takes place influences us. Thus, some training in listening seems to be desirable. As an

English manual points out, "Good listening habits are taught, not caught." With this thought in mind, we are including a separate section in this dimension on the reception of messages.

Communication and Human Motivation

Man is the masterpiece of creation, made in the image of God, yet he is always doing a balancing act between being an angel and a wild jungle beast. So much of his life is made up of pulls and counter-pulls. He has a genius for paradoxical behavior. He can fly to the moon, yet suffers a mammoth knowledge gap about himself. "Know thyself," the slogan of Socrates, is packed with mysteries which modern man has yet to discover. C. G. Jung in his book *The Undiscovered Self* makes much of the point that "man is an enigma to himself." Regarding psychology, he writes: "There seems to be a curious hesitancy. Not only is it the youngest of the empirical sciences, but it has great difficulty in getting anywhere near its proper object."

A crucial phase of human communication is strongly linked with the phenomenon of human motivation. Biological and psychological drives and pulls influence and constrain our actions and our human relationships. Therefore, the more one can understand himself and others, the better his chances for effective communication. Using this premise, we will take a brief, exploratory look at what makes people do the things they do to themselves and to others.

A motivating force is an invisible dynamo generating deep desires, urges, wants, and needs that create strong tendencies toward various kinds of action and reaction. It is largely man's response to being, and to the world of things and people. Certain motivating forces are biologically innate, others are learned behavior which at times may be redirected or restrained by man's own volition. They will vary in appeal and force among individuals according to sex, heredity, age, environment, training, and health of mind and body. In the broad spectrum of human conduct no single motive stands out as completely self-sustaining and isolated.

Dimension 1: People as Communicators

Motivating forces are mysteriously integrated to make up the dynamics governing the way we think, feel, and act. Here lies the multidimensional makeup of human communication.

Each person has within him his own individualistic patterns of action and reaction which differ from those of any other person. As the saying goes, "Everyone longs to do his own thing in his own way." The most common thing among people is their differences. What is one man's trash may be another man's treasure. At the same time, broad categories of forces affecting human behavior are common to most people.

We feel it is important for both speakers and listeners to be aware of these forces. Speakers should know what moves people so that they can address them accordingly. To be sure, an ethical question arises every time a speaker appeals to human motives; nevertheless, it may not be possible to move people to any kind of action without such an appeal. Of course, appropriate ethical criteria should be applied before the appeal is made.

It is at least as vital that listeners gain insight concerning communication and human motivation. Such knowledge will help a listener perceive a speaker's motivation to speak and will also help him give more mature responses to a speaker's appeals. An understanding of our personal motivations should help us reduce irrationality and irresponsibility. It should aid us in our quest for responsible and ethical communication.

We, therefore, submit a category of motives which we think govern most of human behavior. We hope to identify those basic forces that influence both intra- and interpersonal communication. These dynamos of action should not be viewed as wholly distinct and separate items as one would view peanuts, pencils, and mothballs. They are more like elements of chemistry which may react with one another with catalyzing force. The first four are more of a raw energy-producing type which strike deep in human needs and longings. The remainder, although having some motivational power of their own, mainly serve to restrain, distribute, modify, control, and refine what springs forth from the biological, the psychological, the mental, and the spiritual.

The history-making power of motivating forces comes to us loud and clear in the key words of the preamble of our Constitution familiar to every school child: "life, liberty and the pursuit of happiness." Life is based on the biological, liberty on the psychological, and pursuit of happiness is associated with any and all of the other dynamos of action and reaction.

Biological Motivation

People want to survive and prosper biologically. Man is a species of the animal kingdom governed by laws of biological utility. He must eat, sleep, rest, and avoid injury. He must have clothing, beds, houses, sewers, hospitals, and various kinds of industries. People seek to protect themselves against disease, the elements of nature, and human enemies. Generally we give top priority to the protection of self and kin. Hence we have wars, riots and violence; we claim territory, and search for oil, fibers, and foods. An army, it is said, fights on its stomach, prison riots are born in the mess hall, and hunger is a breeding place for communism. International relations quite often hinge upon trade agreements concerning rice, meats, and grains. Gandhi has said, "For a hungry man, food is God."

Biological drives for health and survival have deep implications for human communication. Note the never-ending flow of television advertisements concerning foods, vitamins, and pills for insomnia, pain, and irregularity. The "fear appeal" has long been known to be a potent factor in persuasion. People buy millions of dollars worth of insurance annually because they fear illness, accident, property loss, or death which leaves loved ones unprotected; a certain amount of insurance may be good common sense, but the large amount of insurance purchased in our modern society is ample testimony to self-preservation as a persuasive force.

People want not only to survive and prosper themselves, but they tend to want the race to survive and prosper. Propagation of the species seems to be a drive that all organisms possess. Life goes on and on. Despite all the furor about birth control and population explosion, the biological phenomenon of babies coming into the world continues. The core meaning of sex remains with the family, yet the strength of the drive is well illustrated by the fact that thousands of children are born out of wedlock and that the crime of rape is soaring. Duels have been fought and wars have been triggered by sex. We are more like animals than we care to admit. On the one hand, sex is purely biological; on the other, it has wide and deep sociological values. Prince Edward of England, for example, gave up his throne for the woman he loved. Sex appeal goes well beyond centerfolds and magazine covers. Its mysterious, compelling, and complex appeal rings out in literature, poetry, song, and even architecture. Witness one of the Seven Wonders of the World, the Taj Mahal, that marvel of beauty which for more than three centuries has immortalized romance and tender love. The deeper, fuller, and more sublimated level of love in the romantic sense opens the way for the blessings of companionship, self-realization, and liberation from loneliness.

Sex is the foremost appeal in advertising, making it clear that it is a fantastically-strong motivational force. Products ranging from deodorants to automobiles are sold on the basis of sex appeal by our country's advertisers.

Psychological Motivation

Man also wants to survive and prosper psychologically. This motive is identified by a score or more of familiar terms. For practical reasons, we will focus most of our attention on ego, self-esteem, pride, self-importance, and personal dignity. These words convey shades of meaning from the level of the egocentric, or conceit, to the more noble and honorable qualities associated with the word *dignity*.

Self-importance is a compelling motive from birth to death, often leaving its mark far beyond the grave. The Great Pyramid of Egypt—built fifty centuries ago, covering thirteen acres, tall as a forty-story building, and composed of 2.5 million stone blocks, some weighing seventy tons—still stands as the largest structure in the world. It is a mammoth monument to kingly vanity. Millions and millions of tombstones in thousands of cemeteries across our nation give silent testimony to man's longing to be remembered. Many people have a great fear of being buried in an unmarked grave, unknown.

By the time a child is a year old he learns to say the words *I, me,* and *mine*—all symbols of self. He soon hungers for attention and longs for self-security. When he starts school, thereby making his first big break from home, he senses new risks to his feelings of self-importance. This can be a bewildering, trying time for him. Should he be laughed at, ignored on the playground, or made to feel unwanted by his peers, he may suffer psychological wounds which leave life-long scars on his personality. Most people in this world of imperfections are plagued one way or another with some kind of inferiority feeling stemming from a physical characteristic, imaginary or real. This ego problem can strongly affect communication with others.

It is difficult for us to realize how firmly the ego is tied to everything we do. The sound of our own name is usually music to our ears. How we crave honor and recognition! Think of the work and furor that revolves around intercollegiate athletics. And what is it all about? Mostly pride and honor. Oscars, Nobel prizes, Congressional medals, and trophies of all sorts are common sources of pride. It is astonishing to see the lengths to which intelligent, educated adults will go to achieve goals no more tangible than the child's gold star for good performance. At one time, people fought duels to vindicate pride. Millions of dollars are presented to institutions to perpetuate the names of the donors. We want peace, but peace with honor. It is difficult to estimate our total output of thinking and energy as *status seekers* and *status keepers.*

If you look for the meaning of pride beyond what the dictionaries tell us, suppose you try answering some of these questions: Did you ever feel hurt? Have you ever felt insulted, neglected, ignored, unwanted? Do you feel better if someone calls you a liar, a dummy, a coward? Do you know the meaning of mental cruelty? Do you know how it feels to be forced into the role of a second-class citizen? If these questions reach you, then you will understand how the human ego can cut deep into all kinds of human relations.

Pride is a tremendous catalyzing force when it is combined with one or more of the other motives. Combine pride with sex and you risk violence; Salomé's sexual desire coupled with the humiliation of rejection explains why the head of John the Baptist was delivered on a platter before King Herod and all his festive guests. Couple pride with conscience and you get a closed mind; with religious prejudice and you might get persecution, even a crucifixion.

Observe the role of pride and dignity in the broader context of society in general. Pride was at work in the U. S. race for the moon. Wars often turn out to be a kind of bloody game, resulting in honor and glory for the winner, humility and disgrace for the loser. When there is a stalemate where neither side can win, diplomats frantically try for a mutually face-saving cease-fire so each side can salvage some honor and glory.

In various ways the ego may be a barrier to truth, void of logic, void of a social conscience, and of dubious value to dignity. Gertrude Franklin Atherton makes the observation that "Women love the lie that saves their pride, but never an unflattering truth." Pride is also a potent force for stabilizing a personal prejudice. Gapi Krishnon comments on this point: "Those who oppose a new idea or a new wave of thought without allowing it a fair trial clearly betray the presence of a lurking idea in their minds born of pride, since they know all that can be known in the world."

Pride may open the floodgates of pain and misery, of feelings of fear, anger, worry, hate, embarrassment, anxiety, humiliation and loneliness. It can also open the floodgates of joy and happiness, create feelings of security, freedom, friendliness, love, achievement, hope, and personal dignity. Personal dignity supplies the dynamics by which we ultimately measure the fullness of life for ourselves and the quality of civilized living. The human ego affects traits of personality and forms character. It lies at the basis of the quality of life for both the individual and society.

It is noteworthy that in 1955 in Montgomery, Alabama, one lone woman with a compelling sense of dignity could not bring herself to stand in the back of a bus. This triggered a renaissance of freedom and dignity among Blacks and minority groups of our country. In the realms of government and politics, this powerful motive at the more noble level has done and is doing wonders to improve the quality of life. This nation was founded on the rock of freedom. The motive of personal dignity gave us the Bill of Rights. Later the civil rights movement tried to secure this guarantee of personal dignity for all Americans.

Thus, on the one hand, the psychological motive of man has no social conscience—it is self-centered. On the other, it has great social value. It helps us to keep our yards, houses, and bodies neat and clean. It helps us to have order and good manners. It gives meaning to the saying, "What is worth doing at all is worth doing well." The need to recognize people's sensitivity, pride, and desire for personal dignity is vital in interpersonal communication. It can mean the difference between enthusiastic, cooperative attitudes and divisive resistance.

Mental Motivation

For centuries man has looked through microscopes and telescopes, bent over test tubes in laboratories and risked his life on uncharted seas because he wanted to know things. The questioning urge that is so characteristic of the curious child never really leaves him. He is forever curious to know, to find out, and wants to make productive use of his findings. Our voyages to the moon and unmanned probes of Mars have been motivated by the simple desire to know what's out there. Adults, even from primitive societies, have always been interested in educating their children. Sometimes the valued education has been very practical; in advanced societies, a general, liberal education is deemed worthwhile.

The knowledge explosion that characterizes the twentieth century accelerates at an increasing rate. The total volume of accumulated knowledge doubles every two or three decades, increasing the need for education as a defense against the growing magnitude of ignorance. We have to escalate our efforts in education just to catch up with the learning that is going on. The American Publishing Association reports that at this writing approximately 45,000 new books are published each year in the United States.

Americans have traditionally believed in education. Enrollments at the college level have reached an all-time high. The total college enrollment in public and private schools combined is near the 10 million mark. Today 63 million Americans, more than 30 percent of the population, are directly involved in education as students and teachers. The rest of the people have a vested interest as parents and taxpayers. Our schools symbolize an important aspect of the American way of life involving an annual expenditure of 90 billion dollars, or nearly 10 percent of our gross national product.

The desire to know is interwoven with the biological and the psychological motives. We need knowledge to survive; we want to know as a matter of pride. People always get a deep feeling of satisfaction from displaying insight into a great variety of subjects. The presentation of information to other people is always abetted when it is linked to their natural curiosity.

Spiritual Motivation

Man has a spiritual side to his nature. Unlike lower animals, he has a soul and hungers for its life and security. To meet this need he has developed intricate systems of religion. "Religion is hard to define," we are told,

> not because there is so little of it, but because there is so much. It has existed in some form or another since human history began, and geographically it covers the whole period, for there are no peoples entirely without it. It has wielded immense political power and swayed the rise and fall of empires. If it has been associated with terrible wars and persecutions, it has also, and most profoundly, been a source of inspiration for the highest good of mankind. Indeed, it is this very permeation of all history and social living that makes the word so difficult to define.[2]

Much has been written about the impact of religion on the founding and development of our culture. Some of man's most significant triumphs among the arts, for example, have been inspired by religious motives. These motives have inspired crusades, colonization movements, and bloody wars. Tyrants have attempted again and again to stamp out or suppress the religious motive, but their efforts have been in vain.

Religion supplies man's emotional needs. This can, of course, be a source of serious trouble, a fountainhead for intolerance and deep-seated prejudice. George Bernard Shaw reflects this fact in his caustic words, "Religion is a great force—the only real motive force in the world, but what you fellows don't understand is that you must get a man through his own religion and not through yours." A person's religious conscience is for the most part an educated thing. It is an intimate, personal matter reinforced by

---

[2] Selwyn Gurney Champion and Dorothy Short, *Readings from World Religions* (Greenwich, Conn.: Fawcett, 1963), p. 9.

his own ego and sense of loyalty toward whatever his beliefs may be. For most of us it is easier for us to change our minds about politics, customs, and laws than about religion. Religion is the last place where most people bend. It took this country 150 years to elect a Catholic to the White House.

Mystical Motivation

Somewhat related to spiritual tendencies are people's inclinations to be intrigued by things which are mystical. Most people, in various ways and to various degrees, are influenced to do things on the basis of intuition, superstition, laws of chance, dreams, signs in nature, premonitions, astrology, and fortune tellers. Ancient Greeks, highly civilized in their day, placed stock in oracles. The armies of France at one time were moved by voices heard by the Maid of Orleans. Shakespeare made wide use of witches, ghosts, dreams, and soothsayers in his plays. Hitler relied much on intuition. Great athletes are known to carry good luck charms and wear items of clothing to insure victory. People for centuries have sought to read the language of the stars. Prominent people in government, business, and the military have been known to consult those who claim to have clairvoyant powers. Science fiction has a great following of readers. The television program *The Twilight Zone* had popular appeal for a long time. Magicians can usually enthrall audiences for hours. Personal charisma, which is at least a semi-mystical quality, has become a powerful election determinant. It is hard to assess the exact impact of charisma in interpersonal communication but we are certain that it is considerable.

Logical Motivation

Despite proclivities for the mystical, people like to think of themselves as being logical. Aristotle viewed man as a *rational animal*, meaning that man had the ability to use the power of reason and that this attribute differentiated people from lower animals. Behaviorists of our time view man as a creature governed by needs, desires, wants, and drives, one who uses logic only to rationalize this behavior and thereby maintains a certain mental balance. Regardless of which thought is correct, we Americans are schooled in the tradition of logical thought and pride ourselves on the ability to think logically and critically. Educated people particularly possess this self-concept. Moreover, we tend to think of people who act solely on the basis of prejudice and emotion as immature and mentally lazy. Demagogues tend to be well aware of our craving to be "logical." Their speeches are often saturated with data of all kinds, much of which is irrelevant or distorted in some sense, yet they bombard their listeners with "evidence" for persuasive effect.

Humans certainly have the ability to reason. Our modern world of science and invention is a tribute to logic. People have split the atom, landed on the moon, increased the life span, mastered the mysteries of computer science and much more, all within the span of a few decades. The logical processes call into play the laws of mathematics, physics, chemistry, electronics, and all other sciences. To act logically calls for special effort, great patience, integrity, willpower, and personal discipline. It presents a challenge for even the mature mind. Henry James may have been correct when he observed that "only one person in ten can think logically and he can do it only one-tenth of the time"; but despite our inability to function rationally all the time, the desire to be logical is a strong factor in human communication.

Motivation for Order

Nature is characterized by order. The intricate and harmonious functioning of the universe represents perfection of order, and the creatures of nature seem to have inherited this instinctual drive. The work of ants, bees, birds, and many other animals is noted for its order. Man, too, seems to need this kind of order. Structure and organization give us a feeling for where we have been, where we are, and where we are headed—a concept that is well-illustrated by the road map. All efforts at *society* represent a drive for order. To assure societal orderliness, people invent laws by which they live. "Law and order" has been a major election-year issue of the past decade. When dissident factors in American society sought to break down the nation's system and create a state of general confusion and chaos, immediately other people developed great concern for law and order. Beyond these official laws and ordinances, habits of action and custom, tradition, organizational policy, and good manners help to bring about efficiency and comfort.

Thirst for order is evident in human decision-making. We follow parliamentary rules in policy-making assemblies, and courtesy demands that not everyone speak at once in small-group discussions. We even tend to achieve a certain orderliness in our casual conversations. We have long been taught that if two people begin speaking at once one should politely give way to the other. Speeches that are well-structured and carefully organized usually are thought to be superior to those that are formless.

Laws may constrict or they may set free, they may be good or they may be bad, they may be archaic or they may be visionary. Rules and regulations may abet or impede the conduct of business. But that man is going to continue to invent laws, customs, rules and regulations to achieve order is certain.

Aesthetic Motivation

"A thing of beauty is a joy forever." People have always derived pleasure from the beautiful. No culture has ever been able to escape the urge for artistic expression. Even primitive people found joy, comfort, strength, and inner harmony in art, from the standpoint of both the producer and the receiver. The aesthetic symbolizes both the need and the desire for a higher level of refinement and perfection of human values that gratify the ennobling spirit of man. We commonly think of this as being oriented to the artistic which reveals itself in many forms, such as art, basketry, pottery, sculpture, literature, music, architecture, theater, dance, films, and decorations of various kinds.

People are forever conscious of beauty in physical nature. Each year thousands of tourists flock to see the scenic wonders of the world. The quest for the aesthetic seems less oriented to the material and biological needs of man than to the mental and the spiritual. This is demonstrated in countless ways in everyday living. We see it on the table where we eat, where even the food must look good to taste good. We are also conscious of the aesthetic in our homes, our yards, the clothes we wear, the books we read, the automobiles we drive, and even our jewelry.

The Greeks recognized beauty as having a connection with goodness. Some philosophers perceive that art might be man's miracle weapon to conquer the lie because beauty is equated with truth. Some think that beauty may even have a therapeutic effect on body, mind, and spirit. Often the nonverbal forms of art-communication, such as painting, sculpture, and architecture, convey messages of lasting value that seem to exceed even the spoken word.

At the same time, people have characteristically admired the beautiful in human expression. The medium of poetry has endured for years. Orations of the past that exemplify exceptional stylistic achievement are read over and over again. Ancient rhetoricians devoted considerable space in their rhetorical writings to a discussion of ornateness and style, elements that produce the beautiful in speech. People a generation ago came to admire Winston Churchill's oratory in part because of the aesthetic quality of his metaphors. John F. Kennedy's Inaugural Address is remembered largely because of its stylistic features, whereas inaugural speeches of lesser aesthetic value have long since been forgotten.

Charitable Motivation

There is a compassionate side to most people. "Blessed are the merciful, for they shall obtain mercy" is reflected in hundreds of human relief organizations. The concept is at work in the United Nations, the Peace Corps, nurses aides, and care for the sick and lonely. Hospitals in America are more heavily supported by private donations and private services than by public taxation. We generally hold a charitable person in high esteem. We may even hold such a person up as an example for others to emulate. Most people want to picture themselves as loving, caring people. An appeal to human charity quite often produces amazing results.

People also tend to be charitable when they are members of

audiences. Seldom do they get up and walk out during a speech, no matter how poor the speaker. As a rule, people tend to be supportive of a speaker and empathize with him to some degree. High-anxiety speakers should realize that people in audiences are pulling for them. They wish the speaker success, not failure.

The Speaker's Image

Ralph Waldo Emerson wrote, "The reason why anyone refuses his assent to your opinion, or his aid to your benevolent design is in you. He refuses to accept you as a bringer of truth, because . . . you have not given him the authentic sign." Emerson echoes the classical theory that the authenticity of what is said, as far as the listener is concerned, lies within the speaker himself.

Americans particularly are an image-conscious people. In our free and open society we embrace the cult of personality. The image game gets pretty lively in social situations. Images are formed at the dinner table by your table manners, dress, and pattern of conversation. When you play poker or bridge the players watch the way you hold your cards, the way you bid or bet, and your eye and facial expressions. In conversations, the personal image often depends more upon nonverbal symbols than upon speech and language. Everyone has a somewhat different image of you than the one you have of yourself. The art and science of image-making in the fields of advertising and politics have been developed to a high level of sophistication. Nationally-glorified heroes sell almost everything and anything over radio and television by their endorsements of life insurance, soaps, and liver pills. Even political campaigns, be they local, state, or national, nowadays center more on the image of the candidate than upon vital political issues; and advertising agencies usually are more important than speech writers.

Who is this speaking? Where is he from? What does he do? What does he know, and why is he here? Although he may be unaware of it, the listener usually asks these and similar questions about the speaker. One might object that it makes no difference who says what. But it does matter, for truth exists only for the listener when he recognizes it and accepts it as such. The speaker's message reaches the listener's mind only as it filters through the prism of the speaker's total self—his deeds, personality, character, poise, and personal mannerisms. If the speaker has some truth to reveal, he must be sure that his image rings authentically in the listener's mind.

Ancient Greek and Roman rhetoricians taught that one cannot separate the person from his speaking performance. In his *Art of Rhetoric*, Aristotle noted that "we might almost affirm that his character [the speaker's ethos] is the most potent of all the means to persuasion." He divided ethos into three components: sagacity, integrity, and good will. By sagacity, Aristotle was referring to the knowledge and wisdom of the speaker; by integrity, he meant moral trustworthiness; and by good will, he meant the intentions of the speaker. Cicero later observed that ethos encompasses "a person's dignity . . . his actions and the character of his life." Quintilian perhaps placed the greatest emphasis upon the speaker's character; he said, "The orator must above all things devote his attention to the formation of moral character and must acquire a complete knowledge of all that is just and honorable."

For our purpose, we can say that ethos consists of those elements of character, personality, and prestige that tend to enhance the authenticity of what the speaker says—in other words, the speaker's total image. Remember that although ethos is said to refer to the speaker's *personal persuasiveness*, in reality a speaker possesses ethos only as it is perceived by the listener. It comes from the impression auditors have formed of him prior to the communication event and the image the speaker projects to them during his presentation. In some instances, the antecedent impression is so strong that it is difficult for the speaker to alter it. The first concern, therefore, would be to acquire a good reputation, for this general image will greatly influence his listeners. It is well known, for example, that in a political campaign a candidate's general reputation tends to be more important to voters than a single speech.

Occasionally, however, a person can alter his image with a

group of people during a single speech, either favorably or unfavorably. Barry Goldwater's image doubtlessly suffered with many television viewers when, in his acceptance speech in 1964, he maintained that extremism in the defense of liberty is no vice. On the other hand, John F. Kennedy's image brightened tremendously in 1960 as a result of the first televised debate with Richard M. Nixon. Many people who had previously been uncertain about Kennedy now viewed him as a confident, capable, dynamic leader. Ethos has enough significance that a person needs to be concerned with it while speaking in order to achieve an image of authenticity with his listeners. We will closely examine three related factors: *trust, status,* and *ethos-building channels.*

Trust

Various communication scholars since Aristotle have structured paradigms on the subject of ethos. We find the approach set forth by Kim Giffin in the *Psychological Bulletin*[3] especially meaningful and useful. Giffin defines trust as a "reliance upon the characteristics of an object, or the occurrence of an event, or the behavior of a person in order to achieve a desired but uncertain objective in a risky situation." Defined in this manner, trust encompasses all the ways in which a listener places confidence in a speaker and finds his message believable and acceptable; it subsumes the three Aristotelian factors of sagacity, integrity, and good will. As Giffin explains, trust involves "at least some elements of risk." A person may be willing to risk trusting a speaker somewhere on a continuum between absolute zero and total blind faith. Giffin identifies expertness, reliability, intentions, personal attractiveness, and dynamism as factors bearing upon trust in speech communication. In other writings, he identifies conformity as a possible sixth factor. We will briefly review each of these factors because we feel that they are of vital concern to a speaker and that, in order to assure maximum success in his communicative endeavors, he needs to develop them.

---

[3] Kim Giffin, "The Contribution of Studies of Source Credibility to a Theory of Interpersonal Trust in The Communication Process," *Psychological Bulletin*, 68, 2 (1967), pp. 104–120.

Expertness

The expert is an authority or a specialist; he is either especially knowledgeable about a subject or possesses special skills, and frequently both. We are familiar with the role of expertness in the field of medicine; we think of the brain or the heart specialist, for example. The surgeon is a good illustration of someone who is an authority and also possesses skill. A judge is thought to be an expert on legal matters, and a scientist on things that are scientific.

Ordinarily, a person is asked to give a speech because someone thinks he possesses some special knowledge; by virtue of being the speaker, people assign to him a degree of expertise. It is dangerous, however, for him to rely solely upon an antecedent impression because his expertness must be projected during the speech also. The first step in that direction is being well informed on the subject and demonstrating that the speech is well prepared. Beyond this, if a speaker is not well-known, it is often useful for him to relate what special experiences he has had in relation to his subject. He can also show his knowledge and research by the types of supporting materials he uses.

Reliability

Does the listener perceive the speaker to be a person of good character? We now come close to Aristotle's concept of integrity as an ethos factor and echo the demands of Quintilian that the orator be a good man. The image factor is one of moral trustworthiness. A listener may place confidence in what a speaker says because he thinks him to be a person of truth, that is, honest and sincere. All the character traits that most Americans think are desirable will have relevance to the speaker's image of reliability. This element will hinge primarily upon his antecedent impression, but the speaker, through his manner and through his speech, can often influence a listener's image of his character.

Good Intentions

The amount of trust an audience will place in the speaker often depends on how they perceive his intentions. If people feel that a speaker's intentions are noble and honorable, they often will trust him even if he has other shortcomings. The speaker's mien and manner of speaking tend to project telltale clues about his intent to the listener. Often a spirit of friendliness will produce an image of good intent. He can also show genuine interest in the people's welfare through what he says; he can demonstrate to them that he is not merely representing vested interests and is in no way trying to dupe them.

Likeableness

Listeners find it easier to trust a person if they like him. The speaker's personality will influence his likeableness. A personality displaying human warmth, friendliness, tact and diplomacy, good humor and humility will usually lead to an image of personal attractiveness. Our manifest personality has some characteristics that are more or less manageable and subject to change and modification; others are more permanent. Those that have some permanence are greatly influenced by our vocal quality, the size of our body, and other related factors. Voice quality ordinarily can be improved somewhat, but most of these features are subject to little change; the same is true to a great extent of basic temperament and intellectual ability. But some characteristics of the manifest personality can be changed in order to enhance the image projected to the audience. Hair style, dress, and physical mannerisms, all of which tend to contribute to the personality, can be altered. The voice qualities of articulation and melody patterns can be changed. *My Fair Lady*, one of the great musical-comedy hits of the 1950s, pivots on the transformation of an ill-spoken flower girl from the slums of London to a charming and beautiful lady with a melodious voice and flawless speech. We can also control the feeling of friendliness we project; we can be tactful, polite, and courteous; we can display humility and a good sense of humor. To a degree, we can even overcome traits such as bashfulness and become more forceful and dynamic.

Dynamism

The implied meaning here is activity, energy, and force. The listener perceives the speaker as a person of action, someone who

Dimension 1: People as Communicators 75

gets things done. People tend to respond more favorably to active personalities than they do to passive ones.

The concept of charisma is difficult to define but challenges our interest. *Charisma* is a Greek word meaning the quality of being able to inspire people. It is not a matter of sex, office, fame, fortune, or special achievement. It is a personal magnetism that some people seem to possess and others do not. In the political world, John F. Kennedy and Dwight D. Eisenhower had it in abundance. In the sports world we point to Babe Ruth, Willie Mays, Jack Nicklaus, and John Hadl. Charisma involves factors other than sheer dynamism, but probably it comes closest to fitting in this category. A charismatic personality is usually a leader, and people ordinarily look to men and women of action for leadership. The development of such an image is, quite obviously, the great hope of any public figure.

Propitious Conformity

The term *conformity* refers to behavior that is in keeping with established laws, conventions, customs, and manners that characterize the culture in which a person lives. Audiences and speech occasions tend to place certain constraints upon a speaker. Anyone who disregards the listeners' customs and manners is likely to arouse distrust and cause a communication failure. All listening groups demand propitious behavior from a speaker. Anyone of whom auditors say inwardly, "He must have a screw loose somewhere," has a trust problem.

Propitious conformity operates on a differential scale. It is not a matter of being absolutely in the middle-of-the-road or at a point at either end of violent extremes. Actually, certain oddities or eccentricities that are genuine trademarks of the speaker's personality may even enhance his appeal to an audience. These factors give "color" to an individual's personality, and a speaker is wise to cultivate them. Perhaps the best example of such a speaker in this century was Will Rogers, whose slightly-eccentric behavior was the hallmark of his style. Propitious conformity, in the final analysis, is a matter of not violating people's sense of taste—be it in terms of subjects, occasions, or personal decorum—for such violations tend to make the speaker repugnant to his listeners.

Status

A second major ethos factor, tangential in many ways to trust, is *status.* The term is used in a broad sense to include position, dominance, role, power, and prestige. It implies an awareness of social distance and attitudinal interaction between producer and recipient of communication. A person's status may change with the role he is playing at a given moment. A company executive communicating with his employees has the role and status of boss at that moment; this same person speaking at a men's club meeting of his church may be greatly respected, but his status will be that of member only. He has moved from a position of dominance in one communication situation to that of peer in the other. The phenomenon of status seems to occur in three different levels of speech communication.

The first level is identified with dominance, power, or designated authority in organizational structures and systems. This might well be called the institutional complex of bosses or chain-of-command. We see how this works as the functions of government are carried out by men appointed or elected to office. Some who have posts by appointment are known as managers, directors, aides, secretaries, chief administrators, or judges. The images of those elected to office come through to us clearly. In the city, the highest image is the mayor; for the state, governor; for the nation, president. The pattern of power roles emerges sharply among the armed services, business firms, corporations, colleges, and public-school administrative bodies. There are some situations where great power and authority are concentrated in a single person, the president of a labor organization during a strike, for instance, or the captain of a ship in time of battle.

These levels of power are oriented more toward anticipated activities than the communication of information and opinion. The purpose is to get done what seems necessary in an expedient and orderly manner. When mutual trust and respect are present, effective communication is likely to occur. On the other hand, this type of status may lead to a communication problem. The listeners may distrust and resent the person who speaks from a position of dominance, or, on the other hand, they may blindly accept any-

Dimension 1: People as Communicators

thing that he says without question, depending upon their disposition. Anyone who speaks from such a position should be aware of this and try his best to understand his listeners, all the while observing their feedback. Far too often, a person of status shows little concern for his listeners if they are from a lower level within the structural hierarchy.

The second level of status concerns hero adulation. Communication seems to be enhanced for a person if he listens to someone whom he admires and respects for outstanding achievement or high honor. The sports world has its baseball Hall of Fame, Olympic winners, and world champions. When Jack Dempsey underwent an emergency appendectomy years after he won the world heavyweight boxing championship, his admirers showered him with gifts, including 1000 pounds of candy and half a carload of flowers. Astronauts, Oscar winners, Nobel Prize recipients, and Miss Americas have no difficulty commanding an audience. Sergeant Alvin York, who single-handedly captured 132 Germans and 23 machine guns in World War I, turned to the professional lecture platform as a result of his spectacular achievement as a soldier. Audie Murphy, a World War II hero, became a highly successful movie star despite admitted acting deficiencies. Following his solo flight from New York to Paris in 1927, Charles Lindbergh, who rarely made a speech, was swamped with invitations to speak before various groups. The hero worship lingered, and more than a decade later the America First Committee capitalized on Lindbergh's favorable image. In his dissertation on the America First Committee, Donald W. Parson writes, "People would come to hear Lindbergh, not because he was a member of America First, or even an isolationist, but because he was a daring aviator, a celebrity, a prominent American."[4] When mingled feelings of good will, respect, and admiration exist among listeners, they are likely to respond favorably to communication from their heroes.

The third level of status grows out of *tradition* and *common practice*. One particular area where this level of status affects communication is within the circle of families and blood relatives. It

---

[4] Donald W. Parson, *The Rhetoric of Isolation: A Burkeian Analysis of the America First Committee*, Minneapolis, University of Minnesota, unpublished doctoral dissertation, 1964.

is operative between husband and wife, parents and their children, aunts and uncles and their nephews and nieces, and so forth. What we call family ties vary greatly from culture to culture. The Chinese, for example, are known for their ancestral worship. Even among the highly educated, families make annual pilgrimages to their parents' graves, not to bring flowers, as is our custom, but to place great varieties of food and imitation gold coins on the grave. As one Chinese university graduate of the Christian faith remarked, "I know there is no logic to this, but some strange power makes me do it."

Outside of blood relationships, status exists between adults and young people, members of a social fraternity, alumni of a university, or members of a religious organization. Status, in these instances, is largely a matter of common practice and understanding.

Traditional status, like hero adulation, is something that happens largely by itself and is difficult to influence. We mention these factors because we feel it is important for a student of speech communication to know that they exist and that they may possibly influence the communication act.

Ethos-Building Channels

The antecedent impression of a speaker is a critical ethos factor. He should not, however, rely on this impression alone; he needs to be concerned with his image in relation to his specific audience and the speech occasion. Ethos may be improved through three primary channels: through advance publicity, what the speaker says, and poised and confident delivery.

Advance Publicity

Have you ever noticed how Billy Graham's crusades are always well publicized in advance? This preparatory publicity generates enthusiasm and interest in the campaign; it also intensifies Billy Graham's image. The advance publicity given a speaker by the press, radio and television, posters, the moderator's introduction, and by word of mouth often is the basis of the impression listeners have of the speaker when they go to hear the speech. It is, therefore, helpful for a person to prepare a data sheet of the things that he would like the public to know about him before he speaks. A concise, well-organized biographical sketch, an outline of his professional experience, and a statement of his special qualifications for speaking on the announced subject are usually welcomed by those who prepare publicity. The speaker may even want to give a page of appropriate data to the moderator who will introduce him. Advance publicity can seldom be totally controlled, but it can usually be influenced.

The Speech Itself

As the speaker begins his speech he must realize that there is no guarantee that his established ethos will be preserved until he has finished. Ethos is always in a state of flux. A person may bring an outstanding antecedent reputation to a speech and find his image deteriorating badly during the speech, perhaps through some unfortunate remark or through poor speech habits. The speaker has the dual challenge of maintaining his established reputation (if it is good) and enhancing or improving his image during the course of his speech. He may employ ethos-building compositional materials and stylistic language usage to this end.

Ethos can be maintained and enhanced through what is said. Identification with the audience's background, beliefs, sentiments, attitudes, and so on, will create common ground between the speaker and the listener. A person can demonstrate expertness by revealing his credentials to the audience, by telling them of his training, his experiences, and his activities. If a speaker can point to his wise and honest decisions of the past, he has the record in his favor. Frequently, reference to authorities gives credibility to the message and enhances a person's ethos as well. One may often show objectivity by demonstrating an awareness of the opposing arguments, perhaps even admitting that these arguments have some merit. Ordinarily, the mere fact that a speaker starts with a point with which the audience emphatically agrees will generate a feeling of trust. Points of agreement can usually be found for most speech topics. A person may sometimes engender meaningful rapport with an audience by praising them for their special achievements, patience, regard for truth, or fairness. Some people tend to think, at least privately, that a person who praises them has particular insight. These are a few examples of compositional ethos-building materials a speaker may consider and choose from, although many other similar choices are available.

The image a listener has of a speaker is partially shaped by his mode of expression. Listeners often trust a speaker, for example, because "he talks their language." President Truman, during his whistle-stop campaign in the 1948 election, got considerable mileage out of his ability to talk the people's language in the agricultural Middle West. At the same time, real verbal craftsmanship will often generate a favorable ethos. General Douglas MacArthur was thought by many to be especially competent because of his command of the language. Adlai Stevenson's image was largely based upon his stylistic eminence. His 1952 acceptance speech at the Democratic convention caused many people to think of him as an intellectual. And how can one separate stylistic craftsmanship from the image of Everett Dirksen, the now-deceased senator from Illinois. On the other hand, poor language usage, or saying the wrong thing, may undermine or even ruin a person's ethos. Frequent grammatical errors or mispronunciations are likely to disqualify a person as being an expert in many people's minds. You can probably think of numerous examples of someone whose image became tarnished because he said the wrong thing. A classic example is Charles E. Wilson, who, as President Eisenhower's Secretary of Defense, suffered considerable loss of ethos through his unfortunate comment, "What's good for General Motors is good for the country." Union members distrusted him ever after. It is quite clear that people form impressions of us not only through what we say but also through how we say it. High school and college oratorical contests are often won by the speaker who demonstrates superiority in the management and use of language.

Poised and Effective Delivery

Poise, confidence, and skill in speech delivery help form the speaker's image in the minds of his listeners. This is especially true if he is relatively unknown. Poise and confidence are earmarks of leadership, and listeners are reluctant to trust the person who is unsure of himself. A skillful delivery denotes competence, and people are unlikely to assign expertness to an individual who speaks badly.

Audiences begin forming impressions of a speaker when they first see him sitting on the platform. They observe his physical appearance, his dress, and his general demeanor. They note how he walks to the lectern and how he looks when he first begins to speak. A speaker may at that instant already have two strikes against him or, on the other hand, be virtually assured of a favorable reception. During the speech, vocal quality and voice usage, bodily posture and meaningful gestures are ethos-building factors. It is difficult to assess just how essential delivery is to a speaker's ethos, but its importance cannot be overstressed. It is certain that poor delivery may act as a kind of saboteur to the speaker's image, and it is probable that effective delivery will be an agent for success in speech communication.

The Speaker's Poise and Confidence

If you have ever experienced a good case of speech fright, you may have wished you could drop through the floor and out of sight. But take heart! Plutarch recorded 2300 years ago that Demosthenes, in his first public address, was afflicted by "weakness in his voice, a perplexed and indistinct utterance and a shortness of breath . . . so that in the end, being quite disheartened, he forsook the assembly." Cicero said of himself, "I turn pale at the outset of each speech, and quake in every limb and in all my soul."

The problem of self-management is interlocked with the emotional disturbance common to most speakers and known as speech fright or sometimes as stage fright. This is a psychological condition caused by worry and feelings of anxiety about oneself as a communicator. These emotions can, in various ways and degrees, interfere with the speaker's mental processes, voice and diction, and gestures and bodily movements. His total personality may take on an image that is unreal, frightened and hesistant, or even fraudulent, lacking above all else the *authentic sign*. Speaking, at its best, is the total person in action. But when speech fright has a good hold on a person, he isn't all there. Such a person experiences a miserable, unpleasant feeling of social discomfort.

The opposite of speech fright is described as poise and confidence. These attributes facilitate one's expressive power, enhance one's personal image, and, at least as important, make speaking an interesting and sometimes exhilerating experience. Feeling comfortable while speaking may not be essential to effective communication, but to the speaker himself it is very important. A definite sense of poise and confidence puts one in a favorable mood to carry on oral communication with a listener or a group of listeners.

We have come to know about speech fright largely by its symptoms: pounding heart, flushed face, cold sweat, trembling limbs, dry mouth, loss of memory, lack of eye contact with the audience, increased pulse rate, sinking feeling in the stomach, and so on. Some of these symptoms are noticed by the listeners, others are known only to the speaker. Some people can hide these symptoms so well that their listeners never know they are experiencing speech fright. Such camouflaging is good for one's image but not for personal comfort.

Certain factors, personal and individualistic by nature, affect different speakers in different ways. Many people experience speech fright in relation to a certain type of auditor and the size of the risk involved in the speaking situation. A college student may, for example, be able to address a high school audience with little fear; yet this same person, when addressing a peer group in the form of a college speech class, may be almost petrified. Someone else may experience virtually no speech fright when addressing a peer group, but the minute people of higher status are in the audience, he is nearly paralyzed with fright. Some may be extremely self-conscious when speaking to children, but find that they can address adults with considerable assurance. The star high school quarterback may address the football team with poise and assurance, but blush and flush, fidget and stammer when talking to a girl. Someone who is generally adroit at self-management may tighten up if his wife or his father is in the audience. Some people have no problem when the speech is of minor importance, but fold up almost completely when the risk is great. A person may, for example, normally speak with ease to his boss but find himself tight and trembling when asking his boss for an

Dimension 1: People as Communicators

increase in salary. A public speaker may ordinarily speak with confidence but tremble badly when speaking on behalf of a very important measure.

There may be causes outside the context of the speaking adventure that temporarily aggravate the speaker's feeling of uneasiness. A student speaker may be momentarily depressed or unhappy because of bad news from home, a notice about a poor grade, sweetheart trouble, loss of sleep, or a nasty cold. When he feels weary or blue, his self-assurance is adversely affected. On the other hand, when good news lifts his spirits and he is charged with physical and nervous energy, he is better able to manage his tension and overcome his inhibitions.

Now comes the difficult question: If a person is afflicted with a speech-fright problem, what can he do about it? We suggest a three-pronged approach—Become knowledgeable about various kinds of tension and probable sources of speech fright. Build constructive attitudes. And use specific tactics employing overt action.

Possible Sources of Speech Fright

The most common source of speech fright that generates the most serious emotional imbalance lies in our self-concept. There is *ego* involvement: Our feeling of *self-esteem* or sense of self-importance is being threatened. Our sense of pride is at stake. We care—in fact, too much—what others may think of us. We worry about others seeing our deficiencies and imperfections, imaginary or real. Hence we feel self-conscious and our conscious self pushes our real self out of the way. Our listeners are kept from seeing our true image.

A second kind of speech fright arises out of *conflict*. Conflict exists when thoughts and feelings are drawn in opposite directions. Examples of conflict in life are endless—the first time we drove a car, our first date, the first time we took an important examination. We have mixed feelings about possible success or failure. The girl who is asked to sing the solo part in the church choir because of the sudden illness of the regular soloist is at first thrilled and flattered. However, after the flush of inner joy subsides, she is seized by a sense of fright. She says to herself, "Oh, dear, what if I should fail?" Sweet thoughts of triumph conflict sharply with bitter thoughts of failure. The strong desire to do and the fear of failure work against each other so strongly that the will to action approaches dead center in risky situations. When thoughts of personal glory conflict with fear of failure, a good case of speech fright can develop. The will to do and the will to run away are both powerful forces.

Sometimes speech fears grow out of the unknown, like being afraid of the dark. We feel unsure about many things connected with the audience, the situation, and even ourselves, and this feeling of uncertainty makes us uncomfortable. The strange and unfamiliar bring on that nervous and uneasy feeling.

Another species of speech fright is of the synthetic type, the product of imagination and foolish notions. Some people imagine the audience to be much larger than it is; they think of listeners as being hostile when they really are friendly; they fear a slip of the tongue or a misstatement that will embarrass them. Some even develop emotional allergies; they feel scared at the sight of a lectern, a raised platform, a microphone. The very term *public speaking* strikes terror in their hearts. Among this group of synthetic fears is the fear of being afraid. Franklin Roosevelt once aptly reminded us that the greatest thing we had to fear was fear itself. In all probability, most of our speech-fright problems stem from our imagination. But although the source of our problems may be synthetic, as in all other cases the feelings of queasiness and uneasiness are strikingly real.

Still another variety of stage fright is characterized by a feeling of dread or aversion to do anything before a group. Some people have a tendency to withdraw from situations in which they are the center of attraction. They may be timid, shy, reticent, and find it distasteful to have any part of the limelight. This problem generally is not a severe one, since a little bit of practice will usually help overcome shyness.

Building Constructive Attitudes

Speech fright is common to most people. If you are troubled by it realize at once that you are not the only one with feelings of discomfort. Most speakers experience at least some of these feelings

Dimension 1: People as Communicators

at one time or another. The person sitting next to you is probably worse off than you are. In a survey of beginning speech students at the University of Kansas, only 3 percent claimed to experience no speech fright whatsoever. So you are not alone.

You should also realize that nature provides a built-in protective device—nervous energy—to contain and preserve the whole man and give order to his whole personality. Nervous energy is often more of an asset than a liability. The bad side of the phenomenon gets all the publicity; its virtues get very little notice. Nervous energy is not something to get rid of, like a wart; it is something to live with, something to control, something to put to good use. Nature provides an extra supply of power and energy for you to harness and control. Even highly experienced people tend to get feelings of excitement from anticipation before some event. It is a feeling of being keyed up and is experienced by actors just before the curtain rises, football players before the kickoff, concert artists before the recital, and public speakers before the chairman introduces them. This sense of excitement is nature's way of providing an extra supply of nervous energy for an extraordinary performance. Only as we fail to properly harness this added energy do we get tangled up by tensions and suffer the pangs of stage fright. So we see that some degree of speech fright may be an asset in our speaking venture.

Build a constructive attitude toward yourself. Avoid underrating yourself or the worthiness of your personal resources. This is particularly true concerning physical appearance; size, shape, weight, skin color, or health limitations are no real barriers to effective communication. Today more than ever, people are accepting of others because of what they are rather than what they look like. If you have something worthwhile to say and say it in an interesting manner, people will be interested in listening to you. If you feel that you are not as bright as most of your classmates, keep in mind that the smartest people in the world seldom are the best speakers. Anyone with a degree of talent and ability can develop an interesting and meaningful speech with effort and imagination. Remember that speech fright stems from a person's telling himself that he is inadequate, not from others telling him. So try to understand yourself; determine why you have speech fright; and then build your own brand of self-reliance. Always keep in mind that people admire a fighter, someone who stands and meets the challenge, whereas they hold little respect for someone who flees from the scene. The individual himself feels good about his personal worth when he has met an encounter boldly, but feels worthless when he has backed away.

Be a good self-competitor. Compete with yourself instead of against other members of the class. What matters most is how well you make use of your resources and your abilities. Have you been true to the unique talents available to you? You may make your greatest progress toward self-mastery the day you make your poorest speech grade and the least progress the day you make your best speech grade.

Control of speech fright usually comes gradually. One should not expect a complete overnight breakthrough. The important thing is to develop the will and desire to overcome, then seize every opportunity to speak. Like one who is learning to swim needs water, so one who is learning to speak must have listeners. Therefore, welcome the listener, the audience.

In your kit of attitude builders, consider the following points: You don't need gimmicks or tricks. You don't have to be clever or tell jokes. No one expects you to be perfect. You don't have to be completely at ease to succeed. The audience is usually on your side. Remember, in case of fire, collapsing walls, or flying objects, the speaker's stand is the best place from which to jump and run to safety!

Specific Tactics

In addition to developing a constructive attitude toward yourself as a communicator, consider using some of the following tactics in combating speech fright.

1. *Know your speech well.* The more you minimize the fear of forgetting, the less you have to be afraid of.

2. *Get involved with your subject.* The more you wrap yourself up in your subject, the less you are likely to worry about how you look. Direct your mental attention from yourself to the ideas you are trying to communicate.

Dimension 1: People as Communicators

3. *Speak directly to your listeners.* Avoid letting your eyes look at the floor, out the window, or over the heads of the audience. This is sure to intensify your fear. If you look directly at listeners, you will get more involved in talking to them and forget your fears. You will also discover very quickly that people are listening to you and are interested in what you are saying.

4. *Throw your physical self into the venture.* Let your body help you talk. Moreover, express yourself with more than what seems to you to be normal vocal inflection.

5. *Look directly at the more friendly, sympathetic faces in the audience.*

6. *When possible, use the blackboard and visual aids;* they will help you develop the type of bodily action that uses up excessive nervous energies.

7. *Don't let little mistakes throw you off course.* If you stumble, make an occasional grammatical error, mispronounce a word, or get tangled up on a phrase, don't focus on the mistake but keep thinking about the idea you are trying to communicate. Most listeners will notice small mistakes a lot less than you will.

8. *Stand tall, walk tall.* Take full, brisk strides when walking to the podium. Give yourself an air of confidence.

9. *If great tension grips you, admit it to the audience.* Tell them about it. They will be sympathetic, and such an admission quite often is the most vital antidote for curing speech fright.

10. *Above all, develop the will to communicate.* An athlete with the will to win is likely to perform well. A speaker with a will to communicate is on the road to successful speech communication.

The Reception of Messages

Listening is just as vital to interpersonal communication as its counterpart, speaking. People commonly think that listening is simply a matter of doing it; it is innate; one does not need to learn to do it. This thought is reflected by the fact that educators have for centuries recognized the need to improve the skills of reading, speaking, and writing but have largely neglected the art and skill of listening. A significant educational awakening concerning listening improvement occurred after World War II, reaching its peak in the late 1950s and early 1960s. However, listening training still does not receive anywhere near the amount of attention that the other three language-arts skills do. In an earlier day, the traditional emphases may have been wise; today, however, because of the tremendous amount of information and misinformation we receive from so many sources, the art and skill of listening seem more vital than ever. Moreover, in today's pressure-packed society, people may have a greater need to be listened to than in an earlier age. The biggest favor one can do a person at times is to give him an accepting and sympathetic ear. A criminology professor of one of the authors once related that when he had his shoes shined in Atlanta, Georgia, he struck up a conversation with the shoeshine person. The conversation became quite intense, with the man showing a great desire to talk about certain aspects of his life. Instead of turning off the conversation, the criminologist listened sympathetically, responding in an accepting manner from time to time. The discussion reached its climax when the shoeshine person told the professor that he had virtually decided to commit suicide, but that after their conversation he had decided on another course of action. It seems that the professor had been the first person to show a real interest in listening to him.

This discussion has already suggested several purposes for listening, so at this point we would like to explore the subject of purposes more fully. It is important to appreciate from the outset that each purpose calls for a slightly different approach to listening. For example, sometimes we should listen defensively; other times defensive listening creates communication breakdowns. Sometimes evaluative listening is necessary; other times it will constitute a barrier to understanding.

Purposes of Listening

1. *Casual Listening.* This is the most common and effortless listening we do. It is mostly of the informal chit-chat variety used

Dimension 1: People as Communicators

in the home, at work, and at play. It serves social needs. Courtesy and attentiveness are the most important factors of casual listening, since it is primarily a matter of enjoying ourselves and not offending those with whom we are conversing.

2. *Listening for Amusement.* Sometimes we like to listen for sheer pleasure. The term *entertainment* is commonly used to describe this type of activity, which is usually easy, relaxing, and refreshing. It normally consists of listening to music or to the electronic media. Elements of entertainment may, however, appear in almost any kind of public speaking also. Enjoyment and appreciation are the critical factors of this type of listening.

3. *Listening for Inspiration.* It is well known that man does not live by bread alone. We commonly listen to sermons, eulogies, tributes, and inspirational messages of all kinds to bring strength and renewal to the spiritual side of our nature, a need which never dies. Its meaning was aptly expressed by a college youth who pointed to a church on the corner and called it a filling station. It is a filling station where people go to recharge their spiritual batteries. Effective inspirational listening is more a matter of mood than of cold logic. All it requires is a positive and receptive attitude.

4. *Listening for Information.* Sometimes we listen to learn and to extend our horizon of knowledge. A college student is normally engaged in this type of listening when he goes to a lecture class. Jobs and professions frequently require adults to listen for information. This approach requires sustained attention and concentration, ability to sort out vital information, and skill in discerning essential relationships.

5. *Listening for Critical Evaluation.* We listen for critical evaluation when we assess a musical performance, a play, a debate, or political speeches. Critical evaluation of any art form requires the application of a meaningful set of criteria to the performance; it is a matter of assessing the artistic achievement of the performers. This is slightly different from critically listening to a debate or a political speech, since it requires the careful application of measures of meaning and rationality. We will discuss this more fully at a later point.

6. *Listening for Understanding.* Life presents us with many

situations in which it is highly desirable for us to make every effort to genuinely understand other people—a basic step in conflict resolution. Strife, to a great extent, stems from the fact that people make little effort to understand each other. We have just passed through a period when the *establishment* and the *counterculture* were guilty of this failing. The first requisite of listening for understanding is a nonevaluative attitude. We have to stop debating each other long enough to hear what the other is saying; we have to stop calling each other names and focus on issues; and we have to try to see the other person's point of view on the issues and keep our biases from interfering with the effort. This kind of listening is difficult but important to our collective well-being.

7. *Listening for Personal Reinforcement.* This type of listening is different from the others in that it is almost entirely for the benefit of the other person. There are moments when our listening is geared toward giving strength, hope, and courage to someone else. This type of listening is accepting, sympathetic, and nonevaluative. It also is therapeutic, be it the professional therapist listening to a patient or someone listening to a friend.

The Listening Process

Pay attention! Open your ears! How many times as a child did you hear these or similar words? People quite often think of listening as merely paying attention. However, listening is a much broader concept than this.

Listening consists of a five-fold process of aural assimilation: hearing, concentration, comprehension, interpretation and reflection, and reaction. (1) We hear sounds transmitted to us by air waves. (2) We concentrate on these sounds. (3) If the speaker is speaking a familiar language, we recognize and attach meanings to the oral symbols he is using. If a speaker is using a foreign tongue or terminology we do not understand, we cannot listen to his message. The best we can do is pay attention. We must be able to recognize language before we can comprehend it. (4) We interpret the speaker's message. We reflect as to the true meaning of what the speaker is saying and try to relate it to other things he has said or to our own past experiences. If we are listening critically, we are constantly evaluating the speaker's message at this point. (5) We react to the communication. Whether or not we react overtly—by smiling, scowling, clapping, cheering, and so forth—depends on the impact the message has on us. Sometimes a communication touches our emotional nature, and we respond by cheering loudly; at other times we show logical insight through certain facial expressions.

Problems in Listening

Concentration Problems

Listeners are limited in their ability to concentrate and can give complete attention to a stimulus for a few seconds only. The mind moves in waves and spurts. It pays attention to the speaker and then darts away for a brief instant. If we recorded our attention span, it would be a zigzag line. This is particularly complicated by the fact that a person speaks only 125 to 160 words per minute while the listener's mind can think at least three to five times that fast. The listener must, therefore, exert special effort to keep these mental spurts focused on the speaker's message. If the listener is highly motivated or intensely interested, sustaining attention is relatively easy. However, if the speech is boring and the listener's interest and motivation are low, his mind is likely to dart away from the speaker's message for longer and longer periods of time until he has lost all track of the thought line. If neither interest nor motivation are strong, most people can sustain adequate attention for no more than 15 minutes; from that point on, their attention tends to steadily diminish. Poor communication usually results from a speech that lasts 45 minutes or more, though a listener may find it more difficult to sustain attention for a dull 10-minute speech than for a very interesting one that lasts for an hour.

We often have too much on our minds to give full attention to the speaker. Modern living is full of tensions, busy schedules and complex activities which drain our ability to give sustained attention. Did I turn off the gas before leaving home? Why is my bank balance so low? How are things going at home? Do those slight pains I feel in my chest from time to time suggest serious illness? These and a thousand other questions are vying for the attention of our minds. The more complicated our lives become, the more we have to deal with distractions which get in the way when we try to listen.

This multiorientation gives rise to private planning. While someone is speaking—and the problem is often as great in private conversation as it is while listening to a speech—we permit our minds to dart off and plan what we are going to do over the weekend, how we are going to approach the term paper in history, how we are going to finance the car we just purchased, or how we are going to reply to controversial points the speaker is making. Preoccupation with our personal activities is an enemy of effective listening.

Personality Problems

Certain personality traits act as barriers to effective listening. Three traits are especially detrimental. The first is *self-effacement*. These listeners have appropriately been called *compulsive nodders*. They agree to everything the speaker says. Always attentive, nice, sympathetic, and compliant, they nod approval and every few minutes in a conversation insert "that's right" or some variation of that. Such a person led Cicero to cry out, "By the gods, disagree with me, so that there can be two of us!" These people seldom engage in diligent reflection and fail to listen from any position of conviction or assertion. Their principal concern is giving the impression of being attentive and agreeable. Sometimes they are so concerned with their "yesses" that they miss what actually is being said.

Argumentativeness is the opposite of self-effacement. The argumentative personality listens in a defensive and aggressive manner. He cannot afford to be enthusiastic about what anyone says, let alone agree with him. In conversation, discussion, or debate he spends most of his time thinking of what he is going to say as soon as he gets a chance. He seldom reflects on the ideas of others but merely gets cues from the speaker which trigger his own lines of argument. Listening to a speech is difficult for him because it never gives him a chance to speak himself. This, however, does not keep him from debating the speaker. Silently he questions everything the speaker says and goes off on thought tangents of his own. He is thoroughly nonreceptive to anyone else's point of view.

Many people find *daydreaming* a pleasant and convenient escape from reality; James Thurber's Walter Mitty has some great moments through this vicarious device. The daydreamer escapes into fantasy because his mind is undisciplined or because he is disturbed emotionally and seeks a release from his problems. Everyone is given to daydreaming occasionally; perhaps a certain amount of it is time well spent, for it may be relaxing. But an excessive amount is wasteful. Daydreaming problems are not limited to public speaking situations; members of a small group often ease off into a fantasy world and miss out on the group's deliberations. The problem is most pronounced when listening to a dull speech, when it is pleasant, relaxing, and indeed tempting to daydream. The listener must realize that daydreaming is the arch-rival of effective listening.

Skills of Listening

PRIOR TO THE SPEECH find out something about the speaker. Who is he? What has he done? What are his principal interests? What are his positions on controversial issues? Also learn something about his topic. If he is going to speak on semantics, for example, be sure that you discover what is meant by this discipline and what some of its important teachings are. And if the speaker has written a book on this subject, it is useful to skim through it before hearing his speech.

DURING THE SPEECH consider the following practices for listening improvement:

1. *Look directly at the speaker.* Eye contact can be as important for the listener as for the speaker. Your attention is less likely to waver so long as it is focused on the speaker. You may also obtain important meanings from his visual aspects.

2. *Resist distractions.* If noises are made by the audience or by some external agent, listen all the harder. Double your efforts to concentrate.

3. *Approach the speech with a favorable attitude.* A *favorable*

set may be a genuine asset to listening. It has been shown that listeners with this kind of attitude are able to recall significantly more content after the speech than those with an unfavorable attitude. Keep an open mind throughout the speech. Too many listeners hear a few lines of a speech, decide that it is going to be dull or irrelevant to them, and stop listening. Search for items that may be of possible interest to you. Also, try to recognize your emotional feelings about the speaker's topic and make certain that you do not monitor the speech unfairly. If there is a status difference between you and the speaker, remind yourself that the viewpoint of someone from another station in life can greatly broaden your outlook.

4. *Focus on the central thought-line.* Look for the speaker's central idea. Then try to relate his other materials to it.

5. *Concentrate on main points.* Identify the speaker's main points clearly in your mind. If he has not organized his speech, do it for him. Construct a skeleton of the speech in your own mind. Avoid getting sidetracked by details.

6. *Periodically review the progress of the speech.* After each main point is concluded, it is helpful to think back over the rest of the speech. This review will help fix the main ideas in your mind and allow you to see the speech as a whole.

7. *Look for hidden meanings.* This is sometimes called *listening between the lines.* Try to determine if the speaker means everything literally. He may be speaking figuratively or implying something entirely different from what the surface meanings of his words indicate.

8. *Avoid tripping over little things.* The listener faces all kinds of listening hazards that he may trip over. He may be somewhat shocked by the looks of the speaker, his peculiar dress, the way he walks, his hair, unbecoming gestures, or bad grammar. Also, some of the platform fixtures may seem in disarray. There may be lighting or microphone difficulties. Try to avoid overreacting to such fringe elements.

9. *Don't give up on difficult materials.* Difficult materials are often identified with abstract theory, complex problems, complicated processes of logic, technical language, and excessive use of

Dimension 1: People as Communicators

statistics. Quite often with a little more effort you may find that you can cope with these materials.

10. *Encourage the speaker.* Let the speaker know that you want him to have his say. Show by eye contact, facial expressions, and posture that you are interested. Audience feedback often will help the speaker perform at his best. Good listening in a speech class helps everyone make better speeches.

11. *Hear the speaker out.* Should you become distraught or have mixed feelings about the speech, stay with it until the end; this reduces the risk of errors or false impressions about the speaker and his purpose.

AFTER THE SPEECH mentally review and summarize it. Determine what you may have heard in the speech that you especially want to make a part of your storehouse of knowledge and opinion. Repeat the review the next day. This kind of a review will greatly improve your chances of remembering the main ideas.

Tools for Critical Listening

We believe that effective critical listeners ask four important questions about the speaker and his speech: What do you mean? Why are you so concerned about this? Why should I believe this? Why is this important? An easy way to remember these questions is through the words *meaning, motivation, support,* and *importance.*

Our first step in a critical test of a speech is finding the true *meaning* of the speaker, regardless of motives or worthiness of substance. A number of reasons may explain why meaning sometimes is unclear. Apart from the usual problem of selecting words, phrases, and images that will generate relatively-congruent meaning in the mind of a listener, obscurity often occurs for still other reasons. In the first place, a speaker may have perfectly good and honorable intentions but misfire with his intended meaning because he is using language that is too technical, too vague, too scholarly, or too removed from the experience of his auditors. Sometimes the speaker himself may not really be sure exactly what he means, either because he does not understand it properly or because he has not thought it out carefully enough. Propagandists commonly try to bamboozle their listeners with abstract terms that are unclear and often inaccurate. Seldom are they specific. They fail to use *names, numbers, dates* and *places*, but rely on generalities such as *truth, freedom, the people's will, progress, honor,* and *the democratic way of life*. Communist propagandists are fond of using such terms as the *people's party, republic,* and *the workingman's government*. Most of these expressions mean vastly different things to different people, but propagandists never specify the sense in which they are using them. They hope that listeners will provide their own interpretations and will assume that they mean the same thing.

You may already have detected that most of the generalities of the propagandist are *loaded terms*, or expressions with a high degree of emotional connotation. The traditional appeal to *motherhood* and the *family hearth*, for example, can be used by anyone for any kind of purpose. When a speaker has used a lot of abstract terms, ask yourself if he really means what he seems to be saying. Try to discover his real purpose. Many people joined the Communist Party during the 1930s because the party's stated principles were appealing, yet most of these people were quickly disillusioned when they discovered what the communists really had in mind. Finally, beware of slogans and sayings. Such expressions as "Everyman has his price," "You can't teach an old dog new tricks," or "Honest government for honest Americans" are never specific and rarely accurate. They are an extreme form of generality.

The speaker's *motivation* for speaking tends to explain why he takes a certain position on the point at issue. This is why it is wise for the listener to keep asking, "Who are you?" "Why are you so concerned about this?" "Why do you feel as you do?" A person may give the semblance of objectivity, but he really may be speaking from a basic position of bias resulting from a vested interest. It is not wrong, of course, for someone to speak for his own interests, but knowledge of the speaker's motivation helps the listener detect sham objectivity. Propagandists of all sorts commonly try to exploit people's tendency to think emotionally while they pride themselves on their logicality. They do this by giving an impression of objectivity and by accentuating certain "facts" and passing them off as "typical." They may even recognize an opposing argument in

Dimension 1: People as Communicators

order to carry through the semblance of objectivity. All the while, however, they may be using distorted facts and figures to establish a point. At other times they may be emphasizing unimportant or irrelevant aspects of a subject instead of the central issue. The critical listener must look beyond the speaker's apparent objectivity by inquiring into the speaker's motivation if he is to detect such practices.

A speaker makes his ideas *acceptable* through logic and evidence. Thus, in answering the question, "Why should I believe this?" it is generally well to do two things: Evaluate the speaker's supporting evidence and evaluate the speaker's reasoning.

It is important to identify the significant claims a speaker makes and to test his supporting evidence in relation to these claims. Five questions should generally be asked about the speaker's supporting materials:

1. *Does he cite any evidence?* Or is the speaker merely supporting his claims with other assertions? Is he supporting them solely with emotional appeals? Or is he relying on nicety of expression and smoothness of delivery?

2. *Is the evidence he uses accurate and reliable?* Does the speaker report the source from which he got his evidence? How reliable are the sources he cites? Is there any possible distortion in the data he cites?

3. *Is the evidence he uses typical?* Does he use examples that are truly representative of the subject he is discussing?

4. *Is the evidence he uses sufficient?* Does the speaker overgeneralize from isolated instances? Does he base his claim on enough examples?

5. *Is the evidence he uses relevant?* Certain propagandists, Senator Joseph McCarthy, for example, have been masters at citing a lot of factual data that, when scrutinized carefully, did not prove to be relevant to their claims. The demagogue commonly employs a kind of factual smoke screen.

Despite the obvious importance of evidence in speech, we must warn against being overawed by facts. Ideas are important, not a simple listing of facts, but many people have an uncritical respect for facts and for anything that resembles objectivity. Commercial advertisers exploit this trait fully. "Science proves . . . ," they say, or "Eight out of ten doctors smoke Brand X cigarettes." Another great danger of overvaluing the scientific orientation is that it tends to make us ignore the importance of judgments, sentiments, emotions, and creative thinking.

One does not have to be an expert logician to test a speaker's reasoning; common sense, properly applied, will usually tell us if one thought logically follows another. Some specious reasoning, however, occurs in a rather subtle fashion, and a constant vigil is necessary to guard against it. The two most common logical fallacies are false causes and hasty generalizations. The speaker commits a false-cause fallacy when he ascribes something as the cause of an effect, when in reality it is not the cause at all or is perhaps only a minor contributing cause. He may tell his listeners, for example, that we have to curb labor unions because the growth of labor unions has brought with it considerable unemployment. No real causal relationship may exist between labor unions and unemployment; actually, a general business recession probably caused the rise in unemployment. People also commonly commit *post hoc* fallacies, meaning they attribute one thing to be the cause of another merely because it happened immediately after the other. A service station operator may paint his building red, whereupon his business increases; he assumes that the increase is the result of the new color of his physical plant. There may be a causal relationship between the new color and the business increase, but the fact that his leading competitor went out of business at the same time may be the real cause.

A hasty generalization is the result of jumping to a conclusion on the basis of too little evidence. We may know several artists who led immoral lives and conclude that all artists are immoral. Our sampling in this case is wholly inadequate to warrant a universal induction.

Fact-inference confusion also is a common cause of faulty thinking. You may recall that an observation is a *perceived fact*, whereas an inference is a conclusion drawn from a fact. Interpretations are not necessarily congruent with reality. Yet people commonly pass them off as being factual. It is essential for a critical listener to examine key factual statements to determine if they embody hidden inferences. A similar confusion often occurs from value statements. People very often present value judgments as though they were statements of fact. A statement like "It is better to be dead than Red" expresses a value and cannot be verified in physical reality. The statement is not true or false. It is merely acceptable or unacceptable, depending upon a person's values.

For years debaters have used a device known as the *so what* technique. It consists of questioning the *importance* of the opponent's arguments. One side may have carefully developed a point but failed to demonstrate its significance in the larger issue being debated. If the affirmative says that we need to abolish capital punishment because it was opposed by the greatest criminal lawyer of all time, Clarence Darrow, the negative may justifiably ask, "So what? How is this important?"

The "so what" technique is equally useful in critical listening. A speaker may develop a point with meticulous care but fail to demonstrate that it has any real significance. Most commercials using testimonials certainly should receive this treatment. "Joe Namath eats Wheaties." (So what?) A critical listener should keep asking if the speaker's ideas are really important. If a question-and-answer period is held and some of the speaker's arguments have failed to pass the "so what" test, ask him to demonstrate their importance.

Characteristics of People in Audiences

An audience may be favorable to the speaker and to his subject; it may also be neutral, apathetic, or hostile. The typical American audience, with its sense of fair play and its belief in freedom of speech, tends to be courteous and mannerly. Usually there is a kind of host-guest relationship between the speaker and his listeners. It is safe to assume that most audiences will be neutral, which means that they are at least mildly interested in what the speaker has to say. The favorable audience is very friendly toward the speaker and highly-motivated to listen to his speech. The apathetic group, while not actually hostile, suffers from indifference. It has little interest in the speaking situation, and some of its members may even fall asleep. This audience needs to be *jarred* to attention somehow, perhaps by a very startling introduction. The hostile audience, at the least, is unsympathetic to the speaker's subject and quite often to the speaker himself. However, hostile heckling or walking out in the middle of a meeting exhibits a rudeness that is the exception, not the rule.

A second characteristic is that an audience is not a faceless flock; its members differ from one another in countless ways. Listeners will differ in life experiences, in training, education, social status, family background, self-discipline, context of rational and emotional behavior, and so on. Each listener, so to speak, lives in a private, isolated world of his own. Yet he will be influenced to some extent by the responses of other members of the group. Differences in the audience may be of little consequence or they may be of great importance. They may also vary from one subject to another. People may, for example, disagree strongly on political preferences but unite fully on religious or educational matters. An audience is, therefore, a plurality; each member has his own values, his own emotional makeup, and his own motivation to listen. Yet, in most audiences there is a kind of group norm that is discernible. Most of the members may be businessmen, or most of them may be laborers. It is to some unifying norm that a speaker normally tries to relate his presentation.

A third important characteristic of an audience is that its members tend to react to one another. Although every listener resides in his private sphere structured by a social self, each one is somewhat sensitive to persons to the right and to the left of him. Sometimes, in response to a question, people will not raise their hands until they see people around them do so. Every speech teacher knows how the listening mood of a class is governed to a degree by who sits with whom and by who shares the ideas and feelings expressed by the teacher and student speakers. Most listeners will tend to respond favorably to the speaker if the majority of the group is favorable. "If we are to retain our status in the group," Ewbank and Auer assert in their book *Discussion and Debate* "we do what the others do. If our fellows put money in the collection plate, sign the pledge, or cheer the speaker, we tend to conform to the group standard which they set."[5] This is why

---

[5] Henry Lee Ewbank and J. Jeffery Auer, *Discussion and Debate*, 2nd ed. (New York: Appleton-Century-Crofts, 1951), p. 213.

Dimension 1: People as Communicators

television producers often scatter in the audience paid "laughers" or "applauders" who, at specified times, laugh loudly or clap vigorously. Those sitting nearby will usually follow the lead, and soon a swell of applause or laughter is under way. Not only do people react to the majority response of an audience of which they are a part; they also tend to react to particular people in the group. If we see someone whom we especially respect reacting favorably, we are very likely to do likewise. The extent to which auditors influence one another's responses is greatly dependent upon their homogeneity, their group feeling, and their polarization. *Polarization* (see Figure 6) means commonality of focus and feeling. Individual-mindedness is replaced by group-mindedness, which is similar to team spirit. Many factors may produce a feeling of togetherness in an audience. When people identify their welfare with the welfare of those around them, polarization occurs. When people perform as a group, be it singing, saluting the flag, standing for an invocation, reciting a creed, or cheering, they tend to lose a degree of their individuality. Even such a simple technique as having people sit or stand close together helps to polarize them. The greater the polarization, the greater the likelihood of audience response.

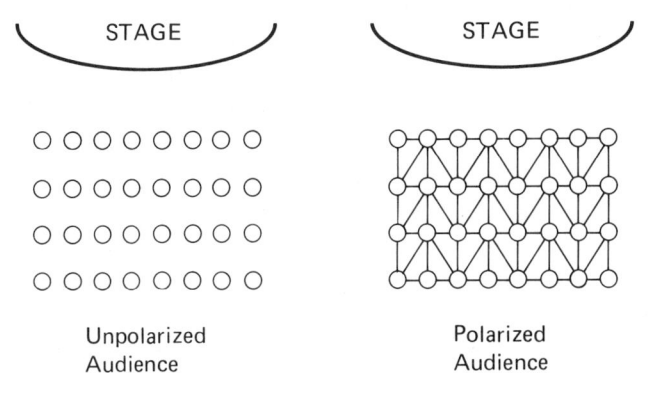

Unpolarized Audience   Polarized Audience

Figure 6—Model of Polarization

dimension two

circumstances of the communication

In the summer of 1967, negotiations for a major summit conference between Premier Kosygin of the USSR and President Lyndon Johnson came to fruition. One of the vital issues surrounding the talks was the site of the event. It was determined that Kosygin should come to the United States, but where in the country were the two heads of state to meet? A meeting in Washington, the nation's capital, would appear to give President Johnson a position of dominance. Camp David was also rejected because it carried the image of a second White House for American presidents. Finally, Glassboro, New Jersey, was selected as the site. Glassboro in no way projected the image that either executive was playing a dominant role. Moreover, Glassboro, being a quiet, restful place amidst peaceful mountains, was considered a good spot to inspire the compassionate and noble nature of man.

The Johnson-Kosygin conference illustrates the vital role that setting and context may play in interpersonal communication. The previous dimension considered people as communicators; this dimension places these people into circumstances that impinge upon their communicative activity. The circumstances of communication involve three key factors: when, where, and why. In order to give a broader perspective, deeper insights, and a keener sense of awareness about this dimension we offer three preliminary observations.

First, this dimension is probably the one most overlooked by the average speech student. It is one that we most likely take for granted. This is not so strange when one considers that many professional communication educators who concern themselves with the development of models of communication tend to overlook it also. The who, what, and how aspects in the context of oral discourse will more likely take preference over when, where, and why in the minds of people. To try to rank communication circumstances as to relative importance in relation to the other basic dimensions of interpersonal communication is not our purpose. Each has its unique potency for chain reaction in the communication process. Yet there are many things to consider concerning what is practical, wise, ethical, humane, and relevant to time, place, and occasion.

Second, by its very nature, this dimension is less manageable and controllable than the others. That is to say, it is less oriented to the art and mechanical skills involved in oral communication. These are external conditions to which speaker and listener must make responsible and meaningful adjustments.

Finally, the ever-present factors of time, place, and occasion often generate the less obvious subtleties that pertain to the inner person—the emotional, intellectual, physical, and spiritual selves of speakers and listeners. Some people, for example, dread getting involved in conversation before 10 o'clock in the morning. They wake up slowly. Some people get upset by color combinations; for example, prominent platform lecturers of the past have actually been known to order their hotel rooms repapered before they would sleep there. A favorite tool of diplomats is a banquet prior to serious negotiations. Restaurants are often judged by their decor and service as well as by the food they serve.

Speeches given at an honors banquet, a high school commencement, or an athletic pep rally will be constrained by the environment and circumstances of the occasion. It also makes a difference where conversation takes place, be it in the home parlor, the principal's office, a bar, over the garden fence, or in the boss's office. Sometimes the most meaningful conversations occur while riding in an automobile. Every speech class is influenced by the size and shape of the room, the podium, windows, furniture, even the cracks in the floor. Able speakers will recognize situational constraints and adjust to them. These constraints fall into three categories: time, place, and occasion.

Time

"Time talks. It speaks more plainly than words. The message it conveys comes through loud and clear. Because it is manipulated less conspicuously, it is subject to less distortion than the spoken language. It can shout the truth where words lie." These words constitute the opening paragraph of Edward T. Hall's book, *The Silent Language*.[1]

"Die Zeit hat eine heilige Kraft," writes Goethe. "Time has a supreme mission." It is the essence of life. There is so much of it, yet so little. Battles are won or lost in a matter of minutes; nations are born or perish in a matter of hours. Better see your doctor in time, it may be a matter of life or death. Many a football game would have a different outcome if playing time were extended another minute.

Next to the weather, time might be a favorite topic of conversation—"Excuse me, could you tell me what time it is"; "Have you time for a cup of coffee"; "good-by now"; and "see you later" are all common expressions. The Old Testament of the Bible speaks about morning and evening time, harvest time, rain time, marriage time, meal time, birth time, death time. Here time is not measured by minutes and hours but by happenings. Its meaning is of *quality* not quantity. We are familiar with such sayings as "A stitch in time saves nine"; "Strike while the iron is hot"; "It is not what you buy, but when"; and "too little and too late." The Bible even says that there is a "time to speak."

All nature vibrates with time messages marked by seasons, daylight, nighttime, ocean tides, cycles and rhythms for the survival of all plants and living creatures. For centuries men have pondered the riddle of the migration of birds and fish. Everything is in varying degrees governed by time.

Time is only a four-letter word, yet it commands more space in Funk and Wagnall's *College Dictionary* than any other single word. It serves to identify life's most moving and trivial experiences. There is a time for laughter and tears; time to eat, sleep, catch the

---

[1] Edward T. Hall, *The Silent Language* (New York: Doubleday, 1959), p. 23.

bus, mail a letter, pay taxes, plant potatoes, pick violets, put out the cat, go fishing.

People as communicators must not forget that time is not a separate, unrelated entity. It registers man's environment and measures meanings in a ratio to experience and happenings. It is a catalyst for communication. It relates to speechmaking at five different levels.

The first level pertains to restrictions imposed upon the speaker by the immediate situation and locale. Time ties strings to the speaker. He is schedule-bound and must adjust to the time allotted him and the others who take part in the meeting. Some schedules are loose and flexible, others rigid, and usually the speaker knows how much time he is expected to use; he almost always knows when he is supposed to stop. More important is the fact that the listeners usually understand these time restrictions and are more conscious of them than the speaker and more insistent that the restrictions be observed. Church is supposed to let out promptly at 12 o'clock; when the minister runs overtime, the worshipers start to shuffle about, rack prayer books, adjust their personal effects, look toward the exits, and think about Sunday dinner. College students who must operate on tight schedules are especially time-conscious and are likely to tune out a class lecture a minute or two before the bell rings. The chances are that anything the lecturer says after the bell rings is a total loss.

The second level concerns events immediately preceding and immediately following a speech. The order of speakers on a program can be very important. Anyone who has ever participated in an oratorical contest, where there may be as many as seven or eight short speeches given in succession, will tell you that it makes a difference whether you speak first, last, or in the middle. Speakers at banquets are often sandwiched between musical numbers or announcements and therefore, must have the ability to expand or contract, or to relate their speech to preceding events.

The third level deals with time constraints imposed by nature. Listener moods, attitudes, feelings, desires, even tastes are influenced by the hour of the day, the day of the week, and the season of the year. The soothsayer's warning to Caesar, "Beware the Ides of March," links motivation to time. For example: A breakfast conference, a noon luncheon meeting, and an evening banquet provide wide variations of psychological overtones. A college dean is disturbed by the popularity of classes meeting at 10 and 11 o'clock in the morning, while 7:30 morning classes and 4:30 afternoon classes are avoided. Experienced actors often change their style of acting for the matinee performance. Night is a better time for emotional release. Preradio evangelists found that soul-saving efforts were more rewarding at night than in broad daylight. There is an old saying that "the moon and the stars must first cast their spell over man and woman before there can be a march to the marriage altar."

Adolf Hitler, a master of propaganda and mass persuasion, was astutely aware of the function of time of day in persuasion. He records in *Mein Kampf* that as a beginner he set a meeting for an important speech at 10 o'clock on a Sunday morning.

> The result was depressing, yet at the same time extremely instructive: the hall was full, the impression really overpowering, but the mood ice cold; no one became warm, and I myself as a speaker felt profoundly unhappy at being unable to create any bond, not even the slightest contact, between myself and my audience, I thought I had not spoken worse than usual; but the effect seemed to be practically nil.[2]

These early experiences led Hitler to conclude:

> The same lecture, the same speaker, the same theme, have an entirely different effect at ten o'clock in the morning, at three o'clock in the afternoon, or at night.
> ... In the morning and even during the day people's will power seems to struggle with the greatest energy against an attempt to force upon them a strange will and a strange opinion. At night, however, they will succumb more easily to the dominating force of a stronger will.[3]

Within this third level, listener responses to external happenings and to personal matters that affect inner equilibrium are significant. We are a news-conscious people. Shocking events of vital interest to the local community, such as a big fire, a sudden storm,

---

[2] Adolf Hitler, *Mein Kampf*, trans. Ralph Mannheim (Boston: Houghton Mifflin, 1943), p. 474.
[3] *Ibid.*, pp. 473, 475.

extreme temperatures, and electric power failures, create interference for effective listening. On a broader scale, race riots, a stock market crash, or the assassination of a president are barriers to communication. Likewise, a new crisis in the Near East, Southeast Asia, or any other part of the world causes the listener to become mentally preoccupied.

Then there are those time-geared personal problems that disturb the self-equilibrium of individual listeners. These are under cover and are not predictable by the speaker. Some listeners may feel drowsy, hungry, or ill. In a speech class one student may be preoccupied with a somber note from home, another with a bad grade, another with an overdrawn checking account, another with a problem with his sweetheart, while another may be racing his mental motors rehearsing his speech. Each listener is in a world by himself, influenced by an event in the context of time.

The fourth level concerns the emergence of ideas, movements, and problems that demonstrate man's effort to adjust to a changing environment. Victor Hugo once wrote, "Greater than an army is an idea whose time has come." Dreams often have a way of coming true, not so much because of what they are but of when they occur. History is a record of ideas whose time had come. Nearly 200 years ago a group of men "brought forth upon this continent a new nation" founded upon the idea of a government of, for, and by the people. Nearly 2000 years ago the Christian Era ushered into this world a new image of the dignity of man. Since World War II we have seen the idea of a better world order with increased chances for world peace take shape in the form of the United Nations. We have also seen a worldwide revolt against colonialism and have seen new nations emerge and take their places in the family of nations. The past decades in American culture have been marked by minority rights, school busing, women's liberation, family planning, drug addiction, pollution control, and so on.

Such concepts are even more evident in the area of science. The development of the radio, radar, atomic energy, and space travel are not the products of any single, isolated mind of a genius. These are products of many minds with ideas whose time had come. The U.S. Patent Office reports that numerous applications for patent rights for the same thing are made at approximately the same time. Thirteen applications for patent rights of the Eskimo Pie arrived in Washington from all parts of the nation, postmarked on the same day. From Eskimo Pies to moon rockets, our lives are touched by ideas whose time has come.

Some speakers are born in the fires of crises. Athens needed Demosthenes because of the threat of Alexander. Churchill was the man of the hour for England when Hitler threatened to conquer her. President Roosevelt's declaration-of-war speech following Pearl Harbor, President Kennedy's speech to the nation at the time of the Cuban missile crisis, and President Nasser's speech offering to resign when his military forces were defeated by the Israelis in 1967 are examples of zero-hour speeches. They represent the moments of decision determining a course of action for a segment of society.

Place

Location, in the context of the physical, social, cultural, and political environment which makes up the total setting, has a strong influence upon the attitudes and feelings of the communicators involved. Change of venue is a well-known legal term used to determine the place where criminal trials may be held to give maximum fairness and justice. The place to hold the peace conference growing out of the Vietnam war was an important issue which took more than a year to settle, and several months of deliberation and debate were devoted to the size and shape of the conference table.

One vital constraint of place is the city or general locale in which the speech is to be given. There are the obvious cultural and vocational differences of place, such as urban-rural, depressed area–prosperous area, and north-south, but more subtle factors may exist as well. For instance, if a person is speaking for education in a city that has just built an ultramodern high school, the element of place may have great effect on how his message is received. Community pride is likely to be strong about such matters. A good question to be answered, therefore, is, "What are the special achievements of the community?" Another area of concern includes those things of which the people of the community are especially aware. Residents of Topeka, Kansas, for example, are intensely aware of mental health, since both the state hospital and the Menninger Foundation are located in that city. A tragedy, a triumph, or a community's aspirations may make one place different from another. Some places—a camp site, a cemetery, a street corner, a city park, a smoke-filled room—have special value connotations. One can only speculate, for example, how much impact the cemetery had on Lincoln's Gettysburg Address, both then and now when we read the speech, but it seems safe to assume that the same words spoken in another place would not have had the same connotative value. Lincoln did, in fact, speak many of the same words in Washington at an earlier time, but hardly anybody knows this. Some people have said that Lincoln's address at Cooper Union in New York City made him president, but he had tried out the ideas of the speech in various Kansas communities at an earlier time, a fact that is also little known.

The type of meeting hall is a second critical aspect of place. The general aura of the building is likely to affect audience response. An old auditorium with an extremely high ceiling has a cold and austere atmosphere, whereas an attractively decorated, more intimate room with plush carpets tends to be cheerful and friendly. Lighting of the hall creates a definite tone. Have you ever tried to tell a joke in the dark? Furthermore, a display of certain symbols, such as a flag, club charter, or group insignia, will tend to polarize an audience and intensify response. Ventilation will surely affect the response to a speech; an uncomfortable audience will find listening difficult.

The third constraint of place is the proximity of the members of the audience to each other. If people are seated close together or are standing in a tight mass, more *elbow rubbing* occurs. Laughter will swell rapidly, and emotional reactions will be encouraged as a result of mutual stimulation. The next time you are a member of a widely scattered audience in a large auditorium, observe how difficult it is for the speaker to get an enthusiastic response, be it applause, emotional reaction, or laughter. If you yourself should have the misfortune of speaking to a scattered audience, try to get them to move in together. Before you begin your speech, either you or the program chairman can ask the listeners to move down front and sit in a group.

A public-address system will influence the reception of the speech. Bad acoustics may deaden what would ordinarily be a dynamic presentation. The speaker may not be able to improve upon the acoustical design of a large auditorium, but proper seating and a public-address system will normally make it possible for him to be heard. It is easier to listen to a speaker whose voice is amplified by a public-address system. Without an amplifying system, the voice will tend to sound flat. In a smaller room with good acoustics, a public-address system is usually not necessary; in fact, any advantages may be outweighed by its disadvantages: The sound may be uncomfortably loud, and the microphone may restrict the speaker's bodily action.

Occasion

The occasion is the raison d'être underlying the speech situation. A high school commencement, a professional convention, a Kiwanis Club meeting, a courtroom trial, a presidential State of the Union message, a church service, a business luncheon—all of these provide speech occasions, and each of these occasions is likely to embody expectations that constrain the speaker's rhetorical choices. Rarely does a speech occur without a specific occasion. A soapbox orator in a city park and a street-corner pitchman must create their own speech occasions, but even these operate in the context of a communicational environment.

There is a reason that the occasion becomes a happening in reality; there are always some underlying objectives, purposes, and motives. We suggest some of the common types of occasions connected with various patterns of audience involvement. The first type falls under the broad category of *regularly scheduled meetings*. Such gatherings are usually identified with some organization or institution sponsoring meetings with regularity as to time, place, and common motives and interests. On the basis of time consumed and number of people involved, this is by far the most common type and covers a broad scope of activities identified with religious, educational, political, community, social, civic, and cultural matters. We see these audience groups in churches, lodges, fraternal organizations, civic clubs, literary clubs, women's clubs, high school and college classrooms, labor unions, and a great variety of specialty groups. They are usually orderly, with a pattern of procedure under directions of some kind of written guidelines and responsible leadership. While there may be a level of the passive attitude and prodding pressures for attendance at meetings, there is usually, on balance, a kind of group consciousness and *esprit de corps*. The speaker is likely to find his listeners courteous, cooperative, friendly, and open to suggestion and polarization. This is where we find the more functional and productive results in speechmaking ventures.

A second type of occasion is where groups meet on *special call*. The time, place, and purpose of the meeting are usually matters clarified by appropriate announcements. Such occasions frequently offer something out of the ordinary. A mood of expectancy, excitement, or perhaps drama frequently characterizes the occasion on special call. Under this type we might mention special political caucuses or conventions, banquets featuring honors and awards, special meetings to nominate or elect some high-ranking official or take action on some hotly contested issue. The meeting might be a sports rally to build school spirit or team morale. This type of occasion may also include the celebration of an historical event or achievement, or the recognition of some prestigious person; we must also include memorial or patriotic services, court trials, funerals, and weddings. This kind of audience is normally highly polarized even before the occasion. Strong emotional overtones may prevail, ranging from the glorified, ennobling spirit to that of bitter conflict and even hostility.

A third type of occasion may be identified by *discussion groups and business meetings*, which symbolize a phenomenon of speech communication germane to the American way of life. The real power and proving grounds of the democratic legislative process rest in the committee system of our law-making bodies. The committee is where the action is. In a discussion group such as a forum, round table, seminar, or parliamentary session, the speakers and listeners interchange roles. The smaller the committee, the more each listener becomes proportionately involved. Some discussion audiences are set up primarily for exploring ideas and learning from each other, with little or no concern for a business meeting. These are brain-storming occasions.

In most discussion situations, there are active differences of opinion among the members. In matters of controversy, many points of view with sharp differences will emerge. When one participant speaks his mind, other members may be busy thinking up contrary proposals. This is no place for a model creative piece, since most of the speaking is done in spurts, and for the most part the messages are realistic and directed for a specific purpose.

The fourth type of occasion involves the *guided and controlled* audience, loosely organized, on the move, for pleasure, sight-seeing, field trips, learning, observing, and so on, under the supervision of a teacher or specially trained qualified guide. The group may be standing, walking, seated in a room, or riding in a bus, boat, train, or airplane. Freshmen in a university may be given a guided tour of the library with demonstrations on how to use it, or a tour of the entire educational plant. Grade- and high-school groups are often taken to visit a factory, museum, zoo, famous monuments, or a capital building. Many college students during vacation time and people with leisure and means take off on tours to see the sights, artifacts, and people in the United States and other lands. Those who are travel-minded will in various ways become involved in tour groups where members are free to ask questions and make comments in a unique open forum. In this kind of audience, one may expect an odd mixture of passive attitudes with a broad range of tastes and interests. Usually curiosity is a prevailing polarizing force. Speaking predominantly features methods of reporting and explaining exemplifying the *show and tell* manner of communication widely featured in grade-school classes.

The fifth type is the *freewheeling* audience-occasion setup usually made up of pedestrians who accidentally come along and become casual listeners. The circus barker, the street-corner agitator, the soapbox orator, the sidewalk vendor, the medicine man, the auctioneer selling distressed goods, or the itinerant religious zealot are examples of this kind of speaking engagement. The collective listeners are a sort of short-ride hitchhiker, and the speakers engage in a kind of oral showmanship.

Success in this kind of oral communication depends almost wholly on attention-getting devices. The speaker normally must have a strong resonant voice and use a lot of exaggerated bodily action and crude slapstick comedy. The freewheeling audience is seldom seated; its members are on the loose. Since they are generally curious onlookers, their reactions to the speaker are highly variable.

dimension three
message preparation: thought and its form

Speech communication, by definition, is a social process. The speaker's messages should generate meaning in the minds of other people. Mere self-expression in a speech, regardless of its artistry, is antithetical to true communication. Therefore, a speaker's major concern is discovering and selecting the ideas he wishes to present to someone. The inclusion of ideas (and their amplification and support, as well as form) or their exclusion constitutes a fundamental variable of all human communication. Our discussion of this dimension will focus on presentations to audiences and will be concerned with the subject of messages—including the speaker's purpose, the specific message to be presented, and amplification and support of the ideas included—and the arrangement of the thoughts the speaker wishes to present.

The Subject

The speaker begins by finding and selecting a subject, that is, a general topic or area of discussion: the population explosion, space science, civil liberties, or whatever. Public speakers are not always free to choose their own subjects. Speech subjects often are prescribed by the sponsoring agent, or they may be limited, in a general sense at least, by the occasion. It is not unusual for a speaker to be invited

Dimension 3: Message Preparation

to speak on a specific subject. An expert on space science may be asked to speak on future space explorations; an authority on communication may be requested to speak on communication barriers in interracial communication; an athlete may be sought for a speech on his athletic experiences. In these instances a speaker may express his own thoughts on the subject, but the choice of the subject is fully constrained by the sponsoring agent.

Sometimes there are no limits placed on the speaker's choice of subject, but the speech situation contains constraints. A high-school commencement may require a speaker to discuss some phase of education. A businessman's luncheon may call for some discussion of business, or a P.T.A. meeting will be concerned with school problems. The speaker in each of these cases may be free to select his specific subject and fulfill audience expectations, but his choice must be made from a general area of interest related to the occasion.

The student, however, usually has complete freedom of choice. To him, finding and choosing a subject is often the most perplexing problem of the whole process of giving a speech. It is not uncommon for a student to spend more time looking for a subject (and generally fretting about the problem of subject selection) than he does in preparing the speech, since he has not yet developed to any degree a vocational interest that readily suggests a large number of topics to him. Choosing the right subject may greatly affect how the speaker is received. We offer the following guidelines to ease the problem somewhat and make intelligent choice likely.

1. *Keep a notebook.* Jot down possible speech subjects and ideas as they occur to you. Very often you will get your best ideas for a subject immediately after the instructor has made the assignment, so be sure to note any thoughts you may have at this time. It is generally helpful to keep a notebook of speech ideas. Many prominent public speakers keep notebooks to which they turn when they are preparing a speech.

2. *Try "brain storming."* Spend twenty or thirty minutes combing your mind for any subjects that may fall within the prescribed area of consideration. Don't evaluate or judge the topics that

come to your mind at this point—work for quantity first, then ferret out and evaluate later.

3. *Talk with others about possible speech subjects.* Very often you may get superb ideas for speeches simply by discussing your problems with someone you know. You may also wish to sound out your friends on any topics you are thinking of using. They will usually give you useful feedback as to the relative merits of your ideas.

4. *Go browsing for ideas.* Glance through newspapers, magazines, and lists of suggested subjects offered by your instructor and in PART THREE of this book. Make note of any ideas that you think might be interesting to discuss.

5. *Think systematically about contemporary issues.* What international issues are especially pressing? What national affairs are in the news? What state and local matters are of concern? In each of these categories investigate the following subcategories: political, economic, social, religious, educational, moral, artistic or aesthetic, and scientific issues.

Having found a general subject, the speaker must then decide on a basic message for his speech. The basic message consists of a single, central idea—often called the theme, the thesis, or the proposition—and the main points of its development. An idea is a thought—what a person feels, believes, or knows—about a subject; it is a product of the mind. When you say you have an idea about an orange, you mean you have a mental image of it which may include its size, shape, color, smell, texture, and taste—images you acquire through the senses. You may also have a mental image of something you want or desire, such as going to a party or going on a trip; or you may have an impression that someone doesn't like you. When you say you have a notion, a concept, or a perception of a thing, a person, a plan of action, a proposal, or a desire, you have indicated that you have an idea. "Interstate highways" may comprise a speech subject, but the thought that "money spent in the construction of interstate highways is money well-spent" is a valuational idea about interstate highways that we try to persuade people to accept. It constitutes a message. "The value construct of the Sioux Indians" may comprise the message for an informative speech on the general subject

Dimension 3: Message Preparation

of the Sioux Indian tribe. Thus, it is the basic message and its development, not the general subject, that determine the worth of a speech. Two people may speak on the same subject, and one may have a stimulating message, the other a worthless one. Not all of us can be great philosophers, but most of us can produce thoughts that should be of some value to our audiences, especially if we select a message appropriate to the audience, to the speaker, and to the occasion.

Select a Message Appropriate to the Audience

The message of a speech first of all should be tested in light of the audience to which it is to be delivered. A speech on "My deer hunting experiences in Colorado" would be inappropriate for the local garden club yet highly provocative to a group of sportsmen interested in deer hunting. Thus, "Will the audience profit from the message?" is an important question to ask. There ought to be some reason why the listeners should wish to add the information the speaker presents to their store of knowledge. Since the college classroom is an intellectual environment, it seems reasonable to expect a student speaker to deal with subjects that any serious-minded college student should be interested in. There is no reason why a college class should want to know how to chop the head off a chicken or why it should listen to someone tell about the peculiar habits of a roommate. On the other hand, college audiences should wish to broaden their knowledge and, in some instances, can profitably be challenged by a subject that may not lie in their immediate range of interest. One may not, for example, be interested in children's literature, but an insightful discussion of what constitutes good children's literature should help one to be a more liberally-educated person. The speaker, of course, will be challenged to arouse the interest of the listener on such a subject. The first test of audience appropriateness is, *Does the message impart worthwhile knowledge to the audience addressed?*

One often hears speech teachers talk about *tired speech subjects*. Virtually every speech teacher has listened to dozens of speeches on juvenile delinquency, capital punishment, and automobile seat belts. In reality, there is no such thing as a tired subject, assuming the subject to be a worthwhile one—it is just that the ideas expressed about that particular subject are shopworn. A speech should be a broadening experience for the audience. The subject of juvenile delinquency is very worthwhile, providing the speaker presents fresh ideas about it. A new and significant point of view is always worth considering, and while it is true that no speaker can always present totally-original ideas, he can present ideas that are new to his listeners. If he cannot meet that challenge, he should find a different subject.

Another useful test of appropriateness is whether the message contains stimulating and motivating ideas on issues of importance to the audience. Any speech that creates audience awareness of and concern for a significant human problem is worthwhile, especially if it contains ideas that will help solve a major problem. Questions concerning important human values also warrant public discussion. Any speech that stimulates a listener to take a careful look at some of his values, or motivates him to formulate new and better values, achieves a valuable purpose. Finally, be aware that the human soul thrives upon inspiration, and any speech that in some way uplifts the human spirit meets the test of usefulness.

Select a Message Appropriate to the Speaker

If the speaker's message should be beneficial to the audience, it is also reasonable to assume that the speaker should benefit from speaking on the subject. It stands to reason, if a speaker is going to prepare diligently for an audience presentation, that this experience should augment his knowledge and broaden his experience. Why waste time researching a subject you don't want to know about?

It is even more important that you analyze your relationship to the audience in regard to the subject. It is imperative that the speaker either know more about the subject than the audience does or have ideas that are new to them. At the very least, he should be more motivated about the subject than his auditors. It would be absurd, for example, for a woman who has neither had children herself nor intensely studied and researched the problem to address a group of mothers on the subject of child-rearing practices. A college student sometimes has no more knowledge about his subject at the outset of his speech preparation than do his classmates,

Dimension 3: Message Preparation

and if he chooses to speak on a certain subject, he must be sufficiently interested to research it. You may not know at this point more about semantics than your classmates, but if you are motivated to read widely you may well be able to present a meaningful classroom speech on the subject. One word of warning, however: Be sure that the subject you choose is one you can cope with. It is unrealistic to try to develop a speech on a difficult economic question, for example, if you possess no background in economics, so it is usually wise to choose a subject from the realm of your personal or professional interests. Also, make sure that necessary and vital information on your subject will be available to you when you prepare your speech. Make a check of library resources and other available sources before you commit yourself to speak on a subject.

Select a Message Appropriate to the Occasion

Possible constraints imposed by the speech occasion were discussed in DIMENSION TWO. It would be good to review them at this time. Your instructor will probably set the occasion for some of your classroom speeches. He may assign a six-minute informative speech. Or, perhaps, he will ask you to present an eight-minute problem-solution speech. These restrictions are not unrealistic ones, since they are not very different from the restrictions we encounter in everyday life. There are moments when only an informative speech is appropriate. There are other occasions when a speech to solve a problem is needed. The class assignments are designed to prepare you for meeting the needs of the speech situations created by our society.

Students commonly select speech subjects that are too broad to be treated adequately in the allotted time. If you are assigned a seven-minute speech and set out to discuss World War II, your speech will be superficial. Rather than deal with generalities, narrow the scope of your subject and focus on some aspect that permits you to speak in depth, "French Collaborationists in World War II" perhaps. Neophyte speakers almost never choose a subject that is too narrow but err frequently in the other direction. An hour is a relatively short time for the examination of most subjects; five or ten minutes is very short. "Juvenile delinquency" is too broad a subject for a short speech, but the proposition that

"Parents should stand trial for their delinquent children" can be meaningfully discussed in five to seven minutes. "Dope addiction" is too broad a subject; "The effects of marijuana smoking" can be treated in a short speech.

The Purpose of the Message

Public speeches are comprised of purposeful messages. The purpose of the message may or may not readily be apparent to a listener, but it will be there. The speaker may state his intention explicitly or he may strategically shield it, but he speaks with an object. There are two broad speech purposes: to inform and to persuade. It is often contended, and with some validity, that it is impossible to separate these general purposes completely. For example, persuasive speeches will have informative elements. Moreover, the effect of a speaker's message may be different from his purpose. A speaker may intend to instruct, only to find that the information he presents causes a shift in audience attitudes toward the subject. Someone may, for example, seek to teach an audience about proper techniques of rose gardening, only to find that the vitality of his presentation has persuaded a listener to plant rose bushes in his flower bed instead of marigolds. The intent was knowledge, the result action. The same effects may occur from informative speeches on scientific, social, economic, or political questions.

Despite the difficulty of drawing hard and fast lines between general speech purposes, it is useful to think in terms of information and persuasion. Although most rhetorical principles apply to all types of speeches, some theoretical aspects apply particularly to specific ends of speech communication.

Speaking to Inform

Many occasions give rise to public address as a medium for imparting knowledge. The speaker, seeking to meet the demands placed upon him, strives to increase or develop an audience's comprehension of an event, a fact, a process, or a concept. At these moments, when a speaker has comprehension as his aim, it may be said that he is speaking *to inform*. It is the speaker's hope that the information he presents will lead to apprehension of knowledge by the listener. He must, therefore, at these moments impart new knowledge or give new and deeper insights into something the listener already knows.

Informative discourse flourishes in the classroom, in the lecture hall, in the Armed Service Training Center, in industrial training centers, in civic clubs, at women's club meetings, and on guided tours of all sorts. The last fifty years has produced a fantastic information explosion. If this vast wealth of knowledge is to be properly disseminated, people must possess proficiency in expository writing and speaking. It is hard to escape the informative oral presentation in most professions. The doctor explains a remedy to his patient, the tax lawyer clarifies tax laws for his client, and the sales manager explains sales techniques to his staff. The ten-minute spoken presentation to a committee has become a standard tool for a company employee.

Informative speeches are of two basic types: reports and "how to" instructional speeches. Speeches on how to fill out a tax form, how to conduct a meeting, or how to use a calculator all meet varying social or business needs. Sometimes demonstrations are given as part of the process. A master teacher may demonstrate how to teach a unit in creative dramatics at a teachers' meeting; a football coach may exhibit the intricacies of blocking; or an artist may show his students the possible use of line and form in painting. In each case the objective is to so present information that the listener can successfully transfer it to a new situation. He should have knowledge and skills he did not previously possess.

Reports also fulfill distinct societal needs. A stockholders' report may be presented at a meeting to enlighten stockholders on the company's annual activities. A professor may report his research at the meeting of a learned society for the purpose of augmenting the knowledge of the field and for generating thinking on a given problem. On the other hand, reports are often given for the purpose of providing bases for action. Fact-finding boards, investigating committees, and boards of inquiry all serve as means of obtaining information to be transmitted to an action agency.

A turnpike feasibility report may be presented to a highway commission, which will then decide upon a course of action. Such an agency will not be interested in persuasion, but in findings—in any and all important pertinent facts that can be used as the basis for intelligent deliberation. The research scientist's report is likely to be based on primary research, whereas other reports may be secondary accounts of existing available knowledge on a given topic. Regardless of the social utility of the report, the objective is to present reliable and pertinent information that will increase the listener's comprehension and knowledge.

Since the rationale for informative speeches is the transfer of meaningful knowledge to the audience, the speaker must make his ideas clear, interesting, and acceptable. What follows is a list of concepts which constitute criteria for judging informative speeches.

Clarity

That ideas be clear and meaningful is important in any speech, but it is critical in speeches of demonstration, instruction, factual reporting, and exposition. Good organization is the first obvious means to rhetorical clarity. In informative discourse, organizational design should lay out the speaker's thoughts as explicitly as possible. Since the rudiments of organization are examined in detail in the next section, no intensive treatment will be given here. A clear style is the second means to clarity, and clarity of language will be dealt with in DIMENSION FOUR. Here we will discuss the compositional factors other than organization and language that help produce meaningful oral discourse. A speaker seeking clarity in imparting knowledge to an audience may choose from the following useful compositional devices.

Define Difficult and Abstract Terms. In private conversation and in informal discussion we are often asked, "What do you mean by that?" In a speaking situation where the listener has little or no chance to check what the speaker means, it is very important, sometimes crucial—particularly when words are used in a special way—that the speaker define his key terms. Through definition we set boundaries that confine the term within a limited area that makes effective communication possible. Frequently, an elemen-

Dimension 3: Message Preparation

tary dictionary definition will suffice; or often simply rephrasing or citing a synonym or two will make our meaning clear. For more difficult terms, however, an intensive definitional analysis is essential.

The first principle of a definition is that it be purposeful and useful; it has no value in itself. A good definition will elicit a meaning which corresponds to that intended by the speaker, and it elicits a meaning in the receiver that is clearer to him than the term being defined. Thus, the speaker must know precisely what meaning he intends to convey, conjecture whether the listener holds erroneous meanings that must be eliminated, and determine how he can most clearly communicate his intended meaning.

The two common approaches to definition are the formal, or Aristotelian, approach and the operational approach. The traditional Aristotelian approach is to define the essence of a term by classifying it in proper categories. The term is categorized according to *genus* and *differentia*. For example, "Man [the term defined] is a rational [differentia] animal [genus]." John Gresham Machen created the following definition of Christianity: "Christianity [the term defined] is that religion [genus] that believes in the atoning power of Christ's death [differentia]." A speech student defined totalitarianism thus: "Totalitarianism [term] is that form of government [genus] that utilizes *all* possible means of control to establish the ultimate supremacy of the state in *all* aspects of the people's lives [differentia]." In order for such a definition to be accurate and meaningful the differentia must identify that single aspect which differentiates the term from all other species of that genus. To say that "Man is a two-legged animal" does not differentiate him from a kangaroo.

Aristotelian definitions have the disadvantage of being static rather than relativistic and may lead to undesirable *allness* thinking. To define a "good Indian" as being a "dead Indian"—as some frontiersmen apparently did—is a classic example of bad categorical definition. Moreover, it is often difficult to find a differentia that will apply to all cases. On the other hand, Aristotelian definitions have the advantage of being exact, clearly excluding specious meanings and specifically limiting the scope of the term.

An operational definition assumes a given point in space and time and sets limits that are useful for that moment. The speaker sets forth what he will take the word to mean in the development of a single discourse. He may, for example, point to the Goebbels German Propaganda Ministry of World War II, identify the essential characteristics of that ministry, and use that as his definition of propaganda in his talk. Operational definitions are useful in that they tend to show direct relationships to the physical world.

The device of negating existing meanings is essential when the audience has prior misconceptions of the term. A speech student whose topic was "What Is Totalitarianism?" used negation as part of her introduction.

> To begin with, totalitarianism does not mean simply any government which is not democratic in nature. To employ such a definition for the term would render it completely meaningless, for to be sure there are many forms of non-democratic rule in our present-day world. Nor does the term *totalitarianism* denote any dictatorship. The dictatorships, for example, of most of South America and South East Asia, overthrown with great regularity as they are, reflect not a totalitarian state, but a situation of intensified political struggle among the members of the power elite of the nation.[1]

In addition to removing misconceptions, negation may be used to make the speaker's meaning vivid. Robert Hutchins, former president of the University of Chicago, tells us that a "university is not a kindergarten, it is not a club, it is not a reform school, it is not a political club, it is not an agency of propaganda. A university is a community of scholars."

A term can often be made meaningful by showing its origin or derivation, by indicating its etymology—the primitive form or root upon which it is based. For instance, the word *transcend* comes from the Latin *transcendere*, "to climb over or to surpass." The word *humanities* stems from the Latin *humanitas*, meaning "humanity or human nature." Etymology is often a good starting point for a definition, with the speaker relating the etymology to usage.

No two words have identical connotative meanings, but they do have synonyms and antonyms. We define *competition* as *rivalry*, *work* as *labor*, *demolish* as *destroy*. Antonyms are words with opposite meanings. Thus, *smart* is the opposite of *stupid*, *weak*

---

[1] Lauralee Peters, "What Is Totalitarianism?," in Wil A. Linkugel, R. R. Allen, and Richard L. Johannesen, eds., *Contemporary American Speeches* (Belmont, Calif.: Wadsworth, 1965), p. 70.

the opposite of *strong, cowardice* the opposite of *bravery*. Antonyms create a useful contrast for the listeners.

Some words can be made meaningful by a proper division of their different kinds of meaning. Martin Luther King, speaking on "Love, Law, and Civil Disobedience," used this technique. Through negation and division Dr. King clarified the kind of love that he felt lay at the heart of the student nonviolent movement:

> Now when the students talk about love, certainly they are not talking about emotional bosh, they are not talking about a sentimental outpouring; they're talking about something much deeper, and I always have to stop and try to define the meaning of love in this context. The Greek language comes to our aid in trying to deal with this. There are three words in the Greek language for love, one is the word Eros. This is a beautiful type of love, it is an aesthetic love. . . . Philia . . . is an intimate affection between personal friends, it is reciprocal love. . . . Agape is more than romantic love, agape is more than friendship. Agape is understanding, creative, redemptive, good will to all men. It is an overflowing love which seeks nothing in return. Theologians would say that is the love of God operating in the human heart.[2]

Often an authority, one who knows a great deal about the term in question, can best explain it. Albert Einstein gives the meaning of the theory of relativity, John Dewey the meaning of reflective thinking, and T. S. Eliot the meaning of poetry. A speaker, by searching the authorities, may often make a term quite meaningful for his listeners.

Meaning can be engendered by comparing the term being discussed with things more familiar to the audience. One speaker used this technique in defining a kilowatt hour: "A kilowatt hour is a unit by which electric energy is measured, just as the bushel is the unit for measuring wheat and corn, the gallon the unit for measuring gasoline, and the pound the unit for measuring butter. It represents one hour's use of one kilowatt of power."

Examples make meaning especially vivid and can profitably be employed in conjunction with other means of definition. The word *demagogue* can be made meaningful by pointing to the careers of highly-successful demagogues and by identifying lead-

---

[2] Martin Luther King, "Love, Law, and Civil Disobedience," in Roy L. Hill, ed., *Rhetoric of Racial Revolt* (Denver: Golden Bell Press, 1964), p. 348.

ing characteristics of their demagoguery. The concept of good mental health can be clarified by pointing to the characteristics of an especially well-adjusted person, either real or imaginary.

Use Illustrations. Illustrations may be the best device for making ideas vivid. Good illustrations not only help to make points clear, but they also have interest value and contain important sensory appeals. Russell Conwell, in his famous "Acres of Diamonds" speech—an address he gave at least 5,000 times at the turn of the century—spent about 80 percent of his time illustrating the message of his speech that everybody has the right and the opportunity to get rich if he has sufficient industry and imagination.

Illustrations are of two types: factual and hypothetical. Factual illustrations are preferable, since they involve reality; however, if no factual illustrations are available, hypothetical illustrations can be extremely effective.

In 1866 Thomas Huxley addressed a group of English workingmen on "The Method of Scientific Investigation" and sought to make the method of science meaningful to this group through a hypothetical illustration.

> Suppose you go into a fruiterer's shop, wanting an apple—you take one up, and, on biting, you find It is sour; you look at it, and see that it is hard and green. You take another one and that too is hard, green, and sour. The shopman offers you a third; but, before biting it, you examine it, and find that it is hard and green, and you immediately say that you will not have it, as it must be sour, like those that you have already tried.
>
> Nothing can be more simple than that, you think; but if you will take the trouble to analyze and trace out into its logical elements what has been done by the mind, you will be greatly surprised. In the first place, you have performed the operation of induction. You found that, in two experiences, hardness and greenness in apples went together with sourness. It was so in the first case, and it was confirmed by the second. True, it is a very small basis, but still it is enough to make an induction from; you generalize the facts, and you expect to find sourness in apples where you get hardness and greenness.[3]

---

[3] Thomas Henry Huxley, "The Method of Scientific Investigation," in Donald C. Bryant and Karl R. Wallace, *Fundamentals of Public Speaking*, 3d ed. (New York: Appleton-Century-Crofts, 1960), p. 484.

Fairy tales, fables, and parables have been used successfully for illustrative purposes. Jesus did much of his teaching through parables. Illustrations often make the difference between a good speech and an ordinary one.

Compare and Contrast. When a speaker uses comparison and contrast he sets two objects, ideas, events, or concepts side by side or one against the other. We are all familiar with the advertiser's trick of showing the difference between old and new, before and after, with movies and television westerns that contrast the hero and the villain, the bully and the timid soul. Thomas W. Phelps, addressing the Bond Club of Buffalo, New York, explained the problem of buying common stocks with this use of contrast:

> When you play football you belong to one team and you stay on that team until the end of the game, win, lose or draw. But when you go into the stock market your sole object is to decide in advance which side is going to win, and to join that side. If any time thereafter you think the other side is going to win you change sides as fast as you can. The object is to be on the winning side as much of the time as you possibly can.[4]

Transform the Abstract into the Concrete. The average listener finds it difficult to pay attention to abstract thought; it tends to be unclear to him. The abstract is vague, the concrete is vivid and appeals to the senses. Cold is abstract; frost-bitten ears are concrete. Beauty is abstract; a prize-winning rose is concrete. Large numbers tend to be abstract; 33 percent is concrete. Generalizations are abstract; a single example is concrete. A graphic, concrete image of the Southern soldier is dramatically portrayed by Henry W. Grady in the following excerpt from his famous speech, "The New South":

> Dr. Talmage has drawn for you, with a master's hand, the picture of your returning armies. He has told you how, in the pomp and circumstance of war, they came back to you, marching with proud and victorious tread, reading their glory in a nation's eyes! Will you bear with me while I tell you of another army that sought its home at the close of the late war—an army that marched home in defeat and not in

---

[4] Thomas W. Phelps, "The Case for Common Stocks," *Vital Speeches of the Day* (May 1, 1948), p. 430.

victory—in pathos and not in splendor, but in glory that equaled yours, and to hearts as loving as ever welcomed heroes home. Let me picture to you the footsore Confederate soldier, as, buttoning up his faded gray jacket, the parole which was to bear testimony to his children of his fidelity and faith, he turned his face southward from Appomattox in April, 1865. Think of him as ragged, half-starved, heavy-hearted, enfeebled by want and wounds; having fought to exhaustion, he surrenders his gun, wrings the hands of his comrades in silence, and lifting his tear-stained and pallid face for the last time to the graves that dot the old Virginia hills, pulls his gray cap over his brow and begins the slow and painful journey.[5]

Had Grady simply stated that the Southern soldier, too, had problems when he returned home from the war, the effect would have been much less compelling. Instead he transformed the abstract into the concrete, and his thought was made more expressive.

Restate and Summarize. Especially-difficult ideas can profitably be restated for purposes of clarity. Sometimes stating the same idea in a slightly different way will turn confusion into comprehension. The statement, "Constructional patterns on the discourse level may reveal some of our most general and least conscious modes of interrelating and evaluating the aspects of our world" may be rephrased more clearly as, "Our language usage reveals how we evaluate the world."

Frequent restatement of your theme often is an effective means of achieving vividness. Many of history's most renowned speeches are strongly thematic, in that the orator carefully related each main idea to his central theme. Albert Beveridge, in his speech on imperialism, "The March of the Flag," which he delivered at the turn of the century, punctuated his main points with the phrase "the march of the flag went on."

Internal summaries, especially as part of transitions between main points, may be used for purposes of clarity. Observe how William Ellery Channing, a prominent rhetorician of the last century, used an internal summary in his speech on "Unitarian Christianity" delivered in 1819: "Having thus given our belief on two

---

[5] Henry W. Grady, "The New South," in A. Craig Baird, ed., *American Public Addresses, 1740–1952* (New York: McGraw-Hill, 1956), p. 183–184.

great points, namely, that there is one God, and that Jesus Christ is a being distinct from and inferior to God, I now proceed to another point, on which we lay still greater stress. We believe in the *moral perfection* of God." Channing used this technique at several points in his speech, thereby achieving a genuine clarity of thought.

Use Extra-Verbal Aids. There is an old Chinese proverb about one picture being worth ten thousand words. However, pictures alone may not be worth much more than words alone. The best way to transmit knowledge to the brain seems to be through the eye *and* the ear. At a recent National Osteopathic Child Health conference in Atlanta, Robert S. Craig of the U. S. Public Health Service reported that "when knowledge was imparted to a person by telling alone, the recall three hours later was 70 percent, and three days later, only 10 percent." He also noted that when showing alone was used "the knowledge recall three hours later was 72 percent, and three days later, about 35 percent." However, he reported, studies show that "when both telling and showing were the teaching tools the recall three hours later was 85 percent, and three days later, 65 percent." This corroborates the studies by H. E. Nelson and A. W. Vandermeer showing that using film instruction supplementary to lecture materials is more effective than lecture alone. They concluded: "The proportion of learning that is attributable solely to listening to the commentary is significantly smaller than that which is attributable to viewing the film with both picture and sound."[6]

The main purpose of visual aids, and the one with which we are now concerned, is clarity. But extra-verbal aids also serve as effective interest devices and enhance the listener's memory. There are many types of visual aids: pictures, graphs, maps, charts, objects, and mechanical devices; live models such as animals, insects, and reptiles; and printed hand-out materials. Charts and graphs are some of the most commonly used visual aids. Pie or circle graphs, picture graphs, lined or curved graphs, and bar graphs all are helpful for making ideas clear. Slides projected on

---

[6] Conwell Carlson, "Best Memory by Eye and the Ear," *The Kansas City Times* (April 19, 1967).

a screen sometimes are especially effective as visual aids. Regardless of the extra-verbal aids used, their importance can hardly be overstressed. Use them at every opportunity.

The following guidelines for the use of visual aids will, if followed carefully, help the speaker achieve effective communication.

1. Be sure that your visual aids are large enough for all to see.
2. Display them in such a manner that everyone can see them.
3. Keep the visual aids as agents of communication while you talk. When you have finished with the ideas related to them, remove them from sight; otherwise, they become counterattractions and stand as your silent competitors.
4. Preserve as much eye contact with your audience as you can when referring to your visual aids.
5. Avoid passing things around in the audience while you are speaking. You will lose a lot of attention if you do. It is much better to pass your visual aids after you have finished speaking.

Interest

Some degree of attention on the part of the audience is an essential minimum condition for imparting knowledge. But it is not merely a matter of paying attention or not paying attention; the degree of attention is important as well. If the level of interest is so low that the attention of the listeners is constantly wavering, they will not get as much from the speech as they will if interest is so high that their attention becomes intense. The speaker should, therefore, develop an awareness of the basic factors of interest that will help him gain and hold the attention of an audience and should learn how to season his speech liberally with them—remembering, of course, that the elements of interest should serve only to make the speech more effective and not be so strong that they obscure the basic message of the speech. If a speaker seeking to impart knowledge or to persuade uses attention devices obviously out of harmony with his ideas or with the spirit of the occasion, he may fail miserably as a speaker, even though he holds the attention of his audience. The best attention arises naturally from challenging ideas, new information, discussion of timely and vital topics, and use of effective language and delivery.

Nevertheless, a speaker must do more than make worthwhile ideas clear; he must make them interesting as well. The following factors help to provoke interest in a speech.

Illustration. Illustrations make ideas vivid; they also make them interesting. All kinds of illustrations are useful, but those that contain a strong *human* element generate the most interest. E. B. White once wisely observed, "Don't talk about man, talk about a man." Note how the following two speakers used illustrations containing a human element to good effect. Karl Menninger, the world-renowned psychiatrist, in an address titled "Healthier than Healthy," says:

> The point I am trying to develop is the old principle that sometimes one illness can, in some way or other, drive out another illness.
> I remember an old story which I am sure you have heard. My dentist told it to me when I was just a little boy. If a tooth was to be extracted he would guarantee that the pain would go away if I would do exactly what he told me. Of course I said, "Well what is it?" He said, "I will give you a hatpin, and when I tell you, stick the hatpin the full length right in your leg and you won't notice that your tooth hurts!" That principle sort of stuck with me and I wrestled with it quite a while![7]

A student speaker makes the following point about happiness:

> In Charles Schultz's popular cartoon depiction of happiness, one of his definitions has special significance for the American school system. The drawing shows Linus, with his eyes closed in a state of supreme bliss, a broad smile across two-thirds of his face and holding a report card upon which is a big bold "A." The caption reads: "Happiness is finding out you're not so dumb after all." For once happiness is not defined as a function of material possessions. . . .[8]

Dialogue. Narration is interesting, but the active verbal interaction of people is more interesting. The novelist uses narration, description, and dialogue, but he usually saves dialogue for the tale's most dramatic moments. Dr. Menninger, in the speech mentioned above, made extensive use of dialogue, thereby making his

---

[7] Karl Menninger, "Healthier than Healthy," in *Contemporary American Speeches* (Belmont, Calif.: Wadsworth, 1965), p. 31.
[8] Carolyn Kay Geiman, "Are They Really Unteachable?," in *Contemporary American Speeches*, p. 123.

ideas clear and interesting. At one point he developed the idea that generous people are rarely mentally ill people and that stinginess is a symptom of some kind of fear. Menninger then recalled:

> I remember I said to a man, "What on earth are you going to do with all that money?" He said, "Just worry about it, I suppose!" I said, "Well, do you get that much pleasure out of worrying about it?" "No, but I get such terror when I think of giving some of it to somebody." I said, "Well, you have quite a symptom there. But you are not alone in it. That is a fairly common symptom at your age. You are older, now, aren't you?" "Yes, I'm fifty-seven now, but I feel just like I did when I didn't have anything."[9]

Action, Suspense, and Conflict. People pay attention to anything moving—trains, meteors, flickering lights, floating clouds. A speaker can effectively utilize this principle by using a blackboard, objects, visual aids, or gestures to describe or give emphasis to thought through physical action. Listening experts even tell us that a fast rate of speech holds attention better than a slow one. Best, however, is a combination of fast speech for narrative and slow speech for emphasis. A speaker can also achieve a sense of action verbally through energetic, dynamic rhetoric. The speeches of most of history's greatest speakers have had this quality. Daniel Webster's oratory was especially known for its energy and vitality. Observe how he swept the audience along in the following passage:

> It is to that Union that we owe our safety at home, and our consideration and dignity abroad. It is to that Union that we are chiefly indebted for whatever makes us most proud of our country. That Union we reached only by the discipline of our virtues in the severe school of adversity. It had its origin in the necessities of disordered finance, prostrate commerce, and ruined credit. Under its benign influences these great interests immediately awoke, as from the dead, and sprang forth with newness of life. Every year of its duration has teemed with fresh proofs of its utility and its blessings; although our territory has stretched out wider and wider, and our population spread farther and farther, they have not outrun its protection or its benefits. It has been to us all a copious fountain of national, social, and personal happiness.[10]

---

[9] Menninger, *op. cit.*, p. 35.
[10] Daniel Webster, "Reply to Hayne," in *American Public Addresses, 1740–1952,* p. 65.

Action is especially effective when it is blended with suspense and conflict. These three vital elements of dramatic action are strong interest factors. The speaker can create suspense by narrating and describing examples vividly, by developing points with increasing clarity, and by accumulating force in the use of supporting evidence. He can develop conflict by setting opposing points of view against each other, by explicitly attacking a statement from the press or from another speech, and by narrating dramatic illustrations.

The Unusual. Robert Ripley found fame and fortune as a collector and publisher of bits of the unusual. His column "Believe It or Not" was syndicated all over the world. His entire work was devoted to the strange and the extraordinary. Unusual tidbits about the speaker's subject, if properly used, can create interest in any speech. Sometimes a speaker can develop his subject in an unusual way. All rhetorical situations are a challenge to the speaker's imagination, and he should tax his imaginative powers in order to achieve the greatest interest value in his speech. Genuine imagination can usually give a new and unusual twist to any subject. Of course, mere sensationalism is never the objective. Unusual elements should serve the basic message of the speech and should not become the prime focus—except perhaps in a speech whose intent is to entertain.

Humor. A proper use of humor grabs the attention of the audience. The best kind of humor is the kind which grows out of the speech situation; it has an element of spontaneity and immediate relevance. Overstatement and understatement are good sources of mirth, and one of the best laugh-makers is an appropriate and relevant story. It is unwise, however, to string together a series of unrelated and irrelevant jokes. The best humor will help further the thought line of the speech.

Acceptability

We commonly associate the problem of making ideas acceptable with persuasive speeches, but it is a factor in informative discourse as well. On the one hand, it is a matter of making arguments acceptable to our auditors; on the other, it is a task of making information acceptable to them.

Audiences tend to accept or reject a speaker's information at three levels: they accept or reject an information statement on face value; they accept or reject an informational statement relative to the speaker who is making it; and they accept or reject an informational statement relative to its original source.

The Face-Value Level. Almost all people will accept certain informational statements at face value, irrespective of their source or who has spoken them. People may read the statement that water freezes at 32° F. in *The New York Times* and in *The Daily Worker* and find the statement equally acceptable, whether it was made by Billy Graham, Jonas Salk, or Alexei Kosygin. Other examples of statements people might find acceptable regardless of source are: Oxygen is necessary for human life; The world is a sphere; George Washington has often been called the father of our country. In each of these instances, neither the source of the information nor the ethos of the communicator is likely to have any bearing on the acceptability of the statements. This, however, is not true of all statements.

The Speaker-Ethos Level. Audiences will find some informational statements acceptable because they trust the speaker making them. Conversely, they will close their minds to certain information because they do not trust the speaker. Receivers of messages often will not accept the information conveyed by certain speakers as true, either because they judge them to be incompetent or because they do not trust their motives. Most Americans during the Cuban missile crisis believed President Kennedy's analysis of missile installation in Cuba during 1962, but found much less acceptable any statement made by the Russians or by Fidel Castro on the same subject. Somewhat similarly, high-school principals often will accept fully the statements of some students regarding the reasons for their absence from school but will distrust fully similar statements from other students; past experience has shown them that the former are totally reliable in reporting such information, whereas the latter have proven to be unreliable.

Dimension 3: Message Preparation

Very often the role the speaker is playing determines his acceptability as a source of information to an audience. Adult audiences may accept any statements a college student makes about college, but find themselves distrusting him when he talks about political questions. The role of the college student as communicator is quite different in those two instances. An authority in his given field will usually find that an audience will accept his informational statements about his field without question. Observe how Carl Rogers, a prominent lecturer in psychology, takes advantage of his role in an address on psychotherapy.

> I would like, in the first part of this talk, to summarize what we know of the conditions which facilitate psychological growth, and something of what we know of the process and characteristics of that psychological growth. Let me explain what I mean when I say that I am going to summarize what we "know." I mean that I will limit my statements to those for which we have objective empirical evidence. For example, I will talk about the condition of psychological growth. For each statement one or more studies could be cited in which it was found that changes occurred in the individual when these conditions were present which did not occur in situations where these conditions were absent, or were present to a much lesser degree. As one investigator states, we have made progress in identifying the primary change-producing agents which facilitate the alteration of personality and of behavior in the direction of personal development. It should of course be added that this knowledge, like all scientific knowledge, is tentative and surely incomplete, and is certain to be modified, contradicted in part, and supplemented by the painstaking work of the future. Nevertheless there is no reason to be apologetic for the small but hard-won knowledge which we currently possess.[11]

Dr. Rogers never cites specific research studies in support of any of the generalizations he presents in his address. He makes the assumption that the audience will not think of his information relative to its source as much as they will relative to him as a reliable authority in the field. A college student speaking on the same subject probably would have to present the same information relative to his source; in other words, he would have to document his generalized statements with specific research findings.

---

[11] Carl Rogers, "What We Know about Psychotherapy," in *Contemporary American Speeches*, pp. 37–38.

The Source Level. When a person playing a role that does not cast him as an authority is presenting information that does not gain face-value acceptance, it is essential for him to document the source of his information. Then, if the audience finds the source of the statements acceptable, they will tend to accept the speaker's informative statements. For example, if a trustworthy speaker reports the number of instances of criminal child molestations that were successfully prosecuted in 1973 in Wichita, Kansas, and documents this data from the *Reader's Digest,* the information may be accepted by many audiences; at the same time, the identical information attributed to the *Kansas Law Review* will probably be accepted by almost everyone. Obviously the speaker should always strive to use the most acceptable sources.

In summary, the speaker needs to relate his message and himself to the audience in informative discourse just as much as he does in persuasive discourse. He needs to discern how much of his information is commonly-accepted knowledge, how willing the audience is likely to accept information relative to him as speaker —especially in terms of his communicative role—and what information he will have to document from the standpoint of his source.

Speaking to Persuade

The informative speaker has comprehension as his aim; the persuasive speaker is interested in decisions of belief and action. Persuasion utilizes information, but its end is influence, not knowledge. It seeks to influence the judgments people make, good or bad, true or false, expedient or inexpedient.

An open society that espouses the marketplace-of-ideas concept is satiated with all types of persuasion—in newspapers and magazines, on radio and television, in books and on billboards, in speeches and in conversation. Some persuasion is ethical, some unethical; some useful, some useless. But occur it does. It takes place in the political arena, in social gatherings, in religious circles, in industrial settings, and even around the family hearth. And not only does it occur, but it is essential that it occur. Social control is vital to a society, and although laws may restrain crime and violence, persuasion builds social cohesion. It legislates and im-

Dimension 3: Message Preparation

plements justice; it also frees people from taboos, makes them aware of important problems, and solidifies social action. At other moments it causes dissension, perpetrates injustice, chains the mind, and misleads. It is a tool for good and evil and is equally available to the just and to the unjust. Since, as Aristotle long ago observed, the wicked learn it and practice it, the noble must learn it for self-defense, for the good of society, and for the advancement of man.

In our discussion of informative discourse, we set forth three factors that the speaker should use as standards for his speech and the critic should use as criteria for judgment. These same three criteria—interest, clarity, and acceptability—apply to persuasive speeches as well. In the first place, persuasive discourse must make clear to the listener what he is to believe or what he is to do. Second, the speech must be sufficiently interesting to gain and maintain the listener's attention. Third, the message of the speech must be acceptable to the listener. However, in a persuasive speech the speaker is concerned with *making arguments acceptable*; information, in such discourse, serves to implement the arguments. The remainder of this section, therefore, is concerned with the strategies used in making arguments acceptable.

Finding the Most Favorable Position for Argument

The first strategy in making arguments acceptable to people is to find the most favorable position for argument. This means knowing the basic value premises the audience holds relative to the speaker's subject. For example, if a person wants to persuade an audience that high-school teachers should have complete freedom of intellectual inquiry in their teaching, he will achieve the best results if he knows the most favorable route to that position with a particular audience. If he is addressing a group of college professors he is probably safe in making the assumption that they believe in academic freedom, and he may use this as a premise from which to reason. On the other hand, another group of people may find the concept of academic freedom unacceptable, so if the speaker uses it as his position for argument he may be doomed to failure. He must either first persuade them that academic freedom is a worthwhile principle or he must use another route to his proposition. If you are going to talk about cheating in college to college students, you can probably assume that they all agree that cheating occurs from time to time. It would therefore be pointless to spend a lot of time documenting cases. It would be more efficient to spend your time talking about solutions or presenting good reasons why people should not cheat. From these examples we can see that a person may prepare a very well-drawn speech from the standpoint of form, but if he argues from the wrong assumption about his audience his speech will not have the right shape for the rhetorical situation. The speaker should, therefore, make every effort to find out what the audience is likely to know and believe about his subject prior to his speech, for it is only through such careful analysis that he is likely to find the most favorable position for argument.

Give Your Argument Logical Credence

Persuasive speech consists of general ideas supported in such a manner that they become vivid and acceptable to the listener. Each such cluster may properly be called a unit of argument. The largest unit of argument is, of course, the entire speech, with the basic message being the general idea, and the main points the supporting data. It is the function of the main points to make the basic message acceptable. Each main point, in turn, is a smaller unit of argument that also has a general idea and supporting data. Very often, still smaller units of argument exist within a main point, and their general ideas are used in support of the main point.

Supporting materials run the gamut in persuasion from factual and reliable data on, say, meteorology, to emotional stories about Spike, the family dog. Ideally, the listener would always demand sound reasoning and factual evidence; practically, he often is moved far more by emotional appeals. People like to think of themselves as logical beings, but in reality they behave emotionally much of the time. Nevertheless, an argument, to be acceptable, must seem logical to them. Sound persuasive strategy thus calls for a judicious blend of logical and motivational materials, with the amount of inclusion of each type depending upon the disposition of the audience, the rhetorical context, and the question for discussion. Any of the following types of data may help to give an argument logical credence.

Examples. Examples are invaluable for making arguments acceptable. They not only give logical credence to the general idea but also make the idea vivid. A word of caution, however, must be issued concerning the use of examples alone. One or two examples do not warrant broad generalizations. This is true even when several examples are cited. When one cites three examples of bad teaching by graduate teaching assistants, he is only demonstrating that *some* graduate assistants do not teach well. But the examples do establish that there may be reason for concern if the examples cited are a fair sample, are typical, and are relatively numerous. These three factors should be used as criteria for judging inferences made from examples.

Statistics. Statistics may represent specific data or they may be generalized averages. The total number of military personnel killed or wounded during World War II, the amount of profit Armour and Company realized last year, and the increase in college enrollments over a five-year period are examples of statistics that give us specific facts. On the other hand, the average income of steelworkers, the average rate of illiteracy among slum children, or the average cost of a college education in a state university provide us with generalized data. Statistics are also expressed as percentages and ratios. Baseball batting averages are good examples of percentages, as are all kinds of standardized test scores. And we are all familiar with the television advertisements quoting "eight out of ten doctors." Statistics are extremely common in our lives; we encounter them every day.

When used in a speech, statistics can bring an idea into sharp focus; they can also be dull and hopelessly abstract. They have the power to make an idea meaningful, and they have the power to deceive. Since Americans tend to be impressed by statistics, they can be powerful supporting data.

In order to achieve maximum effect from statistics, the speaker should present them in the most comprehensible units. This may mean simply presenting the most comprehensible unit, or it may mean presenting the statistics in two forms. For example, when

Jackson County, Missouri, was seeking to pass a $93 million bond issue, which included a $43 million sports complex, the promoters of the measure repeatedly pointed out that it would result in only about a $12 increase for the average taxpayer on a per annum basis. Ninety-three million dollars seems like a staggering figure; $12 per year does not. The same approach to statistics is often used by those opposed to a cause. When a medium-sized Midwestern city sought to increase its levy by 15 mills, the amount of increase seemed small enough; however, when it was presented as an increase in taxes of about $100 per year for the average home owner by the local newspaper, it gave an entirely different meaning to the increase. Usually it is wise to use round figures when dealing with very large numbers. Instead of an exact breakdown of dollars and cents, the round figure of "eight and a half billion" is more meaningful. If a lot of statistics are used in a speech, charts and diagrams to give the listener a visual picture are essential.

Since statistics can be exceedingly deceptive, we should test them carefully for their real meaning before we accept any inferences from them. The following questions provide useful tests:

1. What is meant by the key words used to describe a unit tabulated? What is meant by 6 million unemployed? What is the definition of an unemployed person in this study? Terms like *average home owner, criminals, indigent,* or *amateur athletes* need operational definitions when they constitute units of tabulation.

2. Are the statistics cited from competent and unbiased sources? What are the qualifications of the data compiler? Is there a chance of misrepresentation due to vested interests?

3. Do the statistics cover sufficient cases and length of time? Data covering corn production for only one year, or coal production from only one mine for a period of two months, or the batting average of a baseball player for thirty days, are too limited and unrepresentative to permit sound conclusions.

4. Are the data based on typical units of the whole group? During the political campaign of 1936, when Alf Landon was the Republican candidate for president and Franklin Roosevelt headed

the Democratic ticket, *Literary Digest* conducted a nation-wide poll covering more than a million potential voters and confidently predicted a sweeping Republican victory. Instead, the Democrats won by a landslide. The *Digest* poll failed to include a representative share of typical voters. Its samples were limited to names found in telephone directories, but during the severe economic depression of the 1930s the heavy Democratic support came largely from the great number of people who could not afford a telephone. *Literary Digest*'s subsequent demise was greatly due to its colossal statistical blunder.

5. Are the statistics relevant to the point to be proved? Expert propagandists commonly fill their speeches with all kinds of statistics in order to give the semblance of documentation, but very often their statistics are irrelevant to their claims.

6. If the statistics deal in averages, do they represent the mode, median, or the arithmetical average? In a group of ten numbers the mode is the number occurring the most frequently, the median is the middle number in the group, and the numbers added together and divided by the total numbers, in this case, ten, is the arithmetical average. Suppose a speaker says that the average income of farmers in Lincoln County is $40,000 per year. High income? For one farmer perhaps. One farmer in the county may own thousands of acres and realize a tremendous income. All the other farmers of the county may own only about 200 acres each. The mode income of farmers in the county in such a case gives the truest picture of average income. The mode income may be only $3,500 per year. The larger figure is obviously deceptive.

It is good persuasive strategy to use statistics in conjunction with other forms of data, an example to make the statistics real and vivid, and testimony to give them a ring of authority.

Testimony. Testimony is nothing but a statement. We all make hundreds of statements each day. Some are sound observations, others are logical speculations, and still others are totally unfounded; some are thoughtful value judgments, others are expressions of prejudice. The question is "What are the characteristics of a statement that make it useful supporting data?" The answer lies in an analysis of three different types of testimony: expert opinion, personal observation, and pithy quotations. The rationale for expert opinion as supporting data is that the nuclear scientist is qualified to make statements about nuclear physics, the successful attorney is competent to discuss criminology, and the psychiatrist is prepared to discuss human behavior. It should be kept in mind, however, that expert opinion merely gives credence to an idea; it does not prove it. Expert opinion is not evidence, only supporting data.

The speaker using expert opinion should identify the authorities he cites, because the discerning audience will want to know why it should have faith in the opinions of these authorities. Three factors are especially important—the position of the authority, his special interest and background concerning the subject, and in what source his testimony can be found. Observe how Bert Goss, president of a public-relations firm, handled the qualification of expert opinion in a speech on the effects of antitrust action on public opinion toward business.

> The lead editorial in the current issue of *Fortune* is titled: "Antitrust: The Sacred Cow needs a Vet." This editorial comments on a thought-provoking article in the same issue by Professor Sylvester Petro of New York University School of Law. Professor Petro concludes with this observation:
> "If our economy were to lose its drive, the record ought to show the real cause of the stagnation. Free enterprise and free competition have not failed. The failure would lie in the principle of government control and tutelage that the antitrust laws, properly understood, exemplify so clearly."[12]

Personal observations of fact, if the reporter is a reliable witness, constitute acceptable supporting data for most audiences. The witness in the law court reports what he saw. The journalist reports specific happenings. A member of the State Department may recall past events. The speaker may even recount personal experiences. A personal report is an observation of fact, not a value statement. Such a person need not be anyone of great renown or high position; he must simply be a reliable witness. He

---

[12] Bert C. Goss, "Trial Outside of the Courtroom," in *Contemporary American Speeches*, p. 256.

must be able to report an observation uncolored by value judgments.

The third type of testimony, the pithy quotation, essentially has nothing to do with expertise. The rationale for the pithy quotation as supporting data is that it helps to make an idea especially striking or imaginative. When Grayson Kirk, former president of Columbia University, discusses the problem of imprecise speech and says that Jacques Barzun has referred to this type of speech as an "inelegant algebra," Barzun's testimony serves as an energizer of the speaker's message.

Parallel Cases. Parallel cases, commonly called analogies, draw comparisons between objects, things, principles, happenings, and concepts that are similar in their essentials. Parallel cases function best in making ideas clear and meaningful; however, they can also help to make an argument acceptable. The very existence of a case parallel to the speaker's proposal makes the speaker's argument more plausible. If one were to argue that the consolidation of three school districts would likely result in more efficient use of well-qualified teachers, one could cite similar instances of consolidation and point to the increased efficiency that resulted. If one were to try to predict what Russian reaction would be to a given conflict, one could recall parallel incidents from the past and examine Russian reaction at those moments. Observe how Patrick Henry, in the debate on the adoption of the federal Constitution, argued from analogy to prove that the American colonies did not need a strong federal government.

> The history of Switzerland clearly proves that we might be in amicable alliance with those states without adopting this Constitution. Switzerland is a confederacy, consisting of dissimilar governments. This is an example which proves that governments of dissimilar structures may be confederated. That confederate republic has stood upwards of four hundred years; and, although several of the individual republics are democratic, and the rest aristocratic, no evil has resulted from this dissimilarity; for they have braved all the powers of France and Germany during that long period.[13]

---

[13] Patrick Henry, "Against the Federal Constitution," in Ernest J. Wrage and Barnet Baskerville, eds., *American Forum* (New York: Harper & Row, 1960), p. 20.

The Form of the Message

In his *Institutes of Oratory*, Quintilian wisely observed, "Just as it is not sufficient for those who are erecting a building merely to collect stone and timber and other building materials, but skilled masons are required to arrange and place them, so in speaking, however abundant the matter may be, it will merely form a confused heap unless arrangement be employed to reduce it to order and to give it connexion and firmness of structure."

"Preparing to say something," says Arthur Koestler in *The Act of Creation*, "whether it is a single sentence or a public lecture, is to set a hierarchy in motion." The hierarchy that is set in motion can be thought of as strategic choice. Oftentimes merely placing one phrase ahead of another changes the impact of a statement. A public speaker begins his speech with material that he thinks will obtain listener interest and attention and will lay the groundwork appropriate for his central thought. He decides to use one major idea in the body of his speech prior to another because he feels it will make his thought clearer or more persuasive. He saves certain material for the conclusion of his speech because he thinks it will bring his address to an effective close.

It must be noted that arranging a message is an individualistic undertaking. It is one person's response to a communication exigence. If twenty students were asked to speak for ten minutes on the same subject, we might witness twenty different approaches to that subject. Some, however, would be structuring their presentation in a more strategic manner than others. The more successful ones would tailor their arrangement of ideas to the subject, their purpose, the audience, and the occasion. They might realize that an informative message often calls for a different organizational approach from a speech that seeks to stimulate action, that one needs to approach a hostile audience differently from an extremely friendly one, and that different subjects tend to call for a different division of thought. They might demonstrate awareness of the cardinal principle of speech organization—providing the most meaningful thought progression in terms of their purpose, audience, and occasion. The speaker must shape his message in terms of the constraints that are operating on him.

Dimension 3: Message Preparation

We think that at least five desirable results can come from good organization:

1. *Clarity.* Good organization helps make the ideas clear and readily understood by the listeners.

2. *Efficiency.* Efficiency calls for careful analysis in the selection of message materials and their orderly arrangement. This helps to enrich the speech substance in ratio to time consumed; it entails a level of brevity.

3. *Unity.* Good construction helps the speaker pull things together to establish one central idea and maintain singleness of purpose.

4. *Emphasis.* Structure is a primary vehicle for emphasizing central ideas in any message, and careful organization will highlight the key ideas of a speech.

5. *Impact.* A skillful arrangement of ideas will help lead the listener to desired attitudes, beliefs, and actions. It enhances the persuasive impact of the message.

Since, as we mentioned previously, all human communications have a beginning, a middle, and an end, we can also see that this should be true of speeches. Rhetoricians have long dealt with the introduction of a speech, the body of a speech, and the conclusion of a speech. Whether one wants to approach this tripartite division of messages in such a formal style or not, a speaker needs to make some initial contact with his auditors and lead into his message, present his message, and finally wrap up his message and disengage himself from his listeners. We will, therefore, divide our discussion of arrangement into three sections: the introduction, the body, and the conclusion. Since the body of the speech constitutes the main message, we will take it up first and then deal with beginnings and endings.

The Body of the Message

The body of a speech consists of the basic message; main points of development; statements of support, often called subpoints; illustrative and supporting data; and transitions connecting and relating these materials into a meaningful whole. These components can, of course, be structured and arranged many different ways, but before we examine any arrangement patterns we want to explain and illustrate the five elements of a message that we just mentioned.

The Basic Message

The speaker's message is always made up of a duality: object and subject. In other words, the speaker wants to accomplish something with his audience regarding his subject. The roles of object and subject are so interlocked that one reinforces and influences the other. Thus, before you as a potential speaker fret too much about drawing up a formal outline, make up your mind about two things: What do you want your basic message or your central thought-line to be? And what kind of response do you want from your audience?

A speaker begins the process of arrangement by asking himself what it is that he wishes to accomplish with the audience he is going to address. Is his primary purpose to edify, clarify, energize the mind, spread cheer and joy, give inspiration to more noble attitudes? Is it to establish belief, get action, enhance personal ethos? The speaker's purpose will, to a great extent, govern the pattern and style of message structure. For example, you may decide you want the audience to realize that contributing to the Community Chest not only is their civic duty but also strongly affects the happiness of their families; or you want to clarify your new bookkeeping system so that each employee knows how it works; or you may want to convince parents that the viewing of certain crime-oriented programs is so undesirable for their children that they will carefully monitor the use of their TV in their homes. Whether a speaker expressly states the central idea of his speech to his listeners or not, it is useful for him to formulate a concise statement of what he plans to say. If he does not do this, he may himself be fuzzy regarding his message.

The Main Points

The body of a message consists of one or more main points. Sometimes these points are called *issues*, but since that term is applicable chiefly to persuasive speeches, we use the term *main points* throughout this book. As part of his inventive process, the speaker will analyze his topic, break it down into its key ideas, and then decide which of them to use in his speech and which to exclude. Once this vital inclusion-exclusion decision has been made, the speaker is faced with an equally important question: In what sequence will he arrange his ideas? Only rarely will a good speech have more than four or five main points. A large number of major statements would be hard for a listener to follow and remember. If you have partitioned a topic into more than five main points, try to group some of them under a broader heading, using them as subpoints.

It is desirable that your main points be parallel in their significance. In other words, they should all be on the same level of generalization or classification. Suppose you listed the following under the topic heading, "How to Play Tennis."

1. The history of tennis
2. The rules of tennis
3. The backhand drive
4. The strategy of tennis

Even a cursory examination reveals that the third main point, "The backhand drive," is not on the same level of generalization as the others. Point 3, to be parallel, might be changed to "The fundamentals of tennis."

Main points tend to be most effective if arranged systematically. True, some very effective speeches are often badly organized, but that is not to say that they receive their effectiveness from poor organization. Research evidence shows that systematic arrangement tends to give maximum impact to the speaker's points. The goal is to arrange the main points in such relationship to each other as will achieve the most effective thought-progression. Except for perhaps the hostile listener, the more apparent the design of a speech is to those who hear it, the more effective it usually will be.

Patterns of Arrangement. The best pattern of arrangement is often suggested by the subject itself. If one were to speak on the

United States government, for example, one might have three main divisions, the executive branch, the legislative branch, and the judicial branch. Many subjects have a natural breakdown of categories. Cattle can be classified as dairy and beef; horses as race, riding, and draft; knitting can be discussed according to types of stitches, knit and purl.

In addition to such natural divisions of subjects, certain stock patterns or partitioning designs can often be used. For example:

Local, state, national, and international
Theory and practice
Heredity and environment
Structure and function
Political, economic, and social
Background, characteristics, and accomplishments
Resemblances and differences
Physical, mental, and spiritual
Symptoms, cure, and prevention
Past, present, and future
Causes and effects
Problem and solution
Problem, causes, and solution
Specific and general
Need, plan, advantages

In a speech of description you may be able to arrange your materials geographically, such as east to west, north to south, or bottom to top. Regional dialects, for example, may be discussed as eastern, southern, and general American. A machine may be explained through its inward to outward movement.

Speeches involving either a value or a factual judgment consist of *good reasons* for belief, and the speaker will use *reasons* as the main points of development. A speaker may, in this instance, present three reasons why he feels that "A Democratic Form of Government Is Best":

1. It guarantees rights to the individual
2. It reflects the will of the majority
3. It deepens the citizen's feeling of responsibility

The reasons should always be placed in their most logical order. Sometimes one may be more acceptable to an audience if another

Dimension 3: Message Preparation

has already been developed. Ordinarily, it is wise to begin with the reasons that the audience is most likely to agree with. It should be added that, often, even a *good reasons* approach can be given stock design, such as moving from specific reasons to general. Regardless of how you structure your points, let your arrangement be characterized by system.

The standard classical approach to arrangement divided a speech into six parts: *exordium, narratio, divisio, confirmatio, confutatio,* and *conclusio.* The exordium was designed to attract the listener's attention and gain his good will; the narratio related or narrated the relevant factual information to the proposition to be discussed; the divisio divided and forecasted to the listener the main points to be discussed in the speech; the confirmatio presented the constructive arguments or reasons for belief; the confutatio consisted of a rebuttal of the strongest counterarguments; and the conclusio was the conclusion. This classical approach to arrangement is well suited for most argumentative propositions. For the modern speaker, it raises two pertinent questions: Is it useful to forecast a summary of main points prior to their actual discussion? Is it useful to present, analyze, and refute vital counterarguments in a nondebating situation?

Forecasting versus Unfolding. If a speaker partitions and forecasts his main points, he ends his introduction to the speech with a statement of his thesis, after which he immediately announces his main points to the audience. If, for example, he were speaking on behalf of expanded trade relationships with communist countries, at the close of his introduction he might say:

> I, therefore, want to take the opportunity this evening to explain to you why I feel that expanded trade relationships with Communist countries would be advantageous. In the first place, expanded trade relationships would greatly stimulate the American economy, and secondly, expanded trade relationships would have positive political benefits. Let's take a look, then, at that first reason: Expanded trade relationships would greatly stimulate the American economy.

Such a forecast has potential advantages and disadvantages. Advantageously, stating the main points in advance can (1) increase the clarity of the speech; (2) aid retention; (3) impress the average listener; (4) give an impression of fairness; and (5) act as an aid to appreciative listening in that it tells people how far they have come and how far they have yet to go. To know how much remains, Quintilian wrote, "stimulates us to fresh effort over the labor that still awaits us. For nothing need seem long, when it is definitely known how far it is to the end." Conversely the primary disadvantages of forecasting are as follows: The speaker lacks flexibility; important points he may have omitted in his introduction might occur to him during presentation, and it will be difficult for him to work them in. Moreover, projecting certain points on a controversial subject may arouse the hostility of some listeners, since it does not permit the speaker to begin with points of agreement and gradually lead into the area of disagreement. It may also seem anticlimactic. And finally, it may cause listener impatience, for, as Quintilian explained, "There is in every case some one point of more importance than the rest, and when the judge has become acquainted with it, he is apt to disdain other points as requiring no notice."

In light of the above advantages and disadvantages it would seem that forecasting is good technique for speeches whose purpose is to inform and to secure belief when the audience is neutral or open-minded about the topic. For both types of audiences, clarity, impressiveness, and the high-lighting of good reasons or main points are cardinal virtues. Forecasting permits emphasizing these matters. In other cases, it may be wiser not to forecast and instead unfold the main points as the speaker's thought logically progresses through the speech.

Presenting Both Sides of the Case. Another essential thought that readily emerges from the classical pattern of speech development is the question of what to do with counterarguments. Is it wise to identify the main counterarguments on a controversial subject and to refute them? As a general rule of thumb, it is wise to include the main counterarguments in a controversial speech if the con arguments are likely to be prominent in the listeners' minds. In such instances, including both sides of the case will not only project an element of fairness and awareness by the speaker but will also give him a chance to decrease the importance of chief negative issues. However, whenever counterarguments are included in a speech, it is generally wise to follow the classical speech pattern and present constructive arguments before refuting counterarguments—the theory being that if the audience receives the pro arguments first they will be at least somewhat influenced by them, and it then is easier to refute the counterarguments.

Statements of Support

Main points of a message are developed and explained through a series of supporting statements, often called subpoints. Subpoints answer the question, "Why?" If one argues that Brand A is better than Brand B, one develops the argument through a series of supporting statements that tell why one brand is better than another. This is true even in an informational presentation. If one explains a bookkeeping system and says that column A should always be filled out prior to column B, one goes on to say why this is so. Thus, in a formal debate brief, the word *because* is usually used in outlining supporting statements. Since subpoints are supportive and subordinate, they must be relevant and consequential to the main point.

Primary subpoints are placed on an outline with capital-letter labels.

I. Nongraded high schools have been successful.
   A. Melbourne High School was the first nongraded school.
   B. The Melbourne High School experiment was highly successful.
   C. Other schools using the system have since experienced similar success.

Arabic numbers normally are used to label secondary subpoints—those that explain and support primary subpoints; lowercase letters designate third-level subpoints; and if fourth-level subpoints occur, Arabic numbers are placed in parentheses. For example:

I. Transcendentalism became a concrete movement when the transcendental philosophy spread to America.
   A. New England was the land where the transcendental philosophy had a chance to show what it was and what it proposed.

1. Life in the new world was flexible.
   a. Few prejudices existed.
   b. There were no traditions of philosophy.
      (1) The nation was too young to have developed a philosophical tradition of its own.
      (2) The philosophy taught in the colleges was that of European thinkers.
   c. The search was for new ideas.
2. Able thinkers advanced Transcendentalism in their poems and essays. For example:
   a. Emerson
   b. Alcott
   c. Thoreau
B. In time the movement reached beyond New England.

Illustrative and Supporting Data

Illustrative and supporting data should form the bases for the declarative statements in the message. The main points illustrate and support the basic message; the primary subpoints illustrate and support the main points; the second-level subpoints illustrate and support the primary subpoints; and so forth. However, no matter how far one extends the breakdown of subpoints, at some point claims and declarative statements need to be grounded in data such as specific instances, analogies, statistics, or testimony.

Outlining your speech helps you verify the interest value and the logical adequacy of your main points, inasmuch as it graphically reveals the absence of such data. Some points may be readily acceptable to an audience without specific documentation, but other more controversial ones must be supported with primary data. The speaker should, therefore, scan his outline, identify his significant claims, and determine whether concrete supporting materials are necessary to make them acceptable to his audience. Observe how the section of outline below employs illustrative and supporting data.

1. Ambition and desire are necessary ingredients of success.
   a. Howard H. Kendlen, noted psychologist and author of *Basic Psychology,* says, "Without ambition one has little power, accomplishes little and has little respect."

Dimension 3: Message Preparation

> b. Without ambition Bill Bradley could not have been a three-time All American basketball player and a Rhodes scholar.
> c. Without desire Jim Ryun could not have run a 3:51.3 mile.

The speaker in this instance used a complete-sentence outline. He might also have outlined his point thus:

> 1. Ambition and desire are necessary ingredients of success.
>   a. Quotation from Howard H. Kendlen, noted psychologist.
>   b. Example of Bill Bradley.
>   c. Example of Jim Ryun.

Transitions

Transitions are essential to the total integration of the message. They bridge the gaps between points. Transitions between main points normally terminate the preceding point and forecast the next, with some indication of an interrelationship between them. The words *and, now,* and *so* are inadequate thought bridges and so is the dull repetition of the word or phrase. Search for new and varied bridges. Rhetorical questions frequently make good transitions. At the close of a point you can ask a question that leads into the next point, which will, in essence, answer the question. For example, one might conclude a point by asking, "But can courage alone do it? Obviously not. Imagination is also needed." The next point, then, is imagination. Sometimes a brief restatement of preceding points will provide an adequate thought bridge, as in the following: "Having reviewed the rules of tennis and the basic fundamentals of the game, let's move on to another important consideration, the strategy of the game." Often a simple statement of termination of a point and an introductory statement of the next will be adequate. For example:

1. Having seen three specific reasons for the proposal, let's move on to the fourth and final one.
2. Thus, it is apparent that our city faces an impelling problem. My solution to the problem is a simple one.
3. That is the past. Now let's look at the present.
4. The results of the first experiment are obvious. The second experiment involves a different principle.

The Introduction

In Cicero's words the introduction should render "auditors well disposed, attentive, teachable." Stated differently, the purpose of the introduction is to enlist the attention and good will of the audience and to pave the way for the fullest communication of the speaker's thought and purpose. Most effective introductions have three steps: an interest step, a justification step, and an orientation step.

The Interest Step

When a speaker walks in front of a group of people, pauses, and looks at them, he usually gets their attention. Invariably, he has the fullest attention when he first begins to speak. The introduction should capitalize on this initial attention and envelop the listeners' interest in the speech. To accomplish this end, the speaker may choose to:

1. *Use an appropriate illustration.* Both factual and hypothetical narratives can be effective, as long as they are relevant to the subject and helpful in disclosing the subject in an effective and interesting manner.

2. *Use an appropriate personal experience.* Personal anecdotes quite often comprise the most effective speech introductions. Search in the storehouse of your experiences for incidents that relate to your speech subject.

3. *Use an appropriate quotation.* Quotations chosen should be short and provocative, and relevant to the speech topic.

4. *Use appropriate humor.* Far too many speakers seem to have the idea that one cannot safely begin a speech without first telling the latest joke. Not everyone can relate humorous anecdotes effectively, and, worse yet, far too often the stories aren't funny. But humor suitable to the speech and to the audience and occasion, if well presented, can effectively arouse listener interest and gain good will for the speaker.

Dimension 3: Message Preparation 155

5. *Refer to a pertinent historical event.* A historical reference can be used to contrast the contemporary scene with the past. An effective narration of incidents tends to be interesting.

6. *Refer to major news events.* People are generally interested in important happenings, whether of world or local significance.

7. *Refer to the importance of the occasion.* This approach is particularly useful when speaking at important and distinguished occasions.

8. *Ask rhetorical questions.* Beginning with well-phrased rhetorical questions tends to involve the audience directly and actively with the speaker's ideas.

The Justification Step

The least an audience will expect of a speaker is that he present a subject of importance and that he be qualified to speak on that subject. Often the importance of a speaker's subject is readily apparent to the audience; at other times some kind of justification step in the introduction is vital to the success of the address. At such moments the speaker may wish to point out the relevance of his subject to listeners' individual security or to national welfare. He may be able to relate it to a value of critical importance to his auditors. Listeners must perceive that the speaker's subject pertains to things that matter to them. This is how Gretchen Steffens, a college student, justified her speech by generating concern for her subject.

> When I told my father my oration subject concerned civil rights, he looked at me blankly and said, "Civil Rights—that's not really a current issue—it's now the law of the land." Perhaps many of you, like Dad, may be tired of hearing another oration about the Negro and his problems, feeling that with the passage of the Civil Rights Act, that was the end of them. But is it really? The question that still faces America today is the application of the principles it proclaimed.
>
> True, the Civil Rights Act was an important victory for all of us interested in equal rights for all men. But this victory, as Winston Churchill said of another triumph for freedom, "This is not the end; it is not even the end of the beginning." The problems involving

acceptance of equal rights can prove to be even greater than those faced when enacting the law. Indeed, the words of James Baldwin, prominent Negro author, could very well be true: "The Negroes of this country may never be able to rise to power, but they are very well placed indeed to precipitate chaos and ring down the curtain on the American dream."[14]

Good speeches tend to contain personal elements. The beginning speaker, since he is relatively unknown, will find it especially useful to identify himself with his subject. A speaker who can show a strong identification will have some justification for speaking. You may wish to reveal your experience or training in your introduction in order to generate ethos. Arthur G. Trudeau, in an address called "Morals and Missiles," deliberately revealed his qualifications for speaking on the subject.

It is a great pleasure for me to be here this evening and to join with you in honoring our Army Missile Men. Let me congratulate those who have just received the awards. More and more in these crucial days, the battlefield leans heavily on industry and what it is able to produce. Nowhere is this more clearly seen than in the missile business. Here, industry teamed with the Armed Forces form a major front of national defense and a bulwark to our freedom.

The thoughts I would like to bring you tonight are those of an American who has been privileged to serve our nation for more than 35 years in posts of increasing responsibility in the realm of national defense. My work, especially my experience as a former Chief of Army Intelligence, has provided me unusual opportunities to perceive and appreciate the challenges which face our great Republic and the Free World today, tomorrow and in the foreseeable future.[15]

A skillful speaker often establishes common ground with his listeners in his introduction and thereby achieves a kind of license to speak. He may identify himself with his hearers, their stereotypes and strong beliefs, their heroes, and their community. Observe how Winston Churchill, in a speech before Congress at the outset of World War II, identified himself with America and our American ideals.

---

[14] "The Law of the Land," in *Winning Hope College Orations* (Holland, Mich.: Hope College, 1966), p. 132.
[15] *Vital Speeches of the Day* (April 15, 1960), pp. 404–405.

The fact that my American forbears have for so many generations played their part in the life of the United States and that here I am, an Englishman, welcomed in your midst makes this experience one of the most moving and thrilling in my life, which is already long and has not been entirely uneventful. I wish, indeed that my mother, whose memory I cherish across the veil of years, could have been here to see me. By the way, I cannot help reflecting that if my father had been American and my mother British, instead of the other way round, I might have got here on my own. In that case, this would not have been the first time you would have heard my voice. In that case I would not have needed any invitation, but if I had it is hardly likely that it would have been unanimous. So, perhaps, things are better as they are. I may confess, however, that I do not feel quite like a fish out of water in a legislative assembly where English is spoken. I am a child of the House of Commons. I was brought up in my father's house to believe in democracy; trust the people, that was his message. I used to see him cheered at meetings and in the streets by crowds of workingmen way back in those aristocratic Victorian days when Disraeli said, "The world was for the few and for the very few." Therefore, I have been in full harmony with the tides which have flowed on both sides of the Atlantic against privileges and monopoly and I have steered confidently towards the Gettysburg ideal of government of the people, by the people, for the people.[16]

The Orientation Step

Above all else, the introduction should orient the listener to the message of the speech; it should disclose and clarify what is to follow. Far too often a speaker has an interest-arousing introduction but fails to show any relation between it and his subject. Such an introduction fails to orient the listener. Another common fault occurs when a speaker uses an appropriate introduction but fails to make an adequate transition from it to the statement of the topic. Transitions are always important, but perhaps more so between the introduction and the statement of the topic than anywhere else in the speech. In a speech on "The City and the University," Dr. James M. Hester, president of New York University, uses his introduction as such a transition to build up the importance of his subject and to disclose and clarify his message.

---

[16] *Vital Speeches of the Day* (1941–1942), p. 197.

The future of our cities is a question of extraordinary concern in many parts of America. The core of our growing metropolitan complexes, the central city, where we continue to build magnificent structures for the conduct of business, communications, and the performance of the arts, has become a problem area from which many of our most capable people are alienated. They may use the central city for economic reasons, but few live there and concern themselves deeply with its problems. The result is a defect in our national life that requires vigorous correctives.

Many would agree that the university has become the most potent institution in our civilization. While it is not in and of itself an agency for socal action, it is our most effective device for organizing the efforts of people devoted to advancing the conditions of life.

It would appear obvious, therefore, that we should bring the resources of the university to bear upon the problem of the central city. In universities across the country, institutes of urban studies are attempting to do just that, which is of course, highly desirable. Institutes alone will not, however, in my opinion, solve the problem. A much more dynamic corrective is the proposition you here in San Francisco are considering: building a university in the central city itself.[17]

The Conclusion

Speeches should not just end; they should be brought to a carefully planned conclusion, ending on a note of completeness and finality. The conclusion, in rounding out a creative address, performs three principal functions.

1. *It re-emphasizes the basic message.* The entire purpose of the conclusion is to focus attention on the basic message of the address and, in the process, leave the listeners with a favorable impression. Hence, it is wise to restate the thesis at the outset of the closing remarks. The restatement of the thesis is usually blended with the second function of the conclusion, the summarization step.

2. *It summarizes the main points.* Sometimes you will want to summarize your points by restating them one by one. If it is

---
[17] *Vital Speeches of the Day* (March 1, 1966), pp. 294–295.

important that your auditors remember your main points, a simple recapitulation of them will probably be the best procedure, since research has amply demonstrated that this kind of restatement in a speech is a positive aid to retention. As a rule, it is more effective to crystallize the content of your speech without a routine itemization of your main points. Tie the threads together so that the pattern of your speech is clearly revealed. In summarizing your ideas, be sure to observe Quintilian's warning that the final recapitulation be as brief as possible: "For if we devote too much time thereto, the peroration will cease to be an enumeration and will constitute something very like a second speech."

3. *It effects a climactic ending.* An informative message will end with an appropriate note that rounds off the thought of the discourse. But in persuasive speaking, a final appeal that lifts the address to a climactic close will help to motivate the audience. As in the introduction, special devices may be employed in ending a speech. A few of the more common ones that help bring the speech to a climactic ending are set forth below:

A Terse, Provocative Quotation. Any quotation used in the conclusion of a speech should be short; when possible, one sentence is best. It should capsulize the thought of the speech.

A Short, Pertinent Verse. A poetic quotation or even a verse of the speaker's own creation can be an effective way of terminating a speech. Make certain, however, that the verse is relevant to the central idea of the message.

A Short Illustration. Concluding a speech with a pertinent illustration that makes the central thought of the speech vivid can be as valid as beginning it with one. The illustration used should tell the whole story of the message in a few short lines. As in the case of the introduction, personal anecdotes can often be extremely effective in the conclusion. Moreover, a speaker can often effectively relate his conclusion to his introduction, which gives the speech special unity. This approach can easily be used if an illustration occurred as part of the introduction.

The Outline

An outline for a speech can serve different purposes for different people. Outlines may be formulated in the mind or on paper. Some experienced speakers who are well versed on a particular subject and highly motivated may do as well or better without working out an outline beforehand—it is difficult to imagine Patrick Henry giving his famous speech on Liberty from a carefully written outline. On the other hand, formulating an outline need not be a chore. One primary function of outlining is to act as a kind of mental catalyzer or stimulant to explore ways of enriching the message. Another function is to provide the speaker with a personalized road map to keep him on the right track, to give him a sense of direction and help him avoid repetition. Yet, an outline does not inherently carry an absolute guarantee for your most successful communication. There may be instances when, in light of your subject, audience, occasion, and the subtleties of your inner self, a suitable outline will fail to emerge. Should outlining and structuring annoy you too much and seem to get in your way, select a few of your points or concepts and try to see how much essential matter you can cover by oral or mental rehearsal in a given amount of time. After a few practice runs of this type, some kind of structure will usually emerge. You may even discover that you have eliminated the need for a pencil-and-paper outline because you have structured the message in your mind.

The first thing to remember about outlining is that although the Roman numerals and the A, B, C's help structure the outline they are in no way essential to it. Outlining so often seems like a terribly-mechanical thing because of the stress on proper form, and this is where the problem lies. An outline should be an unfolding process coordinated with the message and purpose of the discourse, not an exercise in form. Outlining should be an interactive process: On the one hand, message materials help to bring the outline into being, but on the other, the outline helps in the composition, structure, and upgrading of the quality of the message itself.

After you have jotted down your speech ideas in outline form, inspect the outline to see if you have done two things: (1) come up with the most desirable thought progression for your message —you may want to speak your thoughts through aloud to see if you like the flow of your arrangement—and (2) included sufficient illustrative and supporting data. What points stand off by them-

Dimension 3: Message Preparation

selves without illustration or evidence? Is your evidence convincing? A careful scrutiny of your outline will help you prepare a speech that is not "like a traveler wandering by night in unknown regions, . . . having no stated course or object, . . . guided by chance rather than design."

dimension four
message presentation: verbal and nonverbal cues

Language is the primary vehicle of human communication. Long ago, primitive man realized that if he could invent a set of vocal sounds and use them consistently and systematically, they would greatly enhance his chances for a social existence. Man was so successful in composing languages that today we are born into a sea of words which create our culture and shape our personal destinies.
We are bombarded every day with verbal cues from radio, television, newspapers, magazines, billboards, junk mail, books, lectures, and conversations. We speak as many as 25,000 words in a single day and hear many more. Our vocabularies grow larger and larger, our dictionaries thicker and thicker. During World War II, about 5000 new words were added to the English language each year; and the United States Air Force alone prepared a dictionary of nearly 600 pages containing more than 16,500 words and phrases which have special meaning for people in that service. Through the miracle of language we can speak of things not immediately present and of abstract concepts such as *justice* and *right*.

Yet, we commonly hear such expressions as: "The whole man talks." "Actions speak louder than words." "Say it with flowers." "Money talks." "A statue has no tongue and needs none." "One picture is worth a thousand words." Such statements would have us believe that we communicate with more than words. Soren Kierkegaard, a nineteenth-century philosopher was keenly aware of this phenomenon.

> If a man were to stand on one leg, or pose in a queer dancing attitude swinging his hat, and in this attitude propound something true, his few auditors would divide themselves into two groups; and many listeners he would not have, since most men would give him up at once. The one class would say: "How can what he says be true, when he gesticulates in that fashion?" The other class would say: "Well, whether he cuts capers or stands on his head, even if he were to throw handsprings, what he says is true and I propose to appropriate it, letting him go."[1]

The flow of nonverbal information surrounds us constantly from all sides every moment of the day. We start out in life among a nonverbal world of pillows, diapers, blankets, and the snuggling and hugging of loving parents. Touch is the language that binds the infant to its mother. Some children, even after they learn to walk and talk, seek ways to move about hugging their "security blankets," like the *Peanuts* character Linus. "Hold my hand" is an expression often heard by grown-ups in moments of anxiety. A gentle pat on the back can be an encouraging message, and a shove may have the opposite effect. For Helen Keller the world of touch was almost totally her salvation, as she shows us in the following example:

> It is known how the artist sees beautiful pictures in his mind before he paints them. Similarly, the spirit projects ideas into thought-images, or symbols; that is the universal and the only true language. If one could convey his joy or faith or his mental picture of a sunrise to another in visible form, how much more satisfactory that would be than the many words and phrases of ordinary language! I have cried when I touched an embossed Chinese symbol which represents happiness, and no amount of description would have produced such an effect upon me. It was a picture of a man with his mouth close to a rice field. How forcibly it brought home the fact that the Chinese are utterly dependent upon the rice they grow, and that when their fields are flooded, and the crops destroyed, starvation for millions of human beings is inevitable. Many ideas crowded into one symbol gain a power which words tend to neutralize.[2]

---

[1] Soren Kierkegaard, *Concluding Unscientific Postscript to the "Philosophical Fragments,"* trans. David Swenson and Walter Lowrie, ed. Walter Lowrie (Princeton, N.J.: Princeton University Press, 1944), p. 182.

[2] Helen Keller, *My Religion* (New York: Swedenborg Foundation, 1960), pp. 74–75.

Sight and hearing also provide us with numerous message cues. The sense of sight functions with miraculous speed and efficiency. People can learn to read ten times faster than they can speak. Seeing gives us information related to space, form, distance, light, shape, movement, color—all with amazing rapidity. We observe people's manners, their dress and the way they walk; how they eat, gesticulate, shake hands, and exchange courtesies. In interpersonal relations, bodily communication is very important. For most people of the Western culture, the way we shake our heads means yes or no; try some time saying yes but shaking your head from side to side and observe the confused look on your receiver's face. Smiles and hand applause mean approval. Thumbs down means "nix on that stuff"; thumbs up is "o.k." Holding a hand high with the index finger up means "We're number one." Two fingers spread out is a symbol for victory; the clenched fist means anger and protest. And there are frowns and "looks that kill."

We also live in a world of sounds, both pleasant and unpleasant. Music is organized sound and as such generates emotions within us. Today, background music is common in stores, offices, and banks. Music can even be an agent of mental therapy.

When addressing a group of people we always need to be cognizant of our nonverbal messages. We often hear the expression, "It isn't what he said, but how he said it that turned me off." Our actions and words should harmonize, for when nonverbal messages contradict the intended meaning of the spoken word, the result for the listener may be confusion, ambiguity, and even mistrust of the speaker. Our dress and general appearance can turn some people off before we ever express an idea to them. The notion of propitious conformity expressed in DIMENSION ONE (page 75) is an essential nonverbal concept. Voice and body should reinforce, amplify, clarify, emphasize, and vitalize the speaker's words. Their purpose is to punctuate ideas, feelings, and images. Intentional nonverbal cues signal the way we want our auditors to view our verbal messages. If we speak with a good deal of urgency, for example, it signifies that we view our message as being particularly crucial.

Our discussion of Message Cues in this dimension will be divided into two parts: Our initial concern will be Communicating with Language, and the latter part, Communicating with Voice

Dimension 4: Message Presentation

and Action, will deal with the speaker's vocal and bodily cues. Most of this section will be prescriptive, rather than descriptive, in that it focuses on concrete things to do when addressing an audience. This is especially true of the section dealing with voice and action.

Communicating With Language

> [We should] bear in mind that nothing is to be done for the sake of words, as words themselves were invented for the sake of things, and as those words are the most to be commended which express our thoughts best, and produce the impressions which we desire on the minds of the judges.
>
> Quintilian, *Institutes of Oratory*

"Speak Up" or "Write Now"

A freshman English composition handbook once used at the University of Kansas was aptly titled *Write Now*. The preface of this handbook contended that we have "one personality for talking and another for writing."

> When we talk we can be ourselves as we really are, but when we take our pens in hand we suffer a . . . change . . ., not rich but strange. We feel that our hair must be combed, our sleeves rolled down and our ties tightened up. When we try to write well we write with one ear cocked for the sound of our words, hoping that they have the ring of the learned or the literary, or that they sound as we think good writing should sound.[3]

Aristotle categorically maintained that the "style of written prose is not the same as that of conventional speaking." The implication of these statements clearly is that certain elements in the oral

---

[3] A. C. Edwards, Natalie Calderwood, and Edgar Wolfe, *Write Now* (Lawrence: University of Kansas Stenographic Bureau, 1952).

situation create a basic difference between speech and writing, and that these elements bear directly on oral style. The same statement could be made for the writing situation.

The speaker has two prime advantages over the writer, his ethos and his delivery. The speaker delivers his ideas and feelings in person. In face-to-face situations the speaker's image tends to be a crucial dimension in the communication event. The listener's response is governed by the degree to which he likes and trusts the speaker. The writer is more of an unknown, impersonal broadcaster. Often his role is anonymous, and his readers are vague entities to him, scattered over wide areas. The words themselves, without significant assistance from their author, have to generate his desired meanings and impact. His written message must stand on its own merit.

The second advantage the speaker enjoys over the writer is delivery, giving him almost unlimited leverage to reinforce, clarify, dramatize, and vitalize his ideas and feelings. As the speaker gets feedback from the audience he can change phraseology, give a new slant and tone to his message, explain the meaning of words that seem to be puzzling people, and repeat key ideas. The writer, on the other hand, has to make advance judgments about his readership. He can check meanings, rearrange the words of a sentence, underline, capitalize, and generally refine and revise both the thought and the composition. But he never gets any direct feedback. The speaker also has the advantage of vocal emphasis; the writer essentially is limited to punctuation, capital letters, spelling, color and style of print, or handwriting.

Both the speaker and the writer have a common concern about proper choice of words, word arrangement, grammar, syntax, and the laws of unity, coherence, and emphasis. Yet an audience is not likely to be concerned over a minor grammatical mistake by the speaker, whereas such an error in writing may reflect seriously upon the author. The speaker may quite effectively use loosely-constructed sentences—in fact, he may speak freely in sentence fragments—but the writer is usually expected to have tightly-drawn sentences.

There are some inherent differences between listening and reading which impel sharp differences in the language and style used by the speaker and the writer. Listening to a speech is, for the most part, a one-shot affair; the listener must catch the message as it is presented. He cannot backtrack or get an instant replay of what was said. The reader can slow down, stop, re-examine certain words and word arrangements, pause to light a cigarette or sip a coke, and even reach for a dictionary to clarify and verify meaning. In light of listener demands, the speaker, unlike the writer, will do well to give priority to short simple sentences, make frequent use of repetition, and use predominantly Anglo-Saxon language. He may even find a judicious recourse to vernacular expressions useful.

Speeches, with rare exception, are for the moment rather than for the ages; they are designed for immediate effect. The public speaker meets his audience and talks to them directly, creating a relationship between communicator and receiver that does not exist in written communication. Whereas the writer usually will speak in an indirect manner, the speaker is always *I*, the audience is *you*, and collectively they are *we*. Since an important principle of public address is audience involvement, an impersonal essay simply does not make a good speech. The speaker will want to make ample use of personal pronouns, for this form of address should help generate and hold attention. Lincoln's farewell speech, delivered at Springfield before departing for Washington, contains 144 words; nineteen of them, or 15 percent, are personal pronouns. The word *we* appears nine times in two sentences in one of Churchill's speeches, and the personal pronoun was a characteristic trademark of Franklin D. Roosevelt. A very good example of this is Mark Antony's speech in Act III, Scene ii, of Shakespeare's *Julius Caesar*:

> If *you* have tears, prepare to shed them now.
> *You* all do know this mantle. . . .
> Oh, what a fall was there, *my* countrymen!
> Then *I* and *you* and all of *us* fell down,
> Whilst bloody treason flourished over *us*.
> Oh, now *you* weep, and *I* perceive *you* feel
> The dint of pity. . . .
> *I* come not, friends, to steal away *your* hearts.
> *I* am no orator, as Brutus is;
> But, as you know *me* all, a plain, blunt man
> That loved *my* friend and that *they* know full well
> That gave *me* public to speak of *him*.

Stylistic Strategies

The attributes of a good oral style—an idea which goes back to the ancient Greeks—are clarity, impressiveness, and appropriateness. We will offer specific rhetorical devices and strategies which, if used wisely, will help you incorporate these attributes in your addresses.

Clarity

As we mentioned in DIMENSION THREE (pages 122–130), clarity is an important element of any speech. In this section, we will look at this strategy from the point of view of organization and language and will offer four methods of developing a clear oral style.

Use Appropriate Words. The speaker, as much as possible, should use words which are familiar to the audience. Saint Paul expressed the importance of this when he said, "Except ye utter by the tongue words easy to understand, how shall it be known what is spoken? For ye shall speak into the air." It is obvious that when addressing children one should use simple words. The idea of simplicity may profitably be extended to most speaking situations. When Churchill paid tribute to the Royal Air Force after the battle for Britain had been won, saying, "Never in the field of human conflict was so much owed by so many to so few," his eloquence largely rose from his use of monosyllabic words. The use of longer words in his statement would only have lessened its impact. The same is true of Lincoln's observation that "A house divided against itself cannot stand" and of Martin Luther King's statement, "It isn't so important how long you live. The important thing is how well you live." The twenty-third Psalm contains 118 words, 92 of which are one syllable. Of the first 118 words in Hamlet's most famous soliloquy, 99 are one syllable; and its first words, "To be or not to be. . . . ," convey incredible force. It is often said that little minds believe that big words signify big ideas, but obscurity of language should not be mistaken for profundity of thought.

The English language as we know it today grew out of the

language used by the scullions who worked in the kitchens of the eleventh century Norman nobility who conquered England. It was often referred to as "Kitchen English." Little by little, the words of the kitchen and such short, crisp words as ox, cow, deer, hunt, and horse began to creep into the Norman French spoken by the educated class. These words—stemming from a combination of ancient tribal dialects shaped and colored by the languages of the invading Angles, Saxons, and Scandinavians—were changed by Norman French into English.

Words learned early in life seem to have stronger meanings than those learned later in life. English words of Anglo-Saxon derivation tend to be the first words children master and tend to have a crisper flavor than English words of Latin derivation. As children, we learned to say *think* instead of *contemplate*, *fire* instead of *conflagration*, and *wish* instead of *desire*. Franklin N. Turner has written,

> Sir Winston's famed blood, sweat and tears that
>   sparked the English nation,
> Would never have endured with
>   sweat dressed up as perspiration.

Simple words retain a power that complex ones lack; they give the speaker his best chance of being understood.

Highly connotative words should be used carefully, especially if the speaker's purpose is to communicate information. Words which are supercharged may cause one listener to tune out, another to get up and leave, and a third to miss the point of the speech. The speaker's analysis of the audience's values should tell him which words are likely to have connotations that will work against him and which ones have the kind of affective quality that will work for him.

Specialized vocabulary unfamiliar to the audience, unless it is essential to the idea expressed, should be avoided. Whenever unfamiliar jargon is used, the speaker should carefully explain and define such terms. It is altogether possible for a social scientist, for example, to speak to a lay audience without their comprehending one single concept he is expressing. Yet it is also possible for such a person to communicate fully, as Dr. Karl Menninger, America's best-known psychiatrist, illustrated in a talk to a lay audience in Chautauqua, New York: "Some patients may have a mental illness and then get well, and then even get 'weller'! I mean they get better than they ever were. They get even better than they were before. This is an extraordinary and little-realized truth—and it constitutes the main point of my talk today."[4] His speech on mental illness that followed was totally free from psychiatric jargon.

Colloquialisms and slang ordinarily tend to degrade the dignity of a speech and often have no meaning to the audience. In some cases, however, a well-chosen colloquialism or slang word may be extremely effective. A few speakers of renown—Al Smith, Abraham Lincoln, Franklin D. Roosevelt, Clarence Darrow, Will Rogers, and Mark Twain—were able to use the raw, folksy, local style to good advantage. Lincoln used the expression "That is cool!" in one of his campaign speeches. When colloquialisms, and sometimes slang, are tastefully used they may be an effective medium for attaining directness, realism, and warmth. It is a matter of talking the language of the people without sacrificing personal dignity and sincerity.

Pomposity and out-and-out pedantry should be avoided. A father warning his eight-year-old son not to eat a rotten apple, would not say, "My lawful and legal heir, I recommend that you refrain from partaking of this fruit, for the process of decomposition has already been inaugurated." He would say, "Son, don't eat the apple. It's rotten." Lincoln began his famous "House Divided" speech with: "If we could first know *where* we are, and *whither* we are tending, we could then better judge *what* to do, and *how* to do it"—a profound statement that is totally unpretentious.

Use Precise Words. Words should convey the speaker's meaning as accurately as possible. Mark Twain once said the difference between the right word and the almost-right word is the difference between lightning and the lightning bug. Grayson Kirk, former president of Columbia University, in an address on the responsibilities of the educated man, held that the first duty of a university

---

[4] Karl Menninger, "Healthier than Healthy," in Wil A. Linkugel, R. R. Allen, and Richard L. Johannesen, eds., *Contemporary American Speeches* (Belmont, Calif.: Wadsworth, 1965), p. 30.

man "is to endeavor to achieve clarity and precision in his spoken and written communication." He went on to say,

> The uneducated man generally is lazy in his speech. When asked to describe something he says, "Oh, I guess it was kind of bluish." He is saying in reality that he has not been observant or that he has not been trained to distinguish anything more than the primary colors. He relies upon such vague descriptive generalities as "that kind of thing" or "you know what I mean." . . .[5]

No two words have fully-identical meanings. They may be listed in Roget's *Thesaurus* as synonyms, but one of the words will be more precise than the other for the speaker's purposes. Webster's *Dictionary of Synonyms* ascribes different shades of meaning to words generally considered synonymous. A good speaker is noted for his precision of description. He is not content with "bluish," or words that generally signify his intended meaning. Notice the difference in the impact of the following two sentences: "He showed a good deal of satisfaction as he took possession of his winnings," and "He grinned as he picked up the money."

Define Difficult and Abstract Words. A review of pages 122–126 in DIMENSION THREE should prove useful at this time. Above all else, be sure to remember that your definitions are to be useful in terms of the audience you are addressing. A very technical definition that no one understands is as bad as no definition at all.

Develop a Clear Thought Progression. In addition to word choice and word usage, stylistic clarity involves overall thought progression. Effective speech is oriented toward a theme and the development of that theme; one sentence ties clearly into the next; each thought unit relates to the one that follows it. It is altogether possible to construct brilliant individual sentences and still lack an instantly-clear style. Emerson's writings and lectures, for example, tend to be sentence-oriented. Sometimes his sentences achieve rare eloquence, but they stand alone instead of blending smoothly into subsequent sentences. Consider the following three sentences,

---

[5] Grayson Kirk, "Responsibilities of the Educated Man," in *Contemporary American Speeches*, p. 168.

which occur in succession in "The American Scholar": "Undoubtedly there is a right way of reading, so it be sternly subordinated. Man Thinking must not be subdued by his instruments. Books are for the scholar's idle times." Or the three sentences which occur in succession in his essay "Self-Reliance": "Whoso would be a man, must be a nonconformist. He who would gather immortal palms must not be hindered by the name of goodness, but must explore if it be goodness. Nothing is at last sacred but the integrity of your own mind." Oral discourse, to be truly effective, requires clear and energetic thought progression. Transitions and cumulative summaries should be used to tie ideas together and to help show the development of the overall pattern of thought. The following quotation from a speech by Adlai Stevenson illustrates how an idea can be unfolded smoothly and effectively:

> This age has been defined in many ways—as a time of conflict in ideology, as a time of ferment in technology, as a period of revolution in science, as an era when at last the means lie at hand to free mankind from the ancient shackles of pain and of hunger. It is all these things—but I believe the true crisis of our time lies at a deeper level. We have indeed conquered means and resources unknown at earlier ages. We have had thrown open to us frontiers of choice which would leave earlier ages stupefied by their scale and their scope.
>
> But all this freedom and elbow room only thrusts onto us with more force the fundamental issue of truth that is within us. We can use our wealth, our capacity for some vision of truth, some ideal of brotherhood, or we can imprison ourselves within the selfishness of our own concerns and the limitations of a narrow nationhood. This is the dimension of our crisis.[6]

Impressiveness

History records decisive moments when public speakers have influenced human action through their artful use of language. Winston Churchill's mastery of the English language rallied the British people during the dark days of World War II. At Dunkirk, when it looked as though defeat would swallow Britain, Churchill stirred the nation with an eloquent appeal for a new effort: "Let

---

[6] Adlai Stevenson, "The Political Relevance of Moral Principle," in Ernest J. Wrage and Barnet Baskerville, eds., *Contemporary Forum* (New York: Harper & Row, 1962), p. 364.

us therefore brace ourselves to our duty and so bear ourselves that if the British Commonwealth and Empire last for a thousand years, men will still say 'This was their finest hour.'" Most of our renowned presidents have been skillful communicators, possessing the ability to present ideas impressively to their national audiences and thereby exerting a high degree of leadership. Lincoln, Wilson, and Kennedy, for example, showed a fine command of the English language in their public addresses. And Franklin D. Roosevelt dispelled panic in 1933 at a time when our democratic system was undergoing its severest test, confidently telling the nation, "We have nothing to fear but fear itself." Harry L. Hopkins remarked of Roosevelt's first inaugural address: "With that one speech and in those few minutes, the appalling anxiety and fears were lifted, and the people of the United States knew they were going into safe harbor under the leadership of a man who never knew the meaning of fear."[7]

The strange power of language has always caused man to stand in amazement. Small wonder Joseph Conrad once said, "Give me the right word and I will move the world." When Nikita Khruschev said to us, "We will bury you," he sent shock waves of ill will, fear and anger all over America. When Barry Goldwater gave his acceptance speech as candidate for president in 1964 and maintained that extremism in the defense of liberty was no vice, his chances for the White House suffered a severe blow. Generals of past centuries were so keenly cognizant of the power of language that they delivered an oration to the troops prior to sending them into battle. Today, the football coach delivers a message to the team at half time; many a team has charged back out onto the field with newfound energy and enthusiasm after being told to go out and win one for the "Gipper." So we see that, in addition to preserving and imparting knowledge, language can also be used to move people. Its fundamental role in human communication is apparent.

Good oral style reaches beyond simple clarity and sets the message of the speech before the listeners as impressively as the thought warrants. It makes ideas sharp and clear, intense and

---

[7] See B. D. Zevin, ed., *Nothing to Fear, The Selected Addresses of Franklin Delano Roosevelt* (Cambridge, Mass.: The Riverside Press, 1946), xvii.

bright. It possesses vitality, imagination, and distinctiveness. An impressive style sets an address apart as being more than ordinary—it makes its message vivid. There are several rhetorical devices which can help to make a speech impressive.

Linguistic Impressiveness

Imagery. Words that call up, through their meanings and sounds, sensory impressions, emotions, and experiences are words that produce mental images. Such imagery makes us see, hear, and feel the ideas a speaker is presenting. Imaginative expressions and sufficient detail of sight, sound, movement, and the like, are essential for vivid imagery. Most great historical addresses contain striking imagery. William Jennings Bryan electrified a Democratic convention with the phrase, "You shall not press upon the brow of labor this crown of thorns. You shall not crucify mankind upon a cross of gold." Patrick Henry warned his fellow Virginians, "There is no retreat but in submission and slavery! Our chains are forged! Their clanking may be heard on the plains of Boston!" Daniel Webster, in his speech "Seventh of March, 1850," told his fellow senators, "Let us not be pigmies in a case that calls for men." And General Douglas MacArthur's moving "Farewell to the Cadets" of West Point made the meaning of the academy's motto, "Duty, Honor, Country," vivid to the cadets through its imagery.

> From one end of the world to the other, he [the American soldier] has drained deep the chalice of courage. As I listened to those songs, in memory's eye I could see those staggering columns of the First World War bending under soggy packs on many a weary march, from dripping dusk to drizzling dawn, slogging ankle-deep through the mire of shell-pocked roads; to form grimly for the attack, blue-lipped, covered with sludge and mud, chilled by the wind and rain, driving home to their objective, and, for many, to the judgment seat of God.[8]

Metaphors and Similes. A simile is a comparison between two things which uses *as*, *like*, or *so*; a metaphor, dispensing with these connecting words, establishes an identity. Carl Sandburg said that Lincoln could be "hard as a rock and soft as drifting fog"; William

---

[8] Douglas MacArthur, "Farewell to the Cadets," in *Contemporary American Speeches*, pp. 153–154.

Herndon said that Lincoln's "ambition was a little engine that knew no rest." Similes and metaphors can create powerful images. One of the most striking images of our time resulted from a metaphor Winston Churchill used at Fulton, Missouri, in March, 1946: "From Stettin in the Baltic to Trieste in the Adriatic, an iron curtain has descended across the continent." Much of Churchill's oratorical greatness lay in his ability to make his thoughts impressive through expressive figures of speech. In a single address he used the following metaphors: "For the first time we have made the Hun feel the sharp edge of those tools with which he has enslaved Europe"; "The United States . . . has drawn the sword for freedom and cast away the scabbard"; "The stakes for which they have decided to play are mortal"; "The long arm of fate reached out across the oceans to bring the United States into the forefront of the battle." Adlai Stevenson reached an effective climax through an extended metaphor in his 1952 acceptance speech:

> Let's tell them that the victory to be won in the twentieth century, this portal to the golden age, mocks the pretensions of individual acumen and ingenuity. For it is a citadel guarded by thick walls of ignorance and of mistrust which do not fall before the trumpet's blast or the politicians' imprecations or even a general's baton. They are, my friends, walls that must be directly stormed by the hosts of courage, of mortality and of vision, standing shoulder to shoulder, unafraid of ugly truth, contemptuous of lies, half truths, circuses and demagoguery.[9]

Metaphors and similes must be used with discretion, lest they be trite, unimaginative, or obscure. These questions may serve as evaluative criteria: (1) Is the figure fresh and new, or is it tired and overworked? (2) Does it have universal meaning, or will only a few in the audience comprehend the comparison? (3) Is it sufficiently imaginative to make the thought more vivid than a simple statement?

Personification. Inanimate objects and abstractions are personified when they are treated as having personal attributes: "The sun smiled on us"; "The car groaned"; "I heard a forest praying."

---

[9] Adlai Stevenson, "Acceptance Speech," in A. Craig Baird, ed., *American Public Addresses, 1740–1952* (New York: McGraw-Hill, 1956), pp. 292–293.

Sometimes speakers use an extended personification and develop a major idea through the words of an inanimate object. Harry Emerson Fosdick, for example, preached a sermon titled "My Account with the Unknown Soldier." However, keep in mind that personification can easily be overdone, as Stuart Chase demonstrates in the following passage:

> Here is the dual shape of Labor—for some a vast, dirty clutching hand, for others a Galahad in armor. Pacing to and fro with remorseless tread are the Trusts and Utilities, bloated, unclean monsters with enormous biceps. Here is Wall Street, a crouching dragon, ready to spring upon assets not already nailed down in any other section of the country. The Consumer, a pathetic figure in a gray shawl, goes wearily to market. Capital and Labor each give her a kick as she passes, while Commercial Advertising, a playful sprite, squirts perfume into her eyes.[10]

Epigrams. An epigram expresses an old idea in a novel way. It is always terse, frequently witty, and usually memorable. By its use a speaker may be able to stamp an important idea in the minds of the audience. Russell Conwell used this epigram in his famous "Acres of Diamonds" speech: "If you have no capital, I am glad of it. You don't need capital; you need common sense, not copper cents." Mary Elizabeth Lease's well-publicized advice to Kansas farmers of the late-nineteenth century, "You need to raise less corn and more hell," is strongly epigrammatic. In his 1952 acceptance speech, Adlai Stevenson, whose speaking was notably epigrammatic, told his audience that "there are no gains without pains." Wendell Phillips told a nineteenth-century audience: "To be as good as our fathers we must be better."

Slogans. Sometimes an especially-striking phrase can be more effective than pages of argument. Politicians use slogans as catchwords around which to center their actions. Theodore Roosevelt stood for the "Square Deal," Franklin Roosevelt for the "New Deal," and Harry Truman for the "Fair Deal." Woodrow Wilson wanted to "Make the World Safe for Democracy," Warren G. Harding pledged "Back to Normalcy," Herbert Hoover desired "A Chicken

---

[10] Stuart Chase, *The Tyranny of Words* (New York: Harcourt Brace Jovanovich, 1938), p. 25.

in Every Pot." John F. Kennedy anticipated a "New Frontier," and Lyndon Johnson yearned for the "Great Society."

Witticisms. Wit, properly seasoned, helps to produce stylistic impressiveness. A good witticism at the right time may be worth a dozen facts and the most irrefutable logic. A hearty laugh produces an immediate psychological effect, often quickly changing the whole atmosphere of an occasion from one of apprehension or dissatisfaction to one of pleasant anticipation. Adlai Stevenson used wit so cleverly in the 1952 election that his opponents attacked him for it. John F. Kennedy began an address on "The Intellectual and the Politician" at Harvard University, his alma mater, with a witticism:

> Prince Bismarck once remarked that one third of the students of German universities broke down from overwork; another third broke down from dissipation; and the other third ruled Germany. As I look about this campus today, I would hesitate to predict which third attends reunions (although I have some suspicion).[11]

Satire. As a rule, sarcasm offends more often than it pleases; a sunny kind of satire, however, can be most effective. Will Rogers once addressed a bankers' convention and relied exclusively on humorous satire to entertain his audience. David Daggett, a staunch New England Federalist, sought in 1799 to expose what he regarded as Thomas Jefferson's softheadedness toward foreign intellectual influences and to lay bare the foolhardiness of wild experimentation—such as men trying to fly or to travel under the sea—with a satirical address titled "Sun-Beams May be Extracted from Cucumbers, But the Process Is Tedious." In the address, Daggett compared the Jeffersonian intellectuals to the scientists at Lagado, in Laputa, who sought to make a pincushion out of marble and to propagate a breed of naked sheep.

Pithy Quotations and Allusions. Pithy quotations and allusions can dress up an ordinary speech and make a good speech striking. President Kennedy in his speech "The Intellectual and the Politician" used allusion.

---

[11] John F. Kennedy, "The Intellectual and the Politician," in *Contemporary American Speeches*, p. 280.

The politician, whose authority rests upon the mandate of the popular will, is resentful of the scholar who can, with dexterity, slip from position to position without dragging the anchor of public opinion. It was this skill that caused Lord Melbourne to say of the youthful historian Macaulay that he wished he was as sure of anything as Macaulay was of everything.[12]

Adlai Stevenson's speeches were almost always enlivened by quotations and allusions. In a speech on the United Nations he observed, "Chesterton once said that the trouble about truisms is that they are still true." Speaking on "The Political Relevance of Moral Principle," he used a quotation to clinch a point:

We can be made slaves simply by the clutter and complexity of modern living—which notoriously leaves no time for serious thought and offers every means of distraction so that we can avoid such thought. Between aircraft that take us everywhere more rapidly, newspapers that grow in weight and coverage, news that flashes round the globe, ceaseless and competitive entertainment, fashions—God help us!—that change from sack to trapeze and back again, we can fill up every "unforgiving minute" with enough trash and preoccupation to still forever the deeper voices of the soul. Like Matthew Arnold, we can

. . . see all sights from pole to pole,
And glance and nod and hustle by,
And never once possess our soul
　　Before we die.[13]

Sound-Effect Words. Words used orally have a dimension they do not have on the printed page—sound. Even when divorced from their meaning, words have sound appeal. Words in nursery rhymes often have no meaning to children, but a child's attention is arrested by their sound. The use of words whose sounds match their meanings is a poetic device known as *onomatopoeia. Bow-wow, meow, moo,* and *ding-dong* are good examples.

Certain words strike the ear especially pleasantly, even apart from their meaning. For example, the historian Hendrik Willem Van Loon thought the word *cuspidor* has melodic quality! The use of pleasant-sounding words is called *euphony,* a device that is an

---

[12] *Ibid.,* p. 281.
[13] Adlai Stevenson, "The Political Relevance of Moral Principle," in *Contemporary Forum,* p. 362.

especially good friend of the poet. Lexicographer Wilfred J. Funk lists the following among our most beautiful words: dawn, hush, lullaby, murmuring, tranquil, mist, luminous, chimes, golden, and melody. On the other hand, the use of especially unpleasant-sounding words is called *cacaphony*. Edgar Allen Poe spoke of the raven as "this grim, ungainly, ghastly, gaunt, and ominous bird of yore," thereby achieving a strong oral dissonance. A group of speech teachers have proffered the following as especially unpleasant-sounding words: spinach, naughtiness, plutocrat, mash, sap, plump, victuals, phlegmatic, and jazz. It is probable, however, that the ideas these words stand for influenced the selection.

Highly-polished speeches can profit from the sound of the words used. Observe how Robert Ingersoll uses euphony and cacaphony in a contrasting manner to express a thought in his famous eulogy at his brother's grave:

> Life is a narrow vale between the cold and barren peaks of two eternities. We strive in vain to look beyond the heights. We cry aloud, and the only answer is the echo of a wailing cry. From the voiceless lips of the unreplying dead there comes no word; but in the night of death hope sees a star and listening love can hear the rustle of a wing.[14]

Placing words that repeat the same sound adjacent to each other, called *alliteration*, is another useful sound-effect device. The politician's cliché of *peace*, *progress*, and *prosperity* has a definite alliterative effect.

Structural Impressiveness

Parallelism. Parallelism may occur in various forms: A series of sentences may begin in a similar manner or may be similar in form, or phrases within a sentence may be parallel. President Kennedy began four successive short paragraphs in his Inaugural Address with "Let both sides. . . ." At another point he developed a series of thoughts around the following sentence beginnings: "To those old allies . . ."; "To those new states . . ."; "To those people in the huts and villages of half the globe struggling to

---

[14] Robert Green Ingersoll, "At His Brother's Grave," in *American Public Addresses, 1740–1952*, p. 179.

break the bonds of mass misery . . ."; and finally, "To those nations who would make themselves our adversary. . . ." The Reverend William A. Holmes, a Dallas clergyman preaching on the assassination of President Kennedy, constructed numerous parallel passages.

> By our timidity we have encouraged the aggressor; by our paralysis we have given safe conduct to reactionaries; by our confusion we have promoted the clarity of evil; by our small prejudices and little hates we have prepared the way for monstrous and demonic acts that have betrayed us all. We are garbled people, mistaking patriotic cries for patriotism, boisterous boasts for courage, and superficial piety for faith. In this blood-stained history and death, we are under an imperative to whisper unto one another and to God: "Lord, have mercy on us all."[15]

A classic example of parallelism occurs in the peroration of Lincoln's Second Inaugural Address:

> With malice toward none, with charity for all, with firmness in the right as God gives us to see the right, let us strive on to finish the work we are in, to bind up the nation's wounds, to care for him who shall have borne the battle and for his widow and his orphan, to do all which may achieve and cherish a just and lasting peace among ourselves and with all nations.[16]

Antithesis. Antithesis consists of sharply contrasting an idea, ordinarily within a single sentence. When it does occur in a single sentence, we have a *balanced* sentence in which two parts weigh against each other—such as President Kennedy's often-quoted line: "Ask not what your country can do for you—ask what you can do for your country." Twice in his Inaugural Address President Kennedy used two sentences to achieve antithesis: "United, there is little we cannot do in a host of cooperative ventures. Divided, there is little we can do—for we dare not meet a powerful challenge at odds and split asunder." And, "Let us never negotiate out of fear. But let us never fear to negotiate."

---

[15] William A. Holmes, "One Thing Worse Than This," in Charles J. Stewart and Bruce Kendall, eds., *A Man Named John F. Kennedy* (Glen Rock, N.J.: Paulist Press, 1964), p. 38.
[16] In *American Public Addresses, 1940–1952*, p. 117.

Rule of Three. The rule of three consists of using three words in a group, such as the notorious campaign epithet of 1884, "Rum, Romanism, and Rebellion." Sometimes parallel groupings of two are used for structural impressiveness, as in "We must have faith and courage, patience and perseverance."

Rhythm. One commonly associates rhythm with poetry, yet rhythm can be strikingly effective in public address also. Observe, for example, the effect that Lincoln got in his Second Inaugural Address from the rhythm of this sentence: "Fondly do we hope, fervently do we pray, that this mighty scourge of war may speedily pass away." President Kennedy's entire Inaugural Address has a rhythmic quality. It is important, however, to heed Aristotle's admonition, "A metrical structure makes the hearer distrustful by its manifest artifice, and at the same time distracts his attention, making him watch for the recurrence of the beat." The rhythm of a speech should never be definite, but variable; it should never be openly manifest to the listener, but subservient to the thought. Rhythm, properly employed, will give a speech energy and movement.

Energy and Movement. Vital speech holds the listener's attention. Speech should be forceful and compelling, not limp and flaccid. Energy and movement are derived from vigorous language. The classic example is Patrick Henry's "Liberty or Death" address which starts serenely, but builds in force with virtually every succeeding sentence.

Energetic speech is active, not passive, so the active voice is preferable to the passive voice. Verbs that denote action, such as, "We must seize the initiative," are much more arresting than passive ones, "The initiative must be taken by us." The use of active verbs in dynamic speech can hardly be overemphasized.

Sentence structure will also influence the forcefulness of speech. Loose sentences are complex sentences that begin with the main clause and place qualifying material after it. Periodic sentences lead up to the main clause with appropriate qualifying material. Although both types of complex sentences are useful, periodic sentences have more vitality than loose ones. Compare the following two sentences, first the periodic and then the loose:

"Last Saturday afternoon, while I was walking down highway 40 west of town, and as I stopped to watch a hawk making lazy circles overhead, suddenly a truck ran over me." The sentence written loosely might read: "A truck ran over me last Saturday afternoon, while I was out walking down highway 40 west of town and as I stopped to watch a hawk making lazy circles overhead." The first sentence is suspenseful, the second is anticlimatic; the first one moves to a definite finish, the second could run on and on.

The needless use of qualifying words tends to weaken a person's style. Too many of us have the habit of using qualifiers—rather, little, pretty, almost, probably—when they are unessential. Doubtlessly the most overused and consequently the most meaningless word in the English language is *very*. Some speakers don't seem to be able to describe anything without using *very* every time a descriptive word is used. Contrast these two sentences for vigor: "It was brilliant!" and "It was very brilliant!"

Trite words and overworked figures of speech are other stylistic stultifiers. Clothing worn too long can become threadbare, or if worn too often for the same occasion or purpose can become tiresome. The same is true of words and phrases. Some adjectives, for instance, need to be put on a quota basis: nice, lovely, terrific, beautiful, great, fine, swell, wonderful, fabulous, fantastic, and cute. Examples of shopworn figures are "white as a sheet," "mad as a wet hen," "as easy as falling off a log," and "as good as gold." A few speakers, notably Franklin D. Roosevelt, have been able to use trite figures to achieve a desired effect. He could use phrases such as "clear as crystal," "simple as A B C," "the doubting Thomases," and "water over the dam" most effectively in communicating with the national audience. For most people, however, freshness of diction and metaphor adds vitality and color to their speech.

Appropriateness

Style should be appropriate to the speaker himself, to the subject discussed, and to the audience addressed. The cardinal principle of stylistic propriety is embodied in Aristotle's warning that the speaker's artifice should not be apparent, but it should make the *thought* expressed impressive. Style that calls attention to itself defeats its purpose. The purpose of poetry is to stimulate man's imagination; the purpose of speech is to communicate ideas.

The Frenchman Buffon maintained that "Style is the man himself." This statement points up, among other things, the importance of a style appropriate to the speaker. Each speaker must develop his own style. He may—and indeed should—profit from the study of the stylistic excellence of great speakers but will wisely avoid trying to replicate their style, for if he does, it will sound forced, artificial, and insincere. The construction of President Kennedy's Inaugural Address has roots in Lincoln, Ingersoll, Franklin D. Roosevelt, and perhaps others, but the style of the address is Kennedy's own.

Aristotle warns that style should "neither be mean nor above the dignity of the subject, but appropriate." This advice should always be heeded by the speaker. Nothing is more absurd than to treat ornately a subject that calls for a straightforward manner. On the other hand, speeches dealing with lofty subjects in a pedestrian manner are certain to be uninspiring. The style of Daniel Webster's "Seventh of March, 1850" varies in ornateness from point to point within the speech. He deals with the fugitive slave law simply and directly, but he speaks of Americanism sublimely.

The speaker's ability to adapt himself and his ideas to his listeners, to their values, abilities, and backgrounds, lies at the center of effective speech. The language of the speech must, first of all, communicate, and, secondly, it must please and inspire. The right word—and the right use of it—constitutes an effective verbal message cue.

Communicating With Voice and Action

> One thing, I suggest, is clear and certain as well as highly familiar: it is tested and verified billions of times a minute in human experience, entirely trustworthy and reliable. And what is this reassuring

and comfortable truth? It is that *what is said* depends on *how it is said*, and *how it is said* on *what is said*. *What we say* and *how we say it* are inseparable—in utterances which are entire.[17]

This quotation from I. A. Richards is central to our discussion of speech delivery. The best prepared message presented poorly is likely to be ineffective. It seems a pity that a speech full of promise to impart knowledge, give wise counsel, and offer flashes of inspiration should go wasted because of failure of delivery. How ironic that the creator of a speech should also be the one who causes the destruction of his own creation. Voice and action are the means by which speech ideas become alive and meaningful. One research study suggests that about 75 percent of the effectiveness of a persuasive speech may be related to delivery.[18]

Delivery in many ways is difficult to teach. It is something that can't be handled by the usual instructional processes applied to grammar, algebra, or chemistry. There are so many personal equations involving the mental, emotional, physical, cultural, social and motivational makeup of the speaker. Delivery is largely a personal matter. What might work well for one person may not work at all for another. Yet there is great joy and satisfaction in the well-delivered idea—in making messages come alive. Anyone who is content to speak in a dull, listless, lethargic manner will never know this exhileration. Only those who speak with vitality, urgency, and a desire to communicate will experience the gratification that comes from excelling in presentational skills.

Although delivery has no absolutes, we feel that certain general goals and basic standards for vocal and bodily delivery can be identified and that they constitute criteria every speaker should hope to fulfill.

Delivery Goals

1. *Cultivate the Communicative Spirit.* The question most often heard when evaluating a speech is, "Was he communicating?"

---

[17] I. A. Richards, "The Future of Poetry," in *The Screens and Other Poems* (New York: Harcourt Brace Jovanovich, 1960), p. 122.
[18] Paul Heinberg, "Relationships of Content and Delivery to General Effectiveness," in *Speech Monographs* (June 1963), pp. 105–107.

Such delivery is characterized by directness, by the rapport a speaker hopes to establish with a listener. He strives to talk directly with his listeners instead of merely hurling a barrage of words at them. A communicative delivery tends to have a conversational quality. In fact it has been described as elevated conversationality. And while speaking directly to the listener, he is all the while observing his reactions and adapting to them. The experienced, alert speaker is very sensitive to speaker-audience interplay, capitalizing on this force to establish even greater rapport with his listeners. Daniel Webster, in his courtroom speaking, developed a great ability to relate closely to his auditors. As the jury in one court trial retired for its deliberation following the instructions from the judge, the foreman turned to the other men and said, "Gentlemen, it seems as though Mr. Webster is in this room with us as the thirteenth man of this jury, trying to decide this case." Your own communicative attitude is best when you imagine yourself sitting in the audience listening to your speech.

2. *Give It the Dynamic Touch.* We are all familiar with the frantic and feverish arm-waving tactics of certain evangelists and the table-pounding, fist-clenching delivery of some politicians. You may find this style of delivery repugnant. We do, too. However, delivery can be dynamic and energetic without being offensive. Think of the best speakers you have heard and you will probably agree that they invariably have been speakers with a dynamic touch. The dynamic speaker creates a mood of anticipation. There is a lure about his manner, a hint of something special and exciting that may take place any moment. Much of John F. Kennedy's success in speaking was attributable to his vitality and energy. For an effective style of delivery, vitalize and energize the entire speech process. Make what you say and do seem important. Avoid the overly-casual, indifferent, noncommittal attitude. Show that you really care about the listener's respectful attention. It is unlikely that you will overdo it; and if you do, remember that it is a lot easier to tone down your delivery than it is to vitalize it.

3. *Utilize Your Personal Resources.* Woodrow Wilson once said, "The most exciting thing in all the world is the human personality." Delivery is best when the speaker gives generously and deeply of himself. Try to discover what it is you can do best in the

presentation of a speech and exploit it to the fullest. Everyone has certain personality traits mingled with a style for doing things, be it playing tennis or making a speech. This style is unique and is an important phase of your personal resources, something that comes naturally and is genuine. Delivery is more than a mechanical skill of expression: It involves your deeper, inner self made up of thoughts, feelings, and action. These hidden personal resources represent a kind of self-fulfillment from which your individualistic style of speaking emerges. Every speaker would do well to put forth a vigorous effort to develop and improve his own style of speaking. It is your uniqueness that can give life, charm, luster, and credibility to what you say.

4. *Feature the Extemporary Style.* Cicero once said that the speaker should make everything appear as though he just thought of it that very moment on the platform. Freshness and spontaneity are appealing to most audiences, for the speaker always seems on the verge of unveiling a newly-conceived idea. There are, generally, three styles of speaking: manuscript speaking, memorized speaking, and extemporaneous speaking. The extemporaneous speaker prepares his speech well, but he does not take a manuscript to the lectern nor does he memorize his speech word-for-word. He speaks from notes or an outline and will have memorized only the broad, general ideas of his speech. Some people can speak most effectively from a manuscript; others find that they memorize easily and are most successful with a memorized speech; most people, however, are at their best when they speak extemporaneously, which also is the most practical method of speaking. But regardless of how the person speaks—from manuscript, memory, or notes—his speech should sound extemporaneous. It should be spontaneous and communicative.

5. *Strive for Artistic Accomplishment.* To be truly outstanding in public address, delivery must be impressive. The good public speaker, not unlike the accomplished stage performer, acts his part well. He can be dynamic when he wants to be dynamic. He can be calm and reassuring when that is the mood he wishes to project. Strive for polish and finish in your delivery. Use the voice for mood and emphasis, intonation and variety; use your face, hands, and

arms for descriptive and emphatic gestures. Develop carefully the art of acting your part in a speech.

6. *Make Your Delivery Appropriate to the Thought You Are Expressing.* The speaker's manner of delivery should be in harmony with his ideas. Insignificant thoughts should not be presented in an eloquent manner, nor are lofty ideas to be treated matter-of-factly. Voice and bodily activity should always fit the thought; Cicero said, "Every emotion has from nature its own peculiar look, tone, and gesture." However, when treating extremely emotional subjects, it is better to underplay emotion somewhat in delivery; otherwise, the performance may become too painful for the listener. At least part of the speaker's feeling should be *pent-up* emotion. He should communicate strong feeling but demonstrate proper restraint.

Standards for Vocal Communication

The speaker must be heard; he must be understood; he must be pleasing. These are the three standards for effective vocal delivery. While representing distinctive objectives, they tend to complement each other in some degree. The speaker with a well-modulated, pleasing, and melodious voice, for example, will more easily be heard and understood. Sometimes clarity of diction is merely a matter of increased vocal projection. We are presenting these three criteria in an ascending order of importance; nevertheless, all three must be met for a truly satisfactory vocal delivery.

1. *The Speaker Must Be Heard.* The first goal of communication is audibility. If the speaker cannot be heard, communication cannot take place. Despite the elemental nature of this standard, it is amazing how many people are unconcerned as to whether they can be heard. They speak softly in a large room and neither observe nor heed audience feedback. Not being heard may properly be called the unforgivable sin of a public speaker. If at all possible, the speaker should use sufficient force and vocal projection so that he may be heard without undue strain or effort. If the listener must

squirm about, turn his head, or cup his hand behind his ear, the speaker fails to fulfill the first standard of good vocal communication. Nothing is more distressing to the listener than to have to work hard to catch a few words and phrases that now and then come in a thin, weak murmur from the platform. The speaker should at all times be alert to audience cues that tell him they have difficulty hearing him. If a speaker is uncertain of his voice projection, he will do well to ask the audience if they can all hear. To be audible requires adequate and sustained vocal loudness, vocal energy, and proper tone placement. It also requires a concern for being heard.

2. *The Speaker Must Be Understood.* To be understood the speaker must clearly and distinctly utter all words and syllables in a scheme of articulation and pronunciation representing standards to which the audience is accustomed. Diction should be precise, accurate, and clean-cut. Language should be instantly intelligible. The speaker must not mutilate his words by omitting or adding sounds or syllables. Careless, slipshod, indistinct mumbling not only annoys and disturbs the listener but gives the impression that the speaker is fuzzy and careless in his thinking. Being understood, like being heard, is crucial. The speaker who cannot be understood is merely using up the listener's time.

3. *The Speaker Must Be Pleasing.* Just to be heard and understood is not enough. The speaker must go beyond the mere mechanics of projecting his voice and of articulating words and syllables. Since it is important that his vocalization not be dull or unpleasant, he must learn to modulate his tones and control the intricacies of inflection, tempo, volume, and rhythm to make listening easy and enjoyable.

A speaker's vocal expression will obviously be more pleasant and enjoyable if he can keep his ideas moving along fluently and at a comfortable pace. A jerky, hesitant delivery, cluttered up with random, meaningless "uhs" and "ers," can be unpleasant and annoying. This is not to say that he must be glib or race toward his goal. The point is that there should be thought progression without creating the impression either of glib superficiality or of tense, laborious effort.

Avoid monotony. Speech that lacks variety of pitch, rate, force, or melody is monotonous. Nothing is so boring as a one-note, one-rate, one-force, or one-tune speaker; listeners like vocal variety and color. A voice that is rigid, stiff, and unresponsive to changes of mood and meaning is distressing to the ears of any audience; a flexible voice is restful and pleasing. Make listening easy and enjoyable, and you will make communication more effective.

Standards for Bodily Communication

Bodily action includes any possible movements of the body—walking about the platform, posture, shrugging the shoulders, head movements, hand gestures, facial expressions, and eye glances. Bodily action is an important part of the natural code for communicating thought. Henry Wadsworth Longfellow realized this when he wrote, "He speaketh not and yet there lies a conversation in his eyes." The fact is that we do talk with our bodies. It was not a joke when the Italian said, "Let go of my hands, I want to talk." Have you ever observed children at play, particularly when adults are not supposed to be present? Have you noticed how naturally and expressively they use their hands, feet, legs, face, eyes, head, and entire bodies as they chatter and carry on their world of make-believe? Infants learn early in life to express their wants by all kinds of bodily actions. Primitive people develop intricate systems of signs to supplement their vocalization, or even as a substitute for language. Columbus and other explorers must have placed great reliance upon pantomime and signs of all sorts in their efforts to communicate with the native inhabitants of lands they discovered.

A speaker is seen as well as heard, except when talking over the telephone or radio, and even then his vocal expressiveness is influenced by the way he sits or stands and by the bodily actions that release his motor tensions. When facing an audience he cannot escape action as part of the communication code. Every speaker must use both words and action—he cannot use words alone. Emphatic motor responses are natural even when talking to oneself. A person may gesticulate, even violently at times, while talking over the telephone, as amusing as this may be to those observing him.

There are many reasons why we should make effective use of

bodily expression in speech delivery. Some of these reasons have a direct bearing on the clarification, emphasis, and reinforcement of thought; others contribute more indirectly to effective speech communication. They help to give ease and comfort to both speaker and audience, increase speaker confidence, activate his mind, increase audience interest and attention, and establish a closer relationship between speaker and audience. We feel that the following three criteria are basic to effective bodily communication.

1. *Sensitive Facial Expression.* Facial expressions reflect not only the speaker's thoughts, emotions, and attitudes but many other attributes of his character and personality as well. The eyes are the focal point of expression in the face. Imagine how difficult it would be for a speaker wearing dark glasses to make contact with his listeners. A communicative speaker looks directly and constantly at his audience. The downcast glance at the floor, the vague gaze over and above the audience and at the ceiling, and the mechanical sweeping of the eyes from one side of the audience to the other like a water sprinkler are habits that distract and annoy the listener. Avoid such behavior. Instead, talk directly to the members of the audience. Meet the eyes of as many individuals as the situation permits. Some speakers find it helpful to pick out the friendly, sympathetic faces in the audience and talk primarily to them. Others find the indifferent, disinterested listeners a special challenge and make a point of trying to win them over.

Some of history's greatest speakers have been known for their unusual eye appeal. For example, William Pitt, first Earl of Chatham, is said to have influenced many with his strong expressive eyes; in debate he sometimes was able to stare down an opponent. Most good speakers reveal a strong personality through effective eye contact.

The entire face should be sensitive to the idea expressed. A dead-pan expression may be appropriate for certain types of humor, but it is not useful for normal communication. The forehead, the eyebrows, and the mouth are expressive agents that can be made to communicate many different feelings. Think of how much can be said by a smile. A frown, a puzzled look, and a reflective appearance can all be used as aids to communication, or even as single agents of communication.

2. *Appropriate Posture.* Your platform bearing is an important and inescapable part of your speech delivery. Before you utter a word, the audience already is sizing you up. Right or wrong, the audience forms opinions about you by the way you walk to the platform and the way you stand. Both consciously and unconsciously, listeners score points for or against the speaker on the basis of his appearance and posture.

Posture plays an important role in creating the initial image of the speaker, the one that tends to linger in the minds of the listeners. The speaker's physical bearing, which includes the way he stands or moves about on the platform, not only affects the attitudes of the listener toward him but influences his attitudes toward himself, his purpose, and his ideas. Every speaker communicates best when his posture and mental faculties are fully cooperative. The speaker who stands or moves about with arms folded or hands locked behind his back for long periods of time is actually holding back part of his personality. The speaker who habitually stands either rigid or tense or in a deep slouch does not talk with his whole body; thus his mind cannot function with complete freedom. Even the quality and vigor of his voice will be adversely affected by a sagging, drooping posture.

Unfortunately the very word *posture* suggests an uncomfortable pose. Mention the word, and the average person thinks he has to snap to attention and stand like a ramrod with chest out and chin in. This may be all right for a West Point cadet, but it is not good for walking, dancing, eating a meal, playing a game, or giving a speech. Janet Lane, in her book *Your Carriage Madam!*, says: "Really good posture, everyday, useful posture, means being lined up for grace and action, your body carried in perfect balance, your bones lying smoothly in place, and all your muscles working on the right tracks. It means Katherine Cornell leaning back in a chair, or Greer Garson floating down a stairway. . . . It's a diver in the air, an aquaplaner keeping his footing, a tennis player running to the net for the kill, or an old lady who knows how to sit at ease when her work is done—look at Whistler's portrait of his mother."[19]

---

[19] Janet Lane, *Your Carriage Madam!*, 2nd ed. (New York: Wiley, 1947), pp. 6–7.

Usually the speaker makes his speech standing. This means standing erect and tall, not slouching over a table or leaning on the back of a chair or the lectern. Nor does it mean standing rigid and immobile, although the upright position must be kept in mind. It has been said that a speaker should maintain a general *attitude of tallness* as a guard against a droopy, slouchy appearance.

3. *Meaningful Gesture and Movement.* The writer can punctuate his thoughts and give emphasis to them; so can the speaker. Punctuation marks are the vehicle of the writer, movement and gesture the means of the speaker. Some movement on the platform helps the speaker to relax and also, if properly used, helps emphasize the message. A point of transition constitutes an especially good time for movement. A slight forward or backward movement, appropriately connected with the thought, is expressive. Aimless rambling or nervous movement should, of course, be curbed; no movement is probably better than bad movement. But the skillful speaker will find that some physical movement on the platform is a great asset to communicating his ideas, to say nothing of the added attention factor it may provide.

Gestures should be natural and spontaneous. Studied, mechanical movements seem artificial and unreal. Freedom and spontaneity of bodily expressions spring basically from good mental attitudes, while inhibited bodily responses are often conditioned by tensions brought on by feelings of speech fright and apprehension. If this applies to you, it does not mean that you should wait until you feel comfortable and self-confident before you try to use gestures in a speech. On the contrary, you should be encouraged to use more bodily action than usual, especially such action as is used for demonstration and description. Indeed, the action may help bring self-confidence. Don't worry about a little awkwardness —awkwardness and mechanical stiffness are not the same. As you gain experience and strengthen your will to talk, you will improve in spontaneity of bodily expression.

Gestures should be appropriate to the meaning. Hamlet advises us, "Suit the word to the action and the action to the word." Action must be in harmony with the meaning that the words symbolize. Vigorous gestures obviously are not suitable to a mood of serenity,

Dimension 4: Message Presentation

meditation, or patience. Weak and timid gestures are inappropriate for a call to action.

Gestures should be properly timed, definite, and complete. They should be synchronized with the thought that they are emphasizing or describing. A speaker using mechanical gestures sometimes uses them either too soon or too late. So avoid halfhearted, uncertain, droopy, incomplete gestures. Their utter lack of force may spoil the total effect of the idea being expressed by suggesting timidity or uncertainty. Gestures should be made with the whole body; they should be unified with the total physical self. If this is done, they will automatically be definite and complete.

Finally, the effective speaker will use variety in his bodily action. He will move about on the platform; gesture with either or both hands; combine gestures of the open palm, clenched fist, and index finger; and vary his head movements, facial expressions, and eye glances. He will use his whole body, not just his tongue, to express his ideas.

part
three three three three three three three three three
guided
experiences

Participating In a Group

As part of this course you may from time to time be asked to participate in a small group. The purpose of the group may vary, from simple decision-making concerning who is going to talk about what topic in a class symposium presentation to a case analysis or a problem-solving group discussion. Almost all speech departments teach one or more courses in small-group communication. This is probably true of your school. Thus, we are not concerned here with developing anything resembling a complete theory of small groups or the communication that takes place in them. Rather our goal is to set forth a basic set of guidelines for group participation so that anytime you are asked to meet in a small group during the semester, you and your group will function effectively.

In the first place, a small-group discussion is a cooperative venture. It is based on the theory that two or more heads are better than one—providing the two or more heads function together effectively. The purpose is to pool information, insights, or value judgments in search of what is probably true, most desirable, most practical, and what reflects a higher level of wisdom. Always the overriding goal is to find answers that are mutually acceptable. In search of these answers, unless there is a discussion leader, everyone is on an equal basis. The most desirable group mood is one of cooperation in which the spirit of frankness is encouraged. Open-mindedness and the spirit of reflection and inquiry are useful mental sets.

Domination of the group by one or two people is counter to the notion of egalitarianism among its members. In such cases the dominant participants are either trying to strong-arm their opinions on the remainder of the group, or the climate of the group is such that some members are reticent to speak. This situation should be avoided at all times. If someone starts to dominate a group, either the discussion leader (if someone is so designated) or another group member should try to direct questions at other members who have not participated and try to draw them into the discussion. You can seldom hurt the group's chances of success by being an *opinion seeker*. Quite often the reticent members have extraordinarily meaningful insights.

A group discussion is not a place for making speeches. Oral contributions of group members should be short in duration and should be related to what has been said before. It is equally bad if someone proceeds to make a 5- or 10-minute presentation or if someone participates by jumping off the track that the group has been pursuing. Unrelated contributions are amazingly effective in breaking down group processes. This does not mean that a participant should never turn the discussion in a new direction, but that he should do so by showing why it would be logical to change the flow of interaction to a slightly different area. Such people are often called *initiators* in that they propose new ideas, new goals, procedures, or solutions, and are vital to group success.

A group also needs a good *clarifier*. If someone is formally designated as discussion leader, he will commonly fill this function. Otherwise, anyone in the group may profitably take up this role. A clarifier is someone who, as the discussion progresses, makes the relationships among factual information and ideas and suggestions clear. He may also seek to relate the ideas and activities of two or more members. This same person may also be a *prodder* and urge the group to increased activity or to a decision, by perhaps pointing out the time factor and how much is still left to be done.

Another useful person in a group is the *harmonizer*. In any group, differences of opinion are likely to arise. This is not undesirable as long as the differences do not polarize the group into subgroups or become personal. When this begins to happen, a good harmonizer will try to mediate differences, conciliate and reconcile disagreements. Groups cannot succeed if there are competing factions within them.

Group participants should avoid private conversations at all times. The overall group structure is unsuccessful whenever two or three people engage in conversation apart from the remainder of the group. Whenever this starts to happen group processes are breaking down badly. The instant you see signs of private conversations, prod participants to group consciousness and group action.

It may be useful for the group to appoint a *recorder*, someone who keeps a written record of vital ideas the group has covered. Such a record—even though it be in rough outline form—will be useful any time the group wants to review what it has covered before it proceeds to new areas. It will, of course, also serve the more basic function of being the group's "memory."

Finally, all groups need good listeners. It is particularly important to listen for understanding of ideas and points of view presented. Sometimes, if an idea is unclear, it is desirable practice to try to restate what someone else has said and ask if you understand his point accurately. The worst type of group member may well be someone who doesn't listen. He will repeatedly make irrelevant comments because he hasn't been paying attention to what has been said.

Many groups function in a leaderless way, while others have a formal moderator. Sometimes a person in a group may be the leader because of his role—such as the teacher in class discussion—while at other times a person may be designated as group leader or moderator. If you find yourself in either capacity, you should generally try to fulfill the following five objectives:

1. *Get the group started on the right track.* Introduce what you think is the task confronting the group, make appropriate suggestions about what you consider good group procedure, and lead off the discussion with provocative questions. Above all else, try to create a suitable mood and atmosphere for the group at the outset.

2. *Keep the discussion moving.* Most groups from time to time will have a tendency to bog down on certain points. They may even digress into talking about irrelevant issues or totally personal questions. In any event, as soon as you sense this happening, draw the group back to its target.

3. *Insure total and balanced participation.* Don't let anyone dominate the discussion too much, and draw out those who are not participating. Try to get everyone to speak for an equal amount of

time. However, be sure not to discourage anyone who may not be intending to dominate the group but simply is excessively zealous in pursuing the group's target. Try to handle the situation tactfully by pointing out that it would certainly be profitable to hear from those who have not yet spoken or else have spoken very little.

4. *Stimulate, guide, and integrate the discussion of group members.* It is up to you to make transitions to new areas and to summarize and relate occasionally what has already been covered. However, avoid talking too much. A careless leader can easily dominate a group and be a thought-stopper instead of the catalyzer that he is intended to be.

5. *Keep track of the time, and bring the discussion to a termination in sufficient time for a final summary on your part.* After you have summarized what you think the group has decided, ask the group if your summary corresponds with their perception of the group's actions.

These five guidelines are, at best, a partial listing of leadership function in group discussion. Whatever his techniques, the leader should always be flexible and adapt to group needs. At all times he should set the tone for the group—be democratic, ask stimulating questions, be a good listener, clarify and relate ideas, and keep things moving. With such leadership, groups will usually be productive.

Preparing Your First Speech

You may be asked to prepare your first speech before you finish reading this book. For that reason, we have provided this short section on Preparing Your First Speech, in which we hope to provide a few helpful starting points. We will in no way attempt to summarize everything that has been said prior to this point. Rather we will block out a definite plan of action. In addition to following this plan you may want to leaf through the book to search out especially relevant sections and read them.

Step One: As soon as your instructor assigns you a speech, start thinking about possible topics. Our minds tend to be most

Guided Experiences

active when the project is first introduced to us. Note possible subjects that occur to you. Later the same day, try to decide on a topic that you want to speak about. Do not procrastinate about subject selection!

Step Two: Jot down ideas that you already have on your subject; then read for additional ideas. Use your library resources, such as the *Reader's Guide*. Once you have accumulated a few ideas, decide on a specific purpose for your speech and make a skeleton outline. Block out ideas. Note what kinds of materials you need to round out your presentation; this usually means searching for factual and interesting materials. Then finish your outline.

Step Three: Prepare notes for speaking. These notes, which serve merely as an aid to your memory, need take no special form. However, the biggest pitfall of the beginning speaker is an inclination to prepare an elaborate set of notes, more than likely in sentence form or even something which resembles a manuscript. Avoid this temptation, and limit your notes to key or *trigger* phrases. Detailed, voluminous notes will tend to be difficult to follow, and you will either become confused and spend awkward moments looking for the next thought or will follow your notes too carefully and lack directness and eye contact.

It is wise to put your notes on cards rather than on sheets of paper, for paper tends to be too flexible to manage. Usually 4 x 6 cards are the most functional; you cannot get enough on smaller cards, and larger ones tend to be awkward. Try to limit yourself to three cards at most, with notations on one side only. Number your cards; that way if you drop them or get them mixed somehow, it will be easy to rearrange them swiftly.

Notes can be either *content* or *descriptive*. Content notes consist of key phrases, sentences, and visual aids, all of which give the exact materials to be used. Descriptive notes merely give reminders as to what comes next. They might simply say, "Give statistics," whereas content notes might say, "50,000 get inadequate care." For especially-difficult and unfamiliar subjects you may want to make key sentence notes; the sentences may help you word your speech more fluently on the platform.

During the delivery of your speech, do not try to conceal your notes by holding them behind you. There was a time when the speaker was advised to make very small notes which could be hidden in the palm of the hand, in hopes that the audience would be deceived into thinking that he was speaking without notes. This is poor practice. In the first place, the audience will notice your attempt at deception all too easily; and, secondly, the notes will necessarily be so small that you will have a hard time reading them. If you are speaking from a lectern, you may want to lay your notes on it; but if the lectern is low and your notes difficult to see, pick them up and hold them at a more useful height. Notes skillfully used are not distracting to an audience. Feel free to hold them up in your hand so that you can read them without effort. In fact, feel free to gesture with the hand which holds them.

It is true that a speaker achieves maximum effectiveness when he is able to speak without notes. Eye contact is extremely important in speaking, and every time a speaker looks at his notes he breaks contact with his audience. However, unless you feel completely sure of yourself without notes, it is better to use them. They will be less of a handicap than awkward mental blocks or omission of major points.

If, on the other hand, the teacher has assigned you to speak without notes, prepare mental notes somewhat akin to what you might put on paper. Get a picture of a skeleton of your speech in your mind and then fill in the skeleton with a few important thoughts. If you have done this carefully you will be able to draw on your mental notes in much the same way you do from written notes.

Step Four: Rehearse your speech. Oral rehearsal will assist you in making a smooth presentation. If you plan to speak extemporaneously, oral rehearsal will help you work out the wording of your speech so that it isn't memorized but neither is it totally unfamiliar territory. Oral rehearsal will also help you to improve your speech composition. Sometimes what makes good sense on paper in outline form will not come across well in speech. If you recite your speeches beforehand, you will tend to detect these difficulties and improve your speech construction.

Step Five: On the day of the performance, volunteer to speak with a positive mind and walk to the front of the group with purpose, look at them for a brief instant, and then start speaking.

Speak with enthusiasm. If when you finish you decide the performance was not as good as you had hoped, remember that it would be a very dull semester if you had no room for improvement!

A Program of Practical Experiences

Group Projects

Group Counsel

The class should be divided into groups ranging from four to seven students. Each group should be assigned one of the topics given below. Their task is to discuss the topic and to prepare a statement that best represents the group's counsel to the person involved. In case the group splits decisively on the nature of the counsel to be given, a majority and a minority report may be issued. During the next class period the students should present their report and be prepared to answer questions from the floor about the counsel they are giving.

Case 1: A parent has suddenly discovered that his teenage son is involved in the use and the sale of narcotics. This parent wishes to have a conference with his son and give him guidance. The parent is not sure how he should approach his son, nor is he certain as to what he should tell him. This parent has therefore turned to your group and has asked you to give him guidance. What counsel do you as a group have for this parent?

Case 2: A parent of reasonable affluence has discovered that her teenage daughter is involved in a prostitution ring. This parent loves her daughter very much and obviously wants to divert her from her new endeavor. Yet she does not know how to approach her or what to say to her. She has therefore turned to you as a group and asked you for help. What counsel do you as a group have for this parent?

Case 3: A college co-ed has discovered that her best friend is a habitual shoplifter. She is, first of all, concerned about having such a friend but she is also concerned for her friend. She has thought of talking to her friend about her problem but does not know how to approach her or what to say. She has also thought of talking to her friend's parents but is reluctant to because she doesn't think they will be very understanding. What counsel do you as a group have for this co-ed? Should she talk with her friend? What should she say? Should she talk with her friend's parents?

Case 4: John, a college student, wants to major in art; his father wants him to major in business. This particular difference of opinion has led to considerable domestic strain. In fact, the last time John was home his father told him that he would cut off his financial support if he failed to major in business. Since John is now only in his sophomore year, he can see no way of financing his remaining two years without financial assistance from home. Moreover, John otherwise has respect for his parents and hates to displease them. John has asked your group for advice. What counsel do you as a group have for him.

Communication Cases

Students should be asked to write out a one-page statement of an incident that has happened to them or that they know about which involved a communication problem, such as miscommunication or a lack of communication. The teacher should then select the four best cases, divide the class into small groups ranging from four to seven students, and give one case to each group. Each group should then discuss and analyze its case, diagnosing the communication factors and problems they found. After the allotted time during the class hour, the group should report to the class briefly describing the case they dealt with and giving their analysis of it. They also may want to make recommendations.

As an alternative to each student's writing up a communication case, the teacher may want to provide the cases himself.

New Words and Expressions

This project represents an attempt to put our collective ears to the ground and come up with some specific instances from personal experience to show how our language is in a state of flux. Dictionaries are of no use here. Nor do we want smut or offensive gutter language. We want to identify new words and expressions often heard among the rank-and-file of people.

The class may be divided into groups for bull sessions to ferret out a list of precisely 25 words and expressions, no more and no less, often heard today. Committee reports may be heard from the floor at the end of the hour, and the results may be tabulated and appraised.

Group Problem Solving

A topic of current interest should be selected for this project. The class should be divided into groups ranging from four to seven. Each group should spend the class hour analyzing the problem aspect of their topic, examine possible solutions, and decide upon courses of action they would like to propose. (Two class hours may be used for this: one hour for the problem phase and the second for the solution phase.) Each group should then be asked to report its solution or solutions to the class as a whole.

SAMPLE TOPICS

1. The energy crisis
2. Pollution
3. The population explosion
4. Alcoholism and drugs
5. Our national elections
6. Our crime rate
7. Marriage and family
8. A problem within your university

Ethics in Communication

Ask the class to read carefully the student resolution concerning ethics in communication on pages 34–36. Then divide them into three or four groups and ask them to draw up a resolution of their own. This may take them two class periods. During the second period, have each group present its resolution to the entire class and defend it in a forum period. As a last step, the class may want to enter a parliamentary session and try to adopt a class resolution.

Short "Tune-Up" Speeches

These experiences are best suited for getting acquainted with one another, getting the feel of things, creating a congenial class spirit, and initiating successful adventures in oral communication.

Do not expect detailed criticism from your instructor during these early short speeches, but evaluate and criticize your own efforts and share comments with other students between class sessions. In trying to orient yourself to the class, you will contribute to its positive tone and mood.

Introduction of a Classmate

The class will be divided into pairs, and each member of the pair will present a friendly, informal biographical sketch about his partner. Part of the class period, or a get-together between classes, may be arranged for interviewing each other. This speech should be packed with information: name, nickname, home town, family, major course interest in college, hobbies, professional aims, unusual interests, achievements, honors, and so forth. This should not be a mere recitation of facts about each other but a pleasantly composed oral account of an important member of the group. (2–3 minutes)

Short Value-Judgment Speeches

The six separate speaking assignments included here should stimulate you to voice your opinions from your own point of view. These speeches should be carefully thought out in advance, but use notes if you wish. The class should be divided into two groups, each dealing with a separate subject, so that on a given day two areas of subject matter may be covered in a single class period. You may want a quick poll of the half of the class not speaking on your subject to get their ranking of the topics you discussed and to compare their totals with your own. (2–3 minutes)

1. *Six Factors of Life.* Rank the following six factors in order of their importance, and give your reasons for so doing: (1) friends, (2) education, (3) family, (4) money, (5) religion, (6) health. Which do you rank first, second, and so on? Explain your evaluation.

2. *Six Professions in Civilization.* Use the same approach to the following six professions and occupations, evaluating them as to which has contributed most to civilization: (1) preacher, (2) farmer, (3) scientist, (4) artisan, (5) politician, (6) teacher.

3. *Give Up Six Modern Conveniences.* Imagine there are six modern conveniences that you must give up, one at a time, beginning a year from now. They are: (1) the telephone, (2) the radio and television, (3) the automobile, (4) the refrigerator, (5) the bathroom, (6) the washing machine. The decision of what to give up first, second, and so on is up to you. Explain your reasons for your choices and the order of their elimination.

4. *Life and Death on the Desert.* Suppose ten people are stranded in a desert and a helicopter can save only five; the other five must be left to perish. The people are: (1) an army captain, (2) Miss America, (3) a twelve-year-old boy, (4) a wealthy society woman, (5) a noted scientist, (6) a preacher or priest, (7) your college president, (8) a college football hero, (9) a bricklayer, (10) a medical doctor. You are the helicopter pilot. Whom would you save and why?

5. *The "Lighthouse" Speech.* You are to spend two years in a lighthouse where there will be no outside communication except occasional mail. You will be allowed a quota of printed matter: four books that you may bring with you and three publications which will be delivered periodically by helicopter. What books and publications would you choose? Give your rationale.

In the value-judgment speeches it is best that half the class take one of the subdivisions, the other half another. In order to save valuable time, speakers may appear before the class in panels of three or four.

Dreams and Fantasies

The class should be divided into groups of four. Each group should be given one of the topics below. Each person in every group should then prepare a 2–3 minute talk on the subject the group is assigned and present it to the whole class.

1. Suppose you won a television prize for a two-week luxury trip, all expenses paid, to anyplace in the world. Where would you choose to go and why?
2. You, as a college student, suddenly have received a $4000 grant to study for one year any subject of your choice at any place you choose. What would you study and where? Tell why.
3. If you were given your choice to visit only two countries, two months each, all expenses paid, and you had a special interest in music, drama, or painting, which two countries would you choose and why?
4. If you could choose to visit with a famous American for a few days, who would it be and why?

A Potpourri of Speeches

Personal Evaluation of Units in the Text

This assignment aims to serve a dual purpose: provide a meaningful speaking experience, and instigate a discussion concerning certain concepts in the text. Select three of the following sections from which you feel you gained the most benefit. Explain why you chose the three you did in as thought-provoking a fashion as you can. Feel free to work in some critical observations.

1. The communication model
2. The definition of communication
3. The speaker's image
4. Self-concept and self-management
5. Motivating forces

Guided Experiences

6. Types of groups and audiences
7. Circumstances of the communication
8. Judging informative speeches
9. Judging persuasive speeches
10. Structuring the message
11. Language
12. Delivery
13. Some other topic in the text not listed here

Pet Peeve Speech

Most of us secretly harbor annoyances about something. Select the one subject that you feel strongest about, and explain to the class why you are peeved about this subject. Don't be afraid to show your feelings when you are making your presentation. If you feel strongly enough about the subject to fight, let that come through. (4–5 minutes)

Role Playing

These speeches represent a deep challenge, combining personal resources with research. It is good, therefore, if several students use the same subject to get variations of concepts.

1. You have suddenly come under an authoritarian government and by decree you must change your religion within two years and live by it the rest of your life. You have the freedom to choose from the world's major religions. What would be your choice and your rationale?
2. You have been given a grant for the preparation and publication of a handbook counselling parents on how to handle their teenage children. What would you say? Ten million copies will be distributed.
3. Within two or three years you must give up your U.S. citizenship and start a new life as a citizen of another country where the native language is other than English. Which country would you choose?
4. You have been appointed as special aide to the President to give counsel and advice dealing with one of the following prob-

lem areas: (1) the Near East, (2) the energy crisis, (3) pollution, (4) narcotics, (5) city slums, (6) ethics in government, (7) taxation reform. What would you tell the President?

Speeches Based Mainly on Personal Resources

These speeches should be meaningfully related to human values and should feature: down-to-earth realism, genuineness of inner feelings, and language that has an elevating, ennobling appeal. Portions of the speech may be read in order to get the most out of the quality of language. (4–7 minutes)

SAMPLE TOPICS

1. Persons who most influenced my life (other than a parent)
2. Questions concerning God, man, or society that concern me greatly
3. Some experiences that changed the course of my life
4. My personal philosophy for happiness
5. My criteria for being a mature person
6. My concept of an ideal teacher
7. How I face the problem of living with and developing my image
8. How I determine my behavior as moral

Special Single-Subject Speeches

Some speech classes are set up to integrate all or most of the speeches on one broad subject area, such as Western civilization, current social problems, or international relations. We submit a pattern that might cover a third or half of the semester, "International Living." The project involves all students equally in a venture of role playing. The class unit would assume the role of a special committee as part of a world organization similar to the United Nations. Each student would select a country and become its official ambassador. There would be no representative for the United States, and countries not now members of the United Nations would be eligible. The ambassador would stand as the authority and spokesman for his country and be committed to make two rounds of speeches. The first speech would be mainly expository, 12 to 15 minutes in length, giving pertinent information about the nation's political and governmental structure, essential matters about its history, geography, people, resources, military status, cultural heritage, and its present place in world affairs. The second speech would be in the persuasive vein on "My Country and Its Manifest Destiny," integrated with one or two formulated resolutions to be debated and voted on in parliamentary manner. The total time would vary, depending on the size of the class and other considerations related to the course program. Perhaps two or at most three ambassadors could be heard in one class session. (The project can readily be expanded to cover the entire semester by integrating special issues connected with the Near East, Southeast Asia, nuclear expansion, and the population explosion.)

Bring 'em Back Alive

If you could bring back one person from the dead for a personal visit for one day, whom would you choose and why? (4 minutes)

A. An American from the field of:
  1. politics or public office
  2. letters
  3. science and invention
  4. education
  5. the military
  6. public address, oratory
  7. religion

B. A non-American from the field of:
  1. literature
  2. philosophy
  3. painting
  4. politics and public office
  5. theater
  6. science and invention
  7. religion

Speeches about Speeches and Speakers
(5–6 minutes)

SAMPLE TOPICS

1. What I dislike most about the speeches I have heard
2. Some outstandingly-good qualities among some of the better speeches outside of the classroom
3. A speech or speaker I shall always remember
4. How to get the most out of a bull session
5. Some suggestions for managing the art of conversation
6. How one should conduct himself when interviewing for a job or seeking counsel from a qualified counsellor
7. How to say "no" under pressure salesmanship and still observe common courtesies

The Speech to Inform

"How to" speeches featuring a descriptive approach

The objective of the "how to" speech is to make a process or procedure as clear as possible. The elements of clarity discussed on pages 122–130 are especially important to this assignment. The material should be unfolded step by step in a logical order. It may even be wise at certain points in the speech to ask the listeners if they have any questions before going on to the next major step.

SAMPLE TOPICS

How to visit an art museum
How to enjoy an opera
How to travel in a particular foreign country
How to develop your musical appreciation
How to watch a football game
How to study communication behavior among birds and animals
How some large cities manage their water supply
How to winter a sailboat

Guided Experiences

How to understand and appreciate some phenomena in nature —tidal waves, volcanoes, earthquakes, geysers, hurricanes, tornadoes
How to read an annual financial report of a corporation
How to appreciate a bullfight
How to use the Chinese counting system

Whenever possible, visual supports should be employed in these speeches.

Informative Speeches Based on Reading Research

The length of this type of speech should be determined by the instructor. Suggested topics are arranged in two groups, representing relative levels of challenge or degree of difficulty in the mastery or assimilation of the central subject matter. Level One represents simple concrete objects, products, and specimens of animals and plants or of human achievements. Level Two represents religions, laws, organizations, agencies of government, philosophies, processes of production, and theoretical concepts. You may want to limit your speech to one aspect of one of the subjects given below.

LEVEL ONE

diamonds	the circus
volcanoes	squids
coffee or tea	lemons
glass	oysters
tobacco	apples
camels	the Bible
oil	leather
coal	mosquitos
fire	potatoes
windmills	the Suez Canal
eggs	rubber
matches	snakes

LEVEL TWO

Religion

agnosticism	Hinduism
atheism	Judaism
paganism	Buddhism

Calvinism
Mohammedanism
Shintoism
Mormonism

Christian Science
Roman Catholicism
Orthodox Church
Anabaptism

Government Agencies and Services

Social Security Administration
Securities & Exchange Commision
Commodity Credit Corporation
Federal Communications Commission
Federal Trade Commission

U.S. Government Printing Office
Federal Reserve System
Internal Revenue Service
U.S. Department of Justice
Civil Aeronautics Board
U.S. Department of Labor
Atomic Energy Commission
Federal Bureau of Investigation
Maritime Administration

Politics, Government, Economics

Fascism
Communism
British Labour Party
Constitutional monarchy
Imperialism
U.S. federal budget
Martial law
Free enterprise

Capitalism
Inflation
The gold standard
The sterling bloc
International banking
The stock exchange
Co-op movement
City management

Science, Invention, Industry

The sponge industry
Pearl culture
Motivational research
The peaceful use of atomic energy
Deep-sea diving
Jet airplanes
The cork industry

Modern methods of mining coal
Building a superhighway
Hybrid corn
Vitamin pills
Atomic submarines
Skin-grafting
Controlling air traffic
Dealing with atomic waste

Informative Speeches Based on Oral Features

This type of speech is based mostly on research other than that gained from reading or from background experience, although these may provide supplementary supports. Often in life we are called upon to make a report about a trip, a convention, a piece of research, or some project or event we have observed or investigated. Our Sunday newspapers frequently run newsworthy feature articles about some person, event, organization, or civic project. The oral feature report resembles this type of journalism except that it is designed for the class audience instead of a reading public. The materials for this speech should be obtained mainly by personal interviews, observation, and investigation. Use the reporter's tools of inquiry: who, when, why, where, and how.

This speech is of the informative type, and most of what you say should reflect worthwhile knowledge that the listeners did not have before. Trivial topics, such as your roommate's habits, how Jim was the life of the party, or table manners at our house, are not acceptable. (5–7 minutes)

SAMPLE TOPICS

> Our fire chief and his problems
> The city police court
> A typical day in the dean's office
> The workings of a produce market
> The operation of a city paper route

Speeches to Persuade

Speeches on Questions of Fact

The emphasis in this assignment is on rational thinking. The speaker tries to get the listener to accept that his proposition of fact is, in reality, true. Thus, main contentions should be fully documented with reliable evidence and made convincing on the basis of logic. Persuade the listener rationally that he should believe your proposition. This speech might also be called, "What Should We Believe About . . ." (5–7 minutes)

SAMPLE SUBJECTS

> Flying saucers
> The Kennedy assassination
> Extrasensory perception
> Mental telepathy

> Brainwashing
> Child prodigies
> Intelligent life on other planets
> Marijuana

Leprosy, its treatment and causes
Human control of the weather

Police brutality
Cure and control of alcoholism
Vitamin pills
Power of the President

Speeches on Questions of Value

These speeches deal with goodness and badness, desirability and undesirability. In this speech, the speaker may either advocate value standards that he thinks people should accept, or he may take value standards and make a value judgment. In any case, the speaker must show the audience his position is the right one because it is good or desirable. (5–7 minutes)

SAMPLE SUBJECTS

The welfare state is inherently undesirable.
Contemporary art has misplaced values.
Censorship is unjustifiable in a free society.
It is justifiable in a democratic society for the government to withhold information from the public.
Psychological research violates the sanctity of the human being.
Education is the best index of a man's worth.
Television is a "vast wasteland."
The end justifies the means.
Mercy killing is justifiable.
Science is overemphasized in American education.
Americans are too apathetic toward the plight of their fellow man.
What is a good teacher?
What is a good neighbor?
What constitutes a good liberal education?
What constitutes being a good parent?
What characterizes good citizenship?
The value of religion in American culture.

Speeches on Questions of Policy

A policy speech advocates a plan of action. It is usually in the form of *problem-solution*. In it you have a threefold objective: to make people aware of an existing problem, sell your listeners on your solution to the problem, and get the listeners to act on your solution.

Begin your speech with an introduction that leads smoothly and logically into the development of the problem (this is often called the *need* step); outline a specific solution to the problem; show that it is practical by giving evidence that your proposal will do what you say it will; show that it is desirable and that its results will be beneficial instead of harmful; and ask for action from your listeners in the conclusion of your speech. (5–7 minutes)

The following suggestions may be helpful for problem-solution speeches:

1. Make the problem as vivid as possible. Show that it affects your individual listeners.
2. Outline your solution clearly.
3. Support your solution adequately.
4. Spend an adequate amount of time in discussing your solution. A frequent weakness of problem-solution speeches is that so much time is spent on the problem that very little is left for the solution. Approximately one-third of your time should be allotted to development and support of your solution.
5. Tell the listeners exactly what you want them to do about your proposal.

SAMPLE SUBJECTS

The water-pollution problem	Recreation facilities in our large cities
The problem of abortion	
The American Indian	Our overcrowded airports
Drunken drivers	Care of the aged
Latin American relations	The high cost of dying
Divorce	Air pollution
Our overcrowded universities	Inflation
The care of our mentally ill	Our city jails
Alcoholism	Water pollution
Vandalism	

Some policy speeches, as in the case where one speaks in opposition to a proposed course of action, are not in the form of problem-solution. A person may also speak in defense of an existing policy and argue that it should be continued. And he may argue for a new policy on the grounds that it is advantageous. In other words, he cites good reasons for the stand he is taking. (5–7 minutes)

SAMPLE TOPICS

> Legalized gambling
> National lottery
> Abolition of all required courses in college
> Compulsory military service for women
> Legalization of mercy killing
> The feasibility of taxing church property
> A plan for getting out the vote

Speeches of Tribute

For this assignment you are to prepare a speech in which you pay tribute to some person, living or dead. You should have some specific reason for your choice of subject. It helps if you have some connection with the person, if he has affected your life in some way; he may be a relative, a close friend, or a historical or public figure you have always admired. If you choose to pay tribute to a friend or relative not generally known by the public, there should be something about this person's life that holds a message for the listener. Avoid choosing someone merely because you like him. (5–7 minutes)

We offer these suggestions:

1. Avoid making your speech a biographical sketch.
2. Organize your speech around the person's leading characteristics, such as courage, imagination, and integrity. Or discuss his virtues first and his important accomplishments next. As a final point you may want to show what effect his life had on those around him, or what his accomplishments did for mankind.
3. Bring in pertinent biographical data in the development of your main points. They are a type of supporting material.
4. You may want to end the speech by pointing out to the audience what can be learned from this person's life.

SAMPLE SUBJECTS

Horace Mann	Joe Louis
Jonas Salk	Wilma Rudolf
Jane Addams	George Gershwin
Thomas Edison	Ira Gershwin
Satchel Paige	Frank Lloyd Wright
Lou Gehrig	Oscar Hammerstein
Babe Ruth	Ludwig von Beethoven
Clara Barton	Jack Benny
Ralph Bunche	Florence Nightingale
Jim Thorpe	Will Rogers
Billy Graham	Robert E. Lee
Boris Pasternak	Winston Churchill

Manuscript Speaking

Manuscript speaking is becoming more and more common, partly because of the influence of radio, television, and improved public-address amplifiers, and partly because busy industrial executives and government officials must guard themselves against inaccuracies of statement and avoid the possibility of being misquoted. Moreover, men in responsible positions with limited public-speaking experience and training view the manuscript speech as something they can handle with the greatest ease and self-assurance.

A common weakness of manuscript speaking is poor delivery, which may be due, in part, to faulty language style. The language of the speech to be read should resemble as nearly as possible that of extemporaneous speech. Too often, however, it is prepared as an essay to be read aloud. The written speech should really be an extemporaneous speech that has lodged itself on paper; and its words, phrases, and sentences should spring forth with conversational freshness suited to the thought, the occasion, and the speaker.

A principal cause for poor manuscript reading lies in the speaker's failure adequately to utilize and master the essential principles of effective oral reading. Speech delivery from a manuscript calls for special skills and techniques and these suggestions may help you improve your ability to deliver such a speech:

1. *Think and relive the thought as you speak.* Re-experience as fully as possible the true meaning of what you say at the moment of utterance. Live anew the thoughts and feelings, sensing their vitality, reality, and importance. Concentrate on your ideas rather than the words.

2. *Speak with a sense of communication*—a sense of sharing your thoughts, feelings, and attitudes with your audience. *Talk it over* with your listeners; look directly at them so you may sense their reaction. Practice until your eyes rest on the audience at least twice as much of the time as on your manuscript.

3. *Practice your speech aloud at least six or eight times.* Thought progression lies in your ability to keep thinking ahead of your tongue. Practice until you can speak from memory a sentence or more ahead of the spot where your eyes fall at any moment. Mark on your manuscript thought units composed of groups of words, each representing one eyeful of meaning. These will serve as guideposts that will help you to speak with a certain rhythm and with effective pauses, while keeping your thoughts going along with easy fluency.

4. *Keep the manuscript as inconspicuous as possible.* The manuscript should never become a barrier between you and the listener. Be sure it is neat and easily legible. Use a lectern or reading stand where papers can lie flat and your eyes can easily focus on the words without stooping or lowering the head. Glance down with your eyes to pick up the meaning—don't keep nodding your head up and down. Sheets of paper should not be flipped over but slipped aside or under the manuscript.

5. *Develop sound attitudes toward manuscript speaking.* Using a manuscript is not the lazy way out or an easy substitute for the extemporaneous speech. Work hard to overcome poor delivery. Don't think that once the speech is written your job is finished. The key to effective manuscript delivery lies in industrious and diligent rehearsal.

6. *Prepare a clean copy of the manuscript.* After you have written your speech, be sure to prepare a good, clean copy from which you will read. Any markings on the manuscript should be for the purpose of helping you in delivery by indicating thought phrases or words you want to emphasize.

Listening Projects

Study of personal values

Each member of the class should take the Allport-Vernon-Lindzey "Study of Values" inventory. This test is scored in terms of theoretical, economic, aesthetic, social, political, and religious values. Each student may score his own test and be asked to analyze the results carefully. What did he learn about his values? Were there any surprises? The teacher may then want to analyze the scores in terms of the whole class and present this information to them, since knowledge of overall class values will be a big help in terms of audience analysis. (The test is produced by Houghton Mifflin Company.)

Listening for Information

A. First major class speech
   1. After speeches for a given class hour are completed, randomly call on students in the class to repeat the speakers' central ideas.
   2. Ask someone to enumerate the main points of one of the speeches.
B. Second major class speech
   1. Ask each student to write down what he thinks was the main point or central idea of each speech delivered; also ask that they list the main supporting points.
   2. Orally check the students' work (but let them correct their own).
C. Third major class speech
   1. Talk briefly about the art of note taking in connection with this project.
   2. For the first two days of the project, have students take notes on speeches. Ask them to turn them in, and go over them and make comments.
   3. For the next two days of the project, stress mental note taking; no writing is permitted.

4. Ask each student to make a rough outline of a speech on which he took mental notes only. Either go over them in class or correct them outside of class. This exercise could be graded as a short test on listening for understanding.
5. If time permits, give the Dow Listening Test. This test is old but still does a good job of testing main aspects of a presentation instead of the minutia that most listening tests seem to test. (See *Speech Teacher,* November 1955.)

D. Any speech

In conjunction with any speech, either in class or out, ask students to fill out the following two charts as a self-inventory:

Did you do any of these things?	*Not at all*	*A few times*	*Frequently*
1. Daydream			
2. Debate the speaker			
3. Nod compulsively			
4. Listen with emotional filters			
5. Private planning			
6. Become interested in physical distractions			
7. Listen for facts only			
8. Judge delivery instead of content			

Guided Experiences

Did you do these things?	Yes	No
1. Capitalize on thought speed by thinking ahead and reviewing		
2. Look for the speaker's purpose		
3. Look for his central idea		
4. Listen for main ideas		
5. Prepare for the listening occasion by thinking about the speech ahead of time		
6. Review the speech after it was over		
7. Keep an open mind		
8. Look for hidden meanings		

Listening for Critical Evaluation

A Class Speech. Choose any class persuasive-speaking assignment and ask each member of the listening audience to choose one speech and write a critical evaluation of it in terms of the Tools for Critical Listening found under The Reception of Messages in DIMENSION ONE (pages 95–99).

A Campus Speech. Ask students to attend a speech given on campus during the semester that is almost certain to provoke a good deal of controversy. Ask them to write a critical evaluation of it in terms of the Tools for Critical Listening. A television address may also be used.

Analyzing a Speech Manuscript. Pass out the text of a controversial speech and ask the class to write a critical evaluation of it.

index

Abstract, 127
Abstract words, 171
Acceptability, 133
Acceptable ideas, 97
Action, 132
Adams, John Quincy, 7
Advance publicity, 78
Aesthetic motivation, 68
Allen, R. R., 170
Alliteration, 179
Allusions, 177
Analogy, 143
Anglo-Saxon words, 169
Antithesis, 180
Antony, Mark, 167
Appropriateness, 182
  in delivery, 187
Argument, logical credence, 138
  most favorable position, 137
  unit of, 138
Argumentativeness, 92
Aristotelian definition, 123
Aristotle, 6, 8, 25, 33, 48, 66, 71, 73, 137, 165, 181, 182, 183
Arrangement, 144
  classical approach to, 149
  forecasting, 149
  patterns of, 147
  presenting both sides, 150
Atherton, Gertrude Franklin, 63
Attic Orators, 5
Audibility, 189
Audiences, 99
Auer, J. Jeffery, 100
Authentic sign, 81
Authority, 76

Balanced sentences, 180
Barzun, Jacques, 143
Basic message, 146
Baskerville, Barnet, 143, 172
Bassanio, 50
Beveridge, Albert, 128
Bible, 104
Biological motivation, 60
Blair, Hugh, 6
Bodily communication, 189

Body of the message, 145
Boylston Chair of Rhetoric, 7
Bryan, William Jennings, 174
Buffon, 183
Burke, Edmund, 6

Cacaphony, 179
Calderwood, Natalie, 165
Campbell, George, 6
Carlson, Conwell, 129
Carnegie, Dale, 5
Carson, Johnny, 26
Castro, Fidel, 134
Champion, Selwyn Gurney, 65
Channing, William Ellery, 128
Charisma, 66, 75
Charitable motivation, 69
Chase, Stuart, 176
Choice, 15
Churchill, Winston, 5, 69, 108, 168, 172, 175
Cicero, 6, 8, 33, 71, 81, 92, 154, 186, 187
Circumstances, 23
Clarifier, 198
Clarity, 122, 168
Clevenger, Theodore, 36
Climactic ending, 159
Colloquialisms, 170
Common practice, 77
Communication
  defined, 11
  code, 55
Communication skills, 57
Communicators, 21
  constraints, 49
Comparison, 127
Conant, James, 9
Concentration, 91
Conclusio, 149
Conclusion, 158
Concrete, 127
Confidence, 81
Confirmatio, 149
Conflict, 83, 132
Conformity, 75
Confutatio, 149

225

Connotation, 42
Conrad, Joseph, 173
Constraints, 49
Contrast, 127
Conwell, Russell, 176
Craig, Robert S., 129
Credibility, 23
Critical listening, 95
Culture, 50

Daggett, David, 177
Darrow, Clarence, 99, 170
Daydreaming, 93
Debate, 9
Definition, 49, 122
  Aristotelian, 123
Delivery 80
  goals, 184
Demosthenes, 5, 81, 108
Dempsey, Jack, 77
Denotation, 42
Dewey, John, 125
Dialogue, 19, 131
Diction, 188
Dirksen, Everett, 80
Divisio, 149
Dominance, 76
Drummond, Henry, 3
Dyadic, 19
Dynamic delivery, 185
Dynamic process, 13
Dynamism, 24

Edwards, A. C., 165
Egyptians, 5
Einstein, Albert, 125
Eisenhower, Dwight D., 75
Eliot, T. S., 125
Elocution, 7
Emerson, Ralph Waldo, 70
Emotions, 56
Energy, 181
Epigrams, 176
Ethical proof, 25
Ethical standards, 34
Ethics, 31
Ethos, 23, 71, 72, 79
  ethos-building channels, 78
Etymology of communication, 12
Euphony, 178
Ewbank, Henry Lee, 100
Examples, 139
Exordium, 149
Expertness, 73
Expert opinion, 142
Extemporary style, 186
Extra-verbal aids, 129

Face-value level, 134
Facial expression, 190

Facts, 48
False cause fallacies, 98
Feedback, 28
First Amendment, 32
Form, 24, 144
Fosdick, Harry Emerson, 176
Fox, Charles James, 6
Frame of reference, 28, 41
Fromm, Eric, 39
Funk, Wilfred J., 129

Gandhi, 60
Geiman, Carolyn Kay, 131
Gestures, 192
Giffin, Kim, 72
Goebbels, 124
Goethe, 104
Goldwater, Barry, 72, 173
Good intentions, 73
Goss, Bert C., 142
Grady, Henry W., 127
Graham, Billy, 78, 134
Greeks, 5, 69
Group decision, 8

Hadl, John, 75
Hall, Edward T., 104
Hamlet, 23, 192
Harding, Warren G., 176
Harmonizer, 198
Harvard School of Business, 10
Hasty generalization, 98
Heinberg, Paul, 184
Henry, Patrick, 143, 174. 181
Herndon, William, 175
Hero adulation, 77
Hester, James M., 157
Hill, Roy L., 124
Historical events, 155
Historical method, 48
Hitler, 31, 34, 106, 108
Holmes, Rev. William A., 180
Hoover, Herbert, 176
Hopkins, Harry L., 173
Hugo, Victor, 107
Human communication defined, 11
Human relations, 10
Humor, 154
Hutchins, Robert, 124
Huxley, Thomas, 126

Illustration, 126, 131, 152, 154, 159
Image, 70
  mental, 174
Imagery, 174
Impressiveness, 172
  linguistic, 174
  structural, 179
Inferences, 45
Informing, 120

Ingersoll, Robert, 179
Initiators, 198
Inner speech, 17, 29
Instructional speeches, 121
Intentional nonverbal cues, 164
Intentions, 73
Interaction, 15
Interest, 130
Interest step, 154
Internal feedback loop, 29
Interpersonal, 18
  communication, 16, 17, 27
  self, 22
Intrapersonal, 18
Introductions, 154
Isocrates, 6
Issues, 146

James, Henry, 67
Johannesen, Richard L., 170
Johnson, Lyndon, 102, 177
Johnson, Wendell, 32
Judgments, 47
Jung, C. G., 58
Justification step, 155

Keller, Helen, 163
Kennedy, John F., 69, 75, 134, 173, 177, 179, 180, 181, 183, 185
Kierkegaard, Soren, 162
King, Martin Luther, 125, 168
Kirk, Grayson, 143, 170, 171
Knowledge, 54
Koestler, Arthur, 144
Kosygin, Alexei, 102, 134
Krishnon, Gapi, 63
Khrushchev, Nikita, 173

Lane, Janet, 191
Lease, Mary Elizabeth, 176
Lewis, Jerry, 26
Likeableness, 74
Lincoln, Abraham, 109, 167, 170, 173, 180, 181
Lindbergh, Charles, 77
Linguistic impressiveness, 174
Linkugel, Wil A., 170
Listening, 57, 87
  critical, 95
  problems, 91
  process, 90
  purpose, 88
  skills, 93
Literary Digest, 141
Loaded terms, 96
Logical credence, 138
Logical motivation, 66
Longfellow, Henry Wadsworth, 189
Loose sentences, 181

Meaning, 14, 27, 41, 95
Media, 29
Memorized speech, 186
Menninger, Karl, 131, 169, 170
Mental images, 174
Message
  appropriate to occasion, 119
  appropriate to speaker, 118
  basic, 146
  body of, 145
  cues, 25
  nonverbal, 27
  preparation, 24
  presentation, 25
  purpose, 120
Metaphors, 174
Mill, John Stuart, 32
Milton, John, 33
Model of interpersonal communication, 20
Motivation, 56, 58, 96
  aesthetic, 68
  biological, 60
  charitable, 69
  logical, 66
  mental, 64
  mystical, 66
  for order, 67
  psychological, 61
  spiritual, 65
Movement, 181, 192
Murphy, Audie, 77
Mystical, 66

Names, 44
Naming, 44
Narratio, 149
Nasser, 108
National Association of Academic Teachers of Public Speaking, 8
National Council of English Teachers, 8
National Defense Research Committee, 9
National Society for the Study of Communication, 9
Nature of speech communication, 11
Nelson, H. E., 129
Nervous energy, 85
News events, 155
Nicklaus, Jack, 75
Nixon, Richard M., 72
Nonverbal cues, 26, 163, 164
Notes, 201

Observations, 45
  personal, 142
Occasion, 24, 110
Oliver, Robert T., 50, 51
Onomatopoeia, 178

Opinion
  expert, 142
  seeker, 198
Oral style, 168
Order, 67
Organization, 144
Orientation step, 157
Outlining, 159

Parallel cases, 143
Parallelism, 179
Parson, Donald W., 77
Pedantry, 170
People, 13
Perception, 45, 46, 53
Periodic sentences, 181
Personal dignity, 63
Personal experience, 154
Personal observations, 142
Personal persuasiveness, 23, 71
Personification, 175
Persuasion, 136
Peters, Lauralee, 124
Phelps, Thomas W., 127
Phillips, Wendell, 176
Philosophy and Rhetoric, 11
Physical factors, 56
Pithy quotations, 143
Pitt, William, 6, 190
Place, 24
Plutarch, 81
Poe, Edgar Allan, 179
Points, main, 138, 146
Poise, 81
Polarization, 101
Pomposity, 170
Posture, 191
Precise words, 170
Prejudice, 44
Pride, 62
Private planning, 92
Process, 12
Prodder, 198
Progression of thought, 171
Psychological motivation, 61
Publicity, advance, 78
Purpose, 120

Qualifiers, 182
Quintilian, 6, 8, 71, 73, 144, 150, 159, 165
Quotations, 154, 159, 177
  pithy, 143

Reasons, 148
Recall, 17
Recorder, 199
Reliability, 73
Reports, 121
Responsible communication, 30

Restatement, 128
Rhetorical questions, 155
Rhythm, 181
Richards, I. A., 184
Ripley, Robert, 133
Rogers, Carl, 135
Rogers, Will, 170, 177
Role self, 22
Romans, 6
Roosevelt, Franklin D., 84, 108, 167, 170, 173, 182
Roosevelt, Theodore, 176
Rule of three, 181
Rumor, 133
Ruth, Babe, 75

Salk, Jonas, 134
Sandburg, Carl, 174
Sarcasm, 177
Satire, 177
Scientific method, 48
Schulz, Charles, 42
Self
  -effacement, 92
  -hood, 40
  importance, 61
  role, 22
Seneca, the Elder, 4
Sentences
  balanced, 180
  loose, 181
  periodic, 181
Sex, 61
Shakespeare, 23, 167
Shaw, George Bernard, 65
Sheridan, Richard, 6
Short, Dorothy, 65
Shylock, 50
Sight, 164
Similes, 174
Situation, 13
Slang, 170
Slogans, 176
Small group discussion, 19
Smith, Al, 170
Social contexts, 16
Socrates, 58
Sound, 164
  -effect words, 178
Source level, 136
So what?, 99
Speaker-ethos level, 134
Speaker's image, 70
Speaking to inform, 120
  to persuade, 136
Speech Association of America, 10
Speech Communication Association, 10
Speech communication
  defined, 12
  nature of, 11
Speech fright, 81, 83

Spiritual motivation, 65
Sputnik I, 43
Statements of support, 151
Statistics, 139
Status, 76
Stevenson, Adlai, 80, 172, 175, 176, 177, 178
Strategy, 15, 25
Structural impressiveness, 179
Style, oral, 168
Stylistic strategies, 168
Subject, 114
Subpoints, 151
Summarize, 128
Supporting data, 152
  materials, 138
Suspense, 132
Symbolic, 14
Symbolizing, 40

Testimony, 141
Thought, 24
  progression, 171
Thurber, James, 93
Time, 24, 104
Toastmaster's International, 5
Topic, appropriate to audience, 117
Tradition, 77
Transitions, 153
Travis, Lee, 4
Triteness, 182
Truman, Harry, 80, 176
Trust, 72
Turner, Franklin N., 169
Twain, Mark, 39, 170

Unfolding arrangement, 149
Unintentional cues, 26

Unit of argument, 138
Unusual, 133

Values, 48, 52
Vandermeer, A. W., 129
Van Loon, Hendrik Willem, 178
Verbal cues, 26
  messages, 27
Verse, 159
Visual aids, 129
Vocal communication, 188
  delivery, 188

Washington, George, 167
Weaver, Andrew, 4
Webster, Daniel, 32, 174, 183, 185
Weltanschauung, 53
Whately, Richard, 6
White, E. B., 131
Wilson, Charles E., 80
Wilson, Woodrow, 173, 176, 185
Witticisms, 177
Wolfe, Edgar, 165
Words
  Anglo-Saxon, 169
  appropriate, 168
  sound-effect, 178
Wrage, Ernest J., 143, 172
Writing, 165

York, Alvin, 77

Zevin, B. D., 173